Claire Macdonald and her husband run Kinloch Lodge Hotel on the Isle of Skye, which is also the family home for them and their four children. Claire is a well-known exponent of Scottish cooking and travels widely, lecturing and demonstrating recipes.

Claire
Macdonald

OF MACDONALD

More Seasonal Cooking

CORGI BOOKS

MORE SEASONAL COOKING
A CORGI BOOK : 0 552 99288 7

Originally published in Great Britain by Bantam Press,
a division of Transworld Publishers

PRINTING HISTORY
Bantam Press edition published 1987
Corgi edition published 1990

9 10

This book is set in 11/12pt Linotron Baskerville by
Rowland Phototypesetting Ltd, Bury St Edmunds, Suffolk

Corgi Books are published by Transworld Publishers Ltd,
61–63 Uxbridge Road, London W5 5SA,
a division of The Random House Group Ltd,
in Australia by Random House Australia (Pty) Ltd,
20 Alfred Street, Milsons Point, Sydney, NSW 2061, Australia,
in New Zealand by Random House New Zealand Ltd,
18 Poland Road, Glenfield, Auckland 10, New Zealand
and in South Africa by Random House (Pty) Ltd,
Endulini, 5a Jubilee Road, Parktown 2193, South Africa.

Printed and bound in Great Britain by
Cox & Wyman Ltd, Reading, Berkshire.

This book is really dedicated to Peter Macpherson. We have cooked together happily (mostly!) for nearly thirteen years. I can't imagine being able to work so closely with anyone else so enjoyably for that length of time. I put our success down to his – and my – rather over-developed sense of humour!

But it is also dedicated to three other people who all cook at times with Pete and me here in the kitchen at Kinloch – Millie MacLure, Jenny Aldridge, and Angela Pargeter. I am indebted to Pete, Millie, Jenny and Angela for all the fun we have producing the food at Kinloch, with the minimum of temperamental tantrums and the maximum enjoyment, and I am so glad to have the opportunity to thank them in print like this and to dedicate this book to them.

Acknowledgements

I spend my life being indebted to people – I really don't know where I would be without my family and friends, who give me confidence

Top of the list and way out ahead is my husband Godfrey, he of the long-suffering temperament, the cast-iron gut, and the seemingly unlimited source of help and encouragement! Darling, thank you.

My children deserve a more than passing mention – Alexandra, Isabella, Meriel and Hugo. My girls are showing infinitely more common sense than I ever had at their ages, and they are all very supportive and great companions to me.

I say a big thank-you to ALL my friends. I value my friends more than they will ever know! A special thank-you for encouragement and inspiration for this particular book goes to Caroline Fox, and to Char Donaldson, and to my sisters, Liv Milburn and Camilla Westwood. I've had such fun putting this book together, and mostly that fun is thanks to Kate Parkin, who at the time of preparing the hardback edition was Senior Editor at Bantam Press. I would like to thank Kate and indeed everyone with whom I've – so far! – come into contact at Transworld. They all seem to belong to a rare breed of people – *so* nice and able to make work appear not to be work at all but more an enjoyable way of life!

Introduction

I count myself very lucky to be able to make a living by doing what I enjoy most in life – cooking and writing about food. To be perfectly honest, I really should say that better than either of those I like to eat, but they all go hand in hand. We live in a large white house at the foot of a hill, bordered on two sides by a sea loch, Loch Na Dal, on the Isle of Skye. The house is rather remote – a mile down a bumpy road from a main road which doesn't really qualify as 'main'. Living in such a remote place isn't everybody's ideal, but I couldn't think of living anywhere else now. I've grown to love it more than I ever thought I would. We – Godfrey my husband, and our four children, Alexandra, Isabella, Meriel and Hugo – live in one side of our house. The rest is occupied by guests, because our home is also a hotel. Now, this isn't everyone's idea of the ideal lifestyle, but it suits us perfectly. You can't really refer to what we do as our 'work' because it is a way of life, and we enjoy it so much. Most of the time life is extremely hectic, and it is certainly never dull.

Running a hotel involves constant contact with the guests, many of whom have become good friends over the years, spending their holidays with us again and again. We have a marvellous staff, really like an extended family. I share the kitchen with Peter Macpherson – we have cooked together for twelve years now. Neither of us had had a lesson in cooking when we started – I'm ashamed to say that I didn't even take Domestic Science when I was at school. In our early days of running Kinloch as a hotel my lack of training worried me, but as the years pass my confidence grows. There is no teacher quite like experience! The menus Peter and I produce are governed almost

7

entirely by the seasons. We are very lucky to have reliable suppliers – butcher, game dealer, fish merchant, fruit and vegetable wholesaler as well as a producer of organically grown soft fruit and vegetables – whom I count as friends. Nevertheless living on Skye means no strawberries and asparagus in December – thank goodness! I wouldn't want them if they were available – because it is the seasons and the different foods they bring that inspire our work in the kitchen. The time of year – or at least the weather – also dictates what we feel like eating. The thought of a fragrant steak and kidney pie may make us drool in January, but isn't half as appealing on a hot August night. I love the varying seasons because I love change. As I write, it is the very beginning of December, and I am still revelling in the afternoons getting dark early, the cosiness of the fires with the curtains drawn against the chill black outside. But by the end of January I shall be eagerly noticing the longer daylight hours and I shall be hunting out the first snowdrops. Each month of the year brings change and I like to offer our guests interesting and unusual menus so I'm always on the look-out for new flavour combinations.

I love sharing ideas – getting inspiration and new approaches from others – and I see this book as a way of sharing my ideas and recipes. Some of them are variations on a familiar theme, such as the different types of roulade, but I hope none the less appetizing for that. I have loved putting these recipes and notes together, and I do hope that you enjoy reading through the book and working from it as much as I've enjoyed writing it.

MORE SEASONAL COOKING

January

When the double festivities of Christmas and New Year are over and January gets under way, we tend to feel rather bleak – the fun and celebrations are behind us and more dreary old winter stretches out ahead! But January can be helped on its way with delicious food, comforting and warming. And for those who, like me, love marmalade-making, January sees the arrival of Seville oranges. I think Seville oranges should be used far more widely than they are – it's a shame to relegate them to the marmalade jar. This chapter includes several ideas for Seville orange puddings, from the homely *Hot Seville orange pudding* to the more elegant *Seville orange roulade*, worthy of the dinner party table. Seville oranges freeze quite well if you want to postpone the marmalade-making but they do lose some of their pectin content if frozen.

Here at our home-cum-small hotel, Kinloch, we close the hotel after the last of our New Year guests have departed – around the middle of the month! – and I settle down to the peaceful routine of living without guests. Part of the January routine is the task of making enough marmalade to last us through the coming year, some 300 lb/80 kg, and the house is filled with the smell of marmalade which is, to me, the essence of January.

First Courses

Fresh ginger, parsnip and orange soup
Carrot and lentil soup
Tomato, lemon and carrot soup
Cheese beignets with tomato sauce
Crab soufflé
Spinach and garlic tart

Main Courses

Steak, kidney and prune pie
Pot-roasted chicken with root vegetables
Game casserole with forcemeat balls
Pork chops with tomato and grainy mustard sauce

Puddings

Rich Seville orange tart
Seville orange roulade
Baked fruit salad with rum and brown sugar
Hot Seville orange pudding
Steamed ginger pudding with vanilla custard
Marmalade

Fresh ginger, parsnip and orange soup

The flavours of ginger, parsnip and orange are a wonderful combination, complementing each other so well in this most delicious soup. It is a perfect first course, and I like to serve it with tiny croûtons and chopped parsley sprinkled on the top.

Serves 6

3 tbsp oil (I use sunflower)
1 oz/ 25 g butter
2 medium onions, skinned and chopped
1 lb/500 g parsnips, peeled and chopped

1 in/2.5 cm piece of fresh root ginger, peeled and chopped
grated rind and juice of 2 oranges
1½ pt/1 L chicken or vegetable stock
salt and freshly ground black pepper

Heat the oil and butter together in a saucepan. Add the onions and sauté for a few minutes, stirring occasionally, until they are soft and transparent. Add the parsnips and the ginger, and cook for a further 5 minutes. Then add the grated orange rind (keeping the orange juice for later) and the stock. Bring to simmering point, half-cover the pan and simmer for 35 to 40 minutes. Allow to cool a little, then liquidize. For a really velvety smooth soup pour the liquidized soup through a sieve into a clean saucepan. Stir in the orange juice and season to your taste. Reheat to serve.

Carrot and lentil soup

The Scots are great soup eaters and our family is no exception. Best of all during the winter months I love soups with lentils in. *Carrot and lentil soup* really is a meal in itself and makes an ideal lunch. I like to serve it with brown rolls spread with garlic butter and warmed.

Serves 6

---

4 oz/100 g lentils (I use orange lentils which take much less time to plump up than brown and green ones)

2 pt/1.2 L chicken, ham or vegetable stock

3 tbsp oil (I use sunflower)

2 medium onions, skinned and chopped

1 lb/500 g carrots, peeled and chopped

1 garlic clove, skinned and chopped

2 heaped tbsp finely chopped parsley

salt and freshly ground black pepper

Put the lentils and stock in a large saucepan and simmer for 20 minutes. Heat the oil in another saucepan and add the onions. Sauté the onions for about 5 minutes, stirring occasionally so that they cook evenly. Then add the carrots, and the lentils and stock. Half-cover the saucepan with a lid and simmer until the carrots are tender, about 30 minutes. Add the garlic. Leave to cool a little, then liquidize for a creamy smooth soup. Reheat, stirring the finely chopped parsley through the soup just before serving, and season to taste with salt and pepper.

Tomato, lemon and carrot soup

A perfect first course for a winter dinner party. The flavours of tomato, lemon and carrot go together beautifully. I like to serve this soup garnished with a spoonful of yoghurt, a little grated raw carrot, a slice of lemon and some finely chopped parsley – use any or all of these garnishes.

3 tbsp oil (I use sunflower)
1 oz/25 g butter
2 medium onions, skinned and chopped
1 lb/500 g carrots, peeled and chopped
1 × 15 oz/450 g tin of tomatoes

pared rind of 2 lemons and juice of 1 (I use a potato peeler to pare the rind from the lemon, removing as little pith with the rind as possible)
2 pt/1.2 L chicken stock
salt and freshly ground black pepper
natural yoghurt to garnish

Heat the oil and butter together in a saucepan, and add the onions. Sauté the onions, stirring occasionally, for about 5 minutes. Add the carrots, cook for a further couple of minutes, then add the tomatoes, lemon rind (keeping back the juice), and stock (as with all soups, the better the stock, the better the soup). Bring to simmering point, half-cover the pan and simmer for about 30 minutes, until the carrots are tender. Leave to cool a little, and liquidize. Pour the liquidized soup through a sieve into a clean saucepan. It's worth this extra stage to get a really velvety smooth texture. Stir in the lemon juice and season to taste. Reheat to serve and swirl a spoonful of yoghurt into each plateful of soup. Serve with any or all of the garnishes mentioned in the introduction.

Cheese beignets with tomato sauce

This is a great favourite when it is on the menu here at Kinloch. The delicious crispy little balls of deep-fried cheesy goo are complemented by the *Tomato sauce* which accompanies them. They are very easy to make, and very convenient – the sauce can be made a day or two in advance and the cheesy choux paste can be made in the morning for cooking the same evening. The deep frying can be done up to two hours in advance, and the beignets kept warm in a low oven, on a dish lined with absorbent kitchen paper. They lose none of their crispness as they keep warm.

Serves 6   I allow 5–6 beignets per person, trying to make each beignet about the size of a walnut

---

2½ oz/60 g butter
¼ pt/150 ml water
3 oz/75 g flour
1 tsp dry mustard powder
2 large eggs
1 garlic clove, skinned and finely chopped

a dash of Worcestershire sauce
a dash of Tabasco
3 oz/75 g Cheddar, grated
oil for deep frying (I like to use sunflower oil because it is so light and tasteless)
Tomato sauce *(see below)*

Cut the butter into the water in a saucepan. Melt the butter in the water over a low heat. Don't let the water boil before the butter has melted completely. Meanwhile sieve the flour and mustard powder together. As soon as the water and butter begin to boil, draw the pan off the heat and add the sieved flour and mustard. Stir and then beat into a paste until it comes away from the sides of the pan. Allow it to cool slightly and then beat in the eggs, one at a time. Add the garlic, seasonings and grated cheese. Heat the oil in a saucepan to a depth of about 2 in/5 cm and drop in teaspoonfuls of the mixture. When they are golden brown all over, remove them from the oil with a slotted spoon, and keep them warm on a dish on several thicknesses of absorbent kitchen paper.

Tomato sauce

This is a very handy sauce to keep stocked in the freezer – it freezes beautifully, it keeps very well in a covered container in the refrigerator and any left over can be used for pizza, which our children love! It is very low in calories, and goes so well with so many different things – it is a delicious accompaniment for grilled fish or meat, or as a sauce for a green vegetable such as broccoli.

This quantity is enough to serve as an accompaniment for the *Cheese beignets* (see above) for 6

---

2 tbsp olive oil
1 medium onion, skinned and chopped
1 celery stick, chopped (optional)
1 × 15 oz/450 g tin of tomatoes
a pinch of dried basil (I use fresh later in the year when I have it growing)

1 garlic clove, skinned and very finely chopped
salt and freshly ground black pepper
a pinch of sugar

Heat the oil in a saucepan and add the onion and celery. Sauté for about 5 minutes, stirring occasionally so that the vegetables cook evenly. Add the tomatoes and the basil. (If you are using fresh basil leaves, later in the year, don't cook them in the sauce – add them when you liquidize the sauce.) Simmer the sauce for about 15 minutes, then add the garlic, salt, pepper and sugar. Allow to cool a little. Liquidize, pour into a clean saucepan and reheat to serve.

Crab soufflé

Crabs are at their best during the winter months, and this soufflé makes a perfect first course for a dinner party or a main course for lunch or supper. The mystique attached to the making of a soufflé is quite unfounded. If I can make one, anybody can – they really couldn't be simpler. The only thing vital to the success of a soufflé, and which has nothing whatever to do with the cooking, is that your guests should rise as one and go immediately to the table when you announce that dinner is served!

Serves 6 as a first course, 4 as a main course

---

1 lb/500 g crab meat, white and brown mixed
3 oz/75 g butter
3 oz/75 g plain flour
1 rounded tsp dry mustard powder
¾ pt/450 ml milk
a dash of Worcestershire sauce

a dash of Tabasco
salt and freshly ground black pepper
freshly grated nutmeg
1 garlic clove, skinned and finely chopped (optional)
6 large eggs, separated

Butter a 2½–3 pt/1.4–1.7 L soufflé dish. Melt the butter in a saucepan and stir in the flour. Cook for a couple of minutes, then stir in the dry mustard powder. Gradually add the milk, stirring all the time until the sauce boils. Draw the pan off the heat. Season with the Worcestershire sauce, Tabasco, salt, pepper, nutmeg and garlic. Stir in the crab meat, and beat in the egg yolks, one by one.

Whisk the egg whites until very stiff. With a large metal spoon fold them quickly and thoroughly into the crab mixture. Pour the mixture into the buttered soufflé dish and bake in a hot oven – 425°F/220°C/Gas 7/top right oven in a 2 or 4 door Aga – for 40 minutes. Another 5 minutes won't hurt the soufflé if your guests are rather slow off the mark!

If you like, and my sister Olivia does for one, add 2–3 oz/50–75 g grated cheese to the sauce along with the crab meat. Personally, I find it altogether too rich but, as with all recipes, you can adjust the seasonings and cheese to your taste.

17

Spinach and garlic tart

A delicious and convenient lunch or supper dish, or a very good first course. The amount of garlic you use depends on your liking for garlic – my liking could more accurately be described as an addiction! The filling for this tart can be made easily in a food processor, with the egg whites then whisked and folded in by hand. I like to serve it with baked potatoes or warm brown rolls and either a tomato salad or a vegetable with a tomato sauce – spinach and tomato are lovely together.

Serves 6–8 as a main course

---

12 oz/350 g shortcrust pastry
2 lb/1 kg frozen spinach, thawed and well drained
8 oz/250 g cottage cheese
1 large garlic clove, skinned and finely chopped

salt and freshly ground black pepper
freshly grated nutmeg
4 large eggs, 2 whole and 2 separated

Roll out the pastry and line an 8–9 in/20–22 cm flan dish. Prick the bottom of the pastry all over with a fork. Put the flan dish into the refrigerator for at least 30 minutes and then bake blind in a moderate oven – 350°F/180°C/Gas 4/bottom right oven in a 4 door Aga – until the pastry is golden brown (about 10 minutes).

Put the spinach into a food processor and process until smooth. Add the cottage cheese and garlic and blend again. Add the salt, pepper and nutmeg, and, with the processor still going, add the 2 whole eggs and the 2 yolks. If you haven't got a food processor, you can use this method with a liquidiser, pushing the mixture down from time to time with a spatula. Otherwise, use chopped spinach and simply beat the ingredients together in a bowl. Whisk the 2 remaining egg whites until very stiff and fold them thoroughly into the spinach mixture with a large metal spoon. Pour the spinach mixture into the baked flan case, and bake in a moderate oven – 350°F/180°C/Gas 4/bottom right oven in a 4 door Aga – for about 25 minutes, or until the filling feels firm to the touch. The tart will keep warm very well for about 20 minutes, but much more than that and it will begin to dry out.

Steak, kidney and prune pie

Steak and kidney is a traditional British dish for which everybody has their own recipe. Some people add onion, some don't. I like prunes in mine. Prunes and dried apricots go very well with meat dishes, and they enhance steak and kidney pie no end. The rich taste and texture of cooked prunes complement so well the meat flavours. And don't worry about serving it to prune-haters – Godfrey is one, and he loves this dish! Remember to put the prunes in to soak the night before making the pie.

Serves 6–8

---

6 oz/175 g prunes
1 pt/600 ml dry cider
2 lb/1 kg rump steak
1 lb/500 g ox kidney
2 rounded tbsp flour
salt and freshly ground black pepper

2 oz/50 g beef dripping or 4 tbsp sunflower oil
1 onion, skinned and finely chopped
½–1 pt/300–600 ml beef stock or water
12 oz/350 g puff pastry
beaten egg

Soak the prunes in the dry cider overnight. The next day stone and halve the soaked prunes. Set the cider aside. Cut the rump steak and kidney into ½ in/1 cm cubes and coat with the flour, seasoned with salt and pepper. Heat the

19

dripping or oil in a heavy casserole or saucepan, and brown the beef and kidney, a few pieces at a time. Keep the browned pieces warm in a low oven. Sauté the onion in the dripping or oil for 3 to 5 minutes, until it is transparent and soft. Sprinkle on any remaining seasoned flour, cook for a further couple of minutes, and then pour on the dry cider in which the prunes soaked and the stock or water – if you like a runnier gravy, add more liquid. Stir until the gravy boils, then replace the meat, and add the prunes. Cover the casserole or saucepan and cook it on top of the stove, just simmering, with a tightly fitting lid, for 45 minutes. Ladle the meat into a large pie dish, and leave to cool. When the meat is quite cold, roll out the pastry and cover the pie. Trim and decorate with pastry leaves, and cut a few air vents in the centre of the pastry. Brush with beaten egg. Bake in a hot oven – 425°F/220°C/Gas 7/top right oven in a 2 or 4 door Aga – for the first 20 minutes, then lower the heat to 350°F/180°C/Gas 4/bottom right oven in a 4 door Aga and bake for a further 20 to 25 minutes, until the pastry is well risen and golden brown.

Pot-roasted chicken with root vegetables

A true winter dish, making the most of the lovely root vegetables which are in season during the winter months. This is also one of those convenient one-pot dishes where the vegetables are cooked with the meat. All that is needed to accompany the pot roast is a dish of baked potatoes. Any vegetables left over from the pot roast can be liquidized into a delicious soup made with stock from the chicken carcass.

**Serves 4–6 If this is to serve 6, it is really better to use
2 small chickens – use any leftovers for soup**

---

1 large or 2 small chickens,
cleaned, wiped and with
giblets removed

4 tbsp oil (I like to use olive or
sunflower)

4 onions, skinned and thinly
sliced

1 lb/500 g carrots, peeled and
either sliced in rounds or cut in
2 in/5 cm chunks and
quartered

1 lb/500 g parsnips, peeled and
cut to match the carrots

1 lb/500 g leeks, washed,
trimmed and cut into 2 in/5
cm lengths

8 oz/250 g turnips, peeled and
cut into smallish chunks

1 lb/500 g celeriac, peeled and
cut into smallish chunks

2 cloves garlic, skinned and
chopped

salt and freshly ground black
pepper

Heat the oil in a large casserole, and brown the chicken all
over. Remove the chicken and keep it warm in a low oven
while you brown the vegetables. First add the onions to
the casserole and cook for 4 to 5 minutes, stirring occasionally. Then add all the remaining vegetables – it looks a lot,
but they reduce in quantity as they cook, and they do
double duty in flavouring the chicken deliciously and its
accompaniment. Cook the vegetables for 10 minutes or so,
stirring from time to time, then add the garlic and season
with salt and pepper to taste.

Replace the chicken, making a nest for it in the vegetables. Cover the casserole first with foil and then a
tightly fitting lid. Cook in a moderate oven – 350°F/
180°C/Gas 4/bottom right oven in a 4 door Aga – for 1½
hours. Test to see whether the chicken ·is cooked by
piercing a thigh with a sharp knife – if the juices run clear,
the chicken is cooked. Put the casserole back to cook for
a bit longer if the juices are at all tinged with pink. This
dish keeps hot very satisfactorily for an hour or so. The

vegetables make a surprising amount of liquid, and I like to serve baked potatoes to soak up the juices.

Game casserole with forcemeat balls

This game casserole is one of the most delicious and warming dishes that I can think of for the chilly winter months, when food goes such a long way to cheer and comfort us. It is also a very practical way to use up an assortment of game, when there isn't enough of each one to make a meal in itself. The *Forcemeat balls* (see below) which accompany the game casserole are lemon and onion flavoured, and can be made in advance and frozen. Thaw them for a couple of hours before reheating to serve with the casserole. I like to serve them separately, rather than in the casserole itself. They tend to lose their crispness if they sit in with the meat and sauce of the main dish. Serve a purée of root vegetables – celeriac is one of my favourites – and a green vegetable with the casserole.

Serves 6–8

---

an assortment of game, for example: 1 pheasant, 2 old grouse, 1 hare, 2 pigeon
1½ pt/1 L game stock, made from the game carcasses, 3 onions, 3 carrots, 2 bayleaves and a handful of black peppercorns
2 oz/50 g flour
salt and freshly ground black pepper

6 rashers of unsmoked bacon
2 oz/50 g butter
2 tbsp oil (I use sunflower)
2 medium onions
grated rind of 1 orange
grated rind of 1 lemon
4 juniper berries, crushed
¾ pt/150 ml port
2 rounded tsp redcurrant jelly
forcemeat balls *(see below)*

Cut all the meat off the carcasses and put on one side. Put the carcasses into a large saucepan, cover with cold water, and add the 3 onions, cut in half (skin and all), the 3 carrots, roughly chopped, the 2 bayleaves and the peppercorns. Bring to the boil and simmer the stock, with the pan uncovered, for 3 hours. At the end of the 3 hours, skim the stock and strain into a bowl. If you have made the forcemeat balls in advance and frozen them, take them out of the freezer to start defrosting at this point.

Cut the game meat into evenly sized pieces. Coat the pieces with the seasoned flour. Cut the bacon rashers into strips about 1 in/2.5 cm long. Heat the butter and oil together in a large heavy casserole. Brown the floured game, a few pieces at a time, until it is well browned all over. Keep it warm in a low oven. Add the chopped bacon to the buttery oil in the casserole and cook until nearly crisp. Remove the bacon and put it to keep warm with the browned game. Skin and thinly slice the onions, and add them to the casserole. Cook for about 5 minutes, stirring from time to time to make sure that they don't stick. Dust in any remaining seasoned flour to take up any fat left in the casserole and cook for a further couple of minutes. Then gradually pour in the stock, stirring all the time, until the sauce boils. Add the orange and lemon rinds, the juniper berries, the port and the redcurrant jelly. Stir until the jelly is melted, then add the browned game meat and bacon to the sauce in the casserole. Cover the casserole with foil and then the lid, and cook in a moderately hot oven – 350°F/180°C/Gas 4/bottom right oven in a 4 door Aga – for 1½ hours. Like all casseroles, the flavours of this casserole improve and intensify if it is made the day before and then reheated.

Forcemeat balls

These onion and lemon flavoured forcemeat balls can be made well in advance, deep or shallow fried, cooled and frozen. Thaw them for a couple of hours before reheating in a warm oven. They will lose none of their crispness.

Serve them with the *Game casserole* (see above), the *Marinated pigeon breasts with celery and walnuts*, or any game recipe.

---

1 tbsp oil
1 medium onion, skinned and
   very finely chopped
4 oz/100 g fresh breadcrumbs
2 oz/50 g beef suet
1 tbsp finely chopped parsley

grated rind of 1 lemon
a pinch of salt and freshly
   ground black pepper
1 beaten egg
oil for frying (I use sunflower)

Heat the tablespoon of oil in a saucepan and add the onion. Cook until the onion is soft and transparent. Mix the cooked onion with the breadcrumbs, suet, parsley and lemon rind in a bowl. Season with salt and pepper and bind the mixture together with the beaten egg. Wet the palms of your hands and roll the mixture into small balls between them. Each ball should be roughly the size of a walnut. Pour the oil into a frying pan to a depth of about ½ in/1 cm and heat. Fry the forcemeat balls until they are golden brown all over. Drain on several thicknesses of absorbent kitchen paper.

Pork chops with tomato and grainy mustard sauce

The sauce for this recipe can be made in the morning ready to serve with the grilled chops for dinner the same evening. I like to serve a green vegetable with the chops – either stir-fried Brussels sprouts or cabbage. A purée of potato mixed with celeriac makes a delicious accompaniment, too.

Serves 6

---

6 pork chops
2 oz/50 g butter
1 medium onion, skinned and finely chopped
1 rounded tbsp flour

2 rounded tsp tomato purée
2 rounded tsp grainy mustard
¾–1 pt/450–600 ml milk
salt and freshly ground black pepper

Melt the butter in a saucepan and add the onion. Sauté for 5 to 7 minutes, stirring occasionally, until the onion is soft and transparent. Stir in the flour and cook for a minute or two, then add the tomato purée and grainy mustard. Gradually add the milk, stirring all the time until the sauce boils. Season with salt and pepper. If you are not going to serve the sauce immediately, press a dampened piece of greaseproof paper over the surface of the sauce to prevent a skin forming. Reheat to serve.

Snip the fat of the pork chops in several places to prevent them curling up as they cook. Grill the chops until they are cooked through. Hand the sauce separately in a jug or sauce boat, or arrange the chops in a shallow serving dish and pour the sauce over them to serve.

Rich Seville orange tart

I think Seville oranges are so delicious that I like to make the most of them while they are in season. Their sharp, intense flavour is just perfect for this rich tart. This recipe can be made a day in advance and kept overnight in a cool place, ideally a larder.

Serves 6–8

FOR THE PASTRY
4 oz/100 g butter, hard from the
    refrigerator, cut in pieces
5 oz/150 g flour
1 oz/25 g icing sugar

FOR THE FILLING
grated rind and juice of 4 Seville
    oranges
4 large eggs
4 oz/100 g butter
10 oz/300 g caster sugar

If you have a food processor, put all the ingredients for the pastry into the bowl and process until the mixture is like fine breadcrumbs. If you are making the pastry by hand, put the flour and icing sugar together in a bowl. Rub in the butter with your fingertips until you have a crumb-like mixture. Pat the mixture around the sides and bottom of an 8 in/20 cm flan dish. Put the flan in the refrigerator for at least half an hour. Bake in a moderate oven – 350°F/ 180°C/Gas 4/bottom right oven in a 4 door Aga – for about 20 minutes, or until the pastry is golden brown.

For the filling, put the Seville orange rinds in a large bowl. Beat the eggs in a jug. Add the butter and sugar to the orange rind. Sieve in the beaten eggs. Mix all together and rest the bowl over a saucepan of simmering water. Stir until the butter has melted and the sugar dissolved, then take the bowl off the heat. Stir the orange juice into the buttery mixture. Don't be tempted to add the juice along with the rind at the previous stage – it just doesn't work. Pour the mixture of butter, sugar, eggs, orange rind and juice into the baked flan case, and carefully put the flan back in the oven. Bake at 350°F/180°C/Gas 4/bottom right oven in a 4 door Aga for 15 minutes, or until the filling is just set to the touch. Take out of the oven and serve either warm or cool.

Seville orange roulade

This variation on the sweet roulade theme uses Seville oranges. The orange liqueur in the whipped cream filling is purely optional, but well worth trying! It makes a most delicious pud.

Serves 6–8

FOR THE ROULADE	FOR THE FILLING
4 large eggs, separated	*½ pt/300 ml double cream*
4 oz/100 g caster sugar	*1 oz/25 g sieved icing sugar*
grated rind and juice of 2 Seville oranges	*4 tbsp orange liqueur (optional)*
1½ oz/40 g ground almonds	

Line a shallow baking tin or Swiss roll tin with siliconized greaseproof paper. Whisk the egg yolks in a bowl, gradually incorporating the caster sugar. Continue whisking until the mixture is pale and thick. Add the Seville orange rind to the yolk mixture and then add the orange juice. Whisk again until the mixture is thick and has the texture of a mousse. Sieve the ground almonds, and fold them into the yolk and orange combination. Lastly whisk the egg whites until they are very stiff. With a large metal spoon, fold them quickly and thoroughly into the orange mixture. Scrape this out on to the lined tin, and bake in a moderate oven – 350°F/180°C/Gas 4/bottom right oven of a 4 door Aga – for about 20 minutes, until the roulade is firm to the touch. Take the roulade out of the oven, cover with another piece of greaseproof paper and then with a damp tea towel. Leave to cool completely.

Whip the cream for the filling, adding the sieved icing sugar and the orange liqueur if you are using it. When the roulade is quite cold, lay another sheet of greaseproof paper on a work surface and dust it with sieved icing sugar. Turn out the roulade onto it and peel the paper off the back, in parallel strips to the roulade. Spread the roulade with the flavoured whipped cream and gently roll it up lengthwise, like a Swiss roll. Slip it on to a serving plate. Dust with more icing sugar and serve.

Baked fruit salad with rum and brown sugar

The fruits in this delicious fruit salad are a combination of fresh and dried – fresh oranges and pineapple with dried apricots and peaches. You can add chopped stem ginger if you like – I do. Or prunes and bananas. This pud makes a most refreshing end to a rich winter's dinner and any that happens to be left over makes very good eating at breakfast the next day. It can be prepared the day before.

Serves 6–8

---

3 oz/75 g dried peaches
3 oz/75 g dried apricots
3 oz/75 g prunes
1 small pineapple
2 oranges
2 oz/50 g soft brown sugar
3 fl oz/75 ml white or dark rum

2 bananas, which are added just
    before serving
½ pt/300 ml whipped double
    cream, ½ pt/300 ml natural
    yoghurt and soft brown sugar
    to finish (optional)

Put the dried peaches into a saucepan and cover with water. Put the lid on the saucepan. Bring the water to simmering point over a moderate heat. Simmer the dried peaches for 1½ hours, then add the dried apricots and prunes and more water as necessary to cover the fruit. Replace the lid and simmer for a further hour. (I find that dried peaches need much more cooking than any other dried fruit.) Tip the peaches, apricots, prunes and their simmering liquid into an ovenproof dish. Remove the skin from the pineapple and cut the flesh roughly into ½ in/1 cm cubes. Cut the peel off the oranges, and slice them in towards the centre, making pithless orange segments. Stir in the soft brown sugar and the rum, and cover the dish with either a lid or a piece of foil, and bake in a moderate oven – 350°F/180°C/Gas 4/bottom right oven in a 4 door Aga – for 45 minutes, then lower the heat to 200°F/110°C/Gas ½/top right oven in a 4 door Aga and bake for a further 30 minutes.

Take out the dish and leave to cool. Just before serving, slice the bananas into the fruit salad. You can serve it as it is or accompany with a mixture of equal quantities (10 fl oz/300 ml) whipped cream and natural yoghurt, folded together, with 2 oz/50 g brown sugar sprinkled over the top.

Hot Seville orange pudding

This very light sponge pudding has a rich orange curd-like base – the pudding separates to form these two contrasting layers during baking. It is very good and very quick to make. Any which happens to be left over can be successfully frozen.

3 oz/75 g softened butter	*5 large eggs*
8 oz/250 g caster sugar	*2 oz/50 g flour*
grated rind and juice of 3 Seville	*½ pt/300 ml milk*
oranges	

Butter an ovenproof dish. I use a soufflé dish for this pudding. Put the butter into a bowl or food processor and cream it, gradually adding the sugar. Beat the butter and sugar together until pale and fluffy. Beat in the grated orange rinds, and then gradually beat in the orange juice. Separate the eggs and beat in the yolks, one by one. Don't worry if the mixture curdles – it won't affect the end result. Sieve the flour and beat it in in small amounts alternating with tablespoonfuls of milk.

Whisk the egg whites until they are stiff. With a large metal spoon, fold them quickly and thoroughly into the orange mixture. Pour into the buttered dish, and stand the dish in a roasting tin. Add hot water to the tin until it reaches halfway up the sides of the pudding dish. Bake in a moderate oven – 350°F/180°C/Gas 4/bottom right oven in a 4 door Aga – for 45 to 50 minutes, until golden brown on top and firm to the touch. Serve warm or cold, whichever you prefer. This pud warms up very well, so you can serve it warm without having to make it at the last minute.

Steamed ginger pudding with vanilla custard

For me (and my father, from whom I inherit my addiction to all things sweet) there is little to beat a good steamed pud in the middle of winter. I find that almost everybody loves steamed puddings, and watch their glee mount when they discover it is accompanied by proper custard, flavoured with vanilla. We are all so brow-beaten into forsaking all our traditional puddings for the good of our health, that an encounter with such a pudding has become a rare treat.

It is a myth that steamed puddings are complicated to make. They are simplicity itself to put together, and the cooking just takes time. The only cautionary note is that you must keep an eye on the saucepan, taking care not to let the water boil dry or the bowl will crack. I did this once – it's the sort of mistake you don't make twice!

Serves 6–8

---

a little butter for greasing	½ tsp vanilla essence
8 oz/250 g flour	4 fl oz/100 ml ginger wine
2 oz/50 g soft brown sugar	1 large egg
1 tsp bicarbonate of soda	2 fl oz/50 ml milk
a pinch of salt	8 pieces of preserved ginger,
2 rounded tsp dry ginger	drained and chopped
3 oz/75 g beef suet	2 tbsp golden syrup
grated rind and juice of 1 lemon	Vanilla custard (see below)

Butter a 3 pt/2 L pudding bowl. Sieve the flour, brown sugar, bicarbonate of soda, salt and dry ginger together into another bowl. Stir in the suet, lemon rind and juice, vanilla essence and ginger wine. Beat the egg with the milk and add to the mixture, together with the chopped ginger. Spoon the 2 tablespoons of golden syrup into the bottom of the buttered pudding bowl, and pour in the pudding mixture. Cut a circle of siliconized greaseproof paper the same size as the open top of the pudding bowl. Fold a pleat from the centre to the edge of the paper circle and lay it over the pudding mixture like a conical hat inside the bowl. The pleat allows the pudding mixture to rise as it cooks. Cover the top of the bowl with another circle of

31

paper, foil (although foil tends to tear rather easily) or a muslin cloth. Tie string securely round the top of the pudding bowl to hold the paper or cloth in position, and put the bowl in a saucepan with water coming halfway up the sides of the bowl. Cover the saucepan with a lid, and put over a moderate heat, so that the water in the saucepan simmers. Cook for 2 to 2½ hours, topping up the water in the saucepan from time to time. This pudding keeps warm for 1 to 1½ hours sitting in the water in the saucepan after the cooking time is up, with the pan off the heat. Serve it with *Vanilla custard* and with cream too, just to gild the lily!

Vanilla custard

Makes 1 pt/600 ml

---

1 pt/600 ml milk
4 large egg yolks
1 tsp sieved cornflour

2 oz/50 g caster sugar
½ tsp vanilla essence

Put the milk in a saucepan over a moderate heat. Beat together the egg yolks, cornflour and caster sugar. Beat a little of the hot milk into the yolk mixture and then return it to the milk in the saucepan. Stir over a gentle heat until the sauce coats the back of a wooden spoon sufficiently thickly for you to draw a path with your finger down the middle. Remove from the heat and stir in the vanilla essence. Serve warm. This custard will go well with any steamed pudding and is, of course, the vital ingredient in any 'proper' trifle.

Marmalade

Marmalade is a very personal taste; some people like it rather bitter and chunky while others prefer it to be sweeter, more jellied than syrupy, and with the fruit cut more finely. I find that each year my marmalade varies a little. We make gallons of marmalade at Kin.och, and there is great satisfaction, I find, in going into the larder to gaze at the rows of jars.

This is the basic recipe that I follow each year – and I included it in my first book, *Seasonal Cooking*. The citrus fruit other than Seville oranges varies from year to year and from one marmalade-making session to the next, but I prefer not to use satsumas.

Makes 11–12 lb/5–5.4 kg

1½ lb/750 g Seville oranges
1½ lb/750 g other citrus fruit – perhaps a grapefruit, a sweet orange, and the balance of the weight made up with good-tasting tangerines or clementines

6 lb/2.75 kg granulated or preserving sugar

Put the fruit in a large saucepan or jam pan with 4 pt/2.3 L water, and simmer gently for about 6 hours – I put mine in the top left-hand oven of my 4-door Aga overnight, with the pan covered with a lid.

Remove the fruit from the water in the pan and cut each orange, tangerine or grapefruit in half. Scoop out all the pips into a small saucepan, cover with ½ pt/300 ml water and simmer for 10 minutes. Leave to cool, then strain this liquid into the jam pan with the water the fruit cooked in.

While the pips are simmering, cut up the fruit – I put mine in a food processor. Put the cut-up fruit back in the water in the jam pan. Add the sugar and cook on a low heat, stirring occasionally until the sugar has completely dissolved. Then boil furiously, and after 10 minutes pull the pan off the heat to test whether the marmalade is setting. Do this by dripping some of the hot marmalade on to a cold saucer (I put a saucer in the refrigerator); leave it for a few minutes and if, when you push the surface of the sample with the tip of your finger, the skin on top of the marmalade wrinkles, you have a set. If it is still runny, put the jam pan back on the heat, boil vigorously for a further 5 minutes and test again. Always remember to pull the pan off the heat while testing for a set, otherwise it may go too far. Fresh oranges will set quite quickly. Oranges which have been frozen will take longer to set, as they lose some of their pectin in the freezer.

Pot when still hot into warmed jars, and cover with a circle of waxed paper. Seal completely with cellophane and rubber bands when quite cold.

February

Where we live on the Isle of Skye, an island off the north-west coast of Scotland, February brings us some of the best weather of the year. We invariably have two or three weeks of clear, cold days, with the snow-covered mountains looking so beautiful against the blue sky. I reckon our landscapes rival any Alpine scenery! February also brings the first of the year's flowers – snowdrops – one of my favourites, perhaps because they are the first flowers for ages. In February the long wintry days begin to recede, and the daylight hours are noticeably longer. Although I love the winter months, I do get fed up with them, and February does bring the first welcome glimpses of spring. We are closed to hotel guests here at Kinloch during the month of February, but we have lots of friends to stay on an informal basis – visits we really enjoy. We also try to get away ourselves during February – in fact, it is such an action-packed month that in no time at all 1 March is here!

First Courses

Crab au gratin
Egg and prawn mousse
Chicken and prune soup
Celery and pepper soup
Chicken liver and rice balls with tomato sauce

Main Courses

Smoked haddock gougère
Bacon, potato and cheese pie
Marinated pigeon breasts with celery and walnuts
Toad in the hole with onion gravy
Sautéed kidneys with port and grainy mustard sauce

Puddings

Vanilla meringues with hot fudge sauce
Marron glacé iced cream
Hot chocolate soufflé with vanilla sauce
Pineapple tart
Pavlova with Seville orange curd

Crab au gratin

This makes an excellent first course for a dinner party. Or a main course for lunch or supper if you serve it with garlic bread or plain boiled rice (or both!) and a green salad. It is very simple and can be made in the morning for dinner the same night. You can serve the crab in individual ramekins or fish dishes rather than one large serving dish.

Serves 6–8

1½ lb/750 g crab meat, white and brown mixed
2 oz/50 g butter
2 oz/50 g flour
1 pt/600 ml milk
1 rounded tsp ready made English mustard
1 garlic clove, peeled and crushed

salt and freshly ground black pepper
freshly grated nutmeg
2 tbsp fresh breadcrumbs
2 tbsp grated cheese (Lancashire ideally, but Cheddar will do)
1 tbsp finely chopped parsley

Melt the butter in a saucepan and stir in the flour. Cook for a minute or two, then gradually add the milk, stirring all the time until the sauce boils. Boil for a minute, then draw the pan off the heat, and stir in the mustard, garlic, salt, pepper and nutmeg. Stir the crab meat in well, then pour the mixture into a shallow ovenproof dish. Mix together the breadcrumbs, cheese and parsley and sprinkle evenly over the surface of the crab mixture. Brown under a hot grill until the crumb mixture is golden and crisp. Serve.

Egg and prawn mousse

This creamy-textured mousse, with the eggs chopped rather than liquidized, is a first course to rave about, I find. It is also extremely convenient because it can be made the day before and kept overnight in the refrigerator or a cool larder. Here on Skye we are lucky because we can get huge prawns, technically known as Dublin Bay prawns or Norwegian lobsters, which have ferocious but rather spectacular pincers like miniature lobsters. If you can get these prawns, it's worth putting one aside for each guest to use as a garnish, arranged around the edge of the dish on which your bowl of mousse sits. Serve with brown rolls, generously spread with garlic butter and warmed.

Serves 6–8

---

8 hard-boiled eggs, roughly chopped
3 tbsp cold water
1 sachet of gelatine – approximately ½ oz/15 g
1 chicken stock cube
½ pt/300 ml boiling water
2 tsp anchovy essence
a dash of Tabasco
¼ pt/150 ml mayonnaise

¼ pt/150 ml double cream, whipped
freshly ground black pepper (no salt – there is enough saltiness in the chicken stock cube and the anchovy essence)
4 oz/100 g shelled prawns (if they are huge, halve or chop them)
finely chopped parsley and lemon wedges to garnish

Sprinkle the gelatine over the cold water. When the gelatine is spongy, pour on the boiling water and crumble in the chicken stock cube. Stir until the stock cube and the gelatine granules have dissolved completely. Leave to cool completely. When the mixture is quite cold stir in the boiled eggs and put in the refrigerator. After about 20 minutes, when it is just beginning to set, stir in the anchovy essence and Tabasco, and fold in the mayonnaise and whipped cream. Season with black pepper. Finally fold in the prawns, and pour the mousse mixture into a serving bowl. Leave to set. Sprinkle with finely chopped parsley before serving, and garnish each plate with a lemon wedge.

Chicken and prune soup

To anyone familiar with the traditional Scots soup Cock o'leekie, this soup won't sound at all strange with its combination of chicken and prunes. I love it, and it's one of those soups which come into the meal-in-a-soup category. It's very filling and substantial, yet not calorie-laden – the rare and perfect dish! It has to be made a day before it is to be eaten.

Serves 6–8

1 chicken weighing approximately 3½ lb/1.75 kg	*6 carrots, peeled and thinly sliced*
6 leeks (more if they are particularly small)	*18 large prunes*
3 medium onions, skinned and thinly sliced	*2 pt/1.2 L chicken stock*
2 celery sticks, thinly sliced	*salt and freshly ground black pepper*
	3 oz/75 g rice (I use brown rice)

Put the chicken in a large saucepan or casserole which has a lid. Pack the vegetables and prunes all round the chicken and pour the chicken stock over. Cover and cook in a moderate oven – 350°F/180°C/Gas 4/bottom right oven in a 4 door Aga – for 1 to 1½ hours, or until the juices from a chicken thigh run clear when pierced with the point of a sharp knife. If you prefer, the cooking can be done on top of the stove, with the stock gently simmering. Remove the pan or casserole from the heat. Leave to cool completely.

Take the chicken out of the vegetables and stock, and separate all the flesh from the carcass. Cut the chicken into smallish ½ in/1 cm pieces and put to one side. You can stone the prunes at this point if you wish – I do. Skim any fat off the top of the cold stock, add the rice to the vegetables in the stock, and reheat. Cover the saucepan and cook until the rice is tender – about 25 minutes if you are using brown rice. Return the chicken meat to the soup and allow to reheat. Taste and season before serving. Sprinkle each plateful with chopped parsley if you like, and tell your guests to beware of the stones in the prunes unless you have already removed them. Use the carcass to make more delicious chicken stock for future use!

Celery and pepper soup

A simple soup which makes a delicious first course for a dinner party in the winter months. The celery and green pepper combination is excellent. You can either chop the celery and pepper very neatly and leave the soup unliquidized or, as I prefer, you can liquidize and then sieve the soup for a really velvety texture. Serve with tiny crisp croûtons and finely chopped parsley to provide a pretty garnish and a contrasting texture to the smoothness of the soup. The soup can be made a day or two in advance, kept in the refrigerator and reheated to serve.

Serves 6–8

---

2 oz/50 g butter
2 tbsp oil (I use sunflower)
2 medium onions, skinned and chopped
3 medium green peppers, halved, deseeded and chopped
1 good head of celery, washed and chopped, leaves and all

1 large garlic clove, skinned and chopped
2 pt/1.2 L chicken stock
salt and freshly ground black pepper
croûtons and finely chopped parsley for garnish

Heat the butter and oil together in a large saucepan. Add the chopped onion and sauté for about 5 minutes, stirring from time to time to prevent the onion sticking to the bottom of the pan. Then add the green peppers and sauté for a further 5 minutes, stirring occasionally. Next add the celery and continue to cook for another 5 minutes, then add the garlic and pour on the stock. Half-cover the saucepan and gently simmer for about 30 minutes. Test to see if the celery is soft. When it is, draw the saucepan off the heat and allow to cool. Then liquidize and sieve the soup. Reheat to serve, adding salt and pepper to your taste. Sprinkle each plateful with tiny croûtons and finely chopped parsley before serving.

Tomato Sauce

This is such a useful sauce because it freezes well and complements so many things, from fish, grilled meat and vegetables to the chicken liver and rice balls (page 42). It has the added bonus of being very low in calories for those who are conscious of such things!

---

3 tbsp oil, preferably olive oil
2 medium onions, skinned and
chopped
1 celery stick, chopped
2 × 15 oz/450 g tins of tomatoes

1 large garlic clove, skinned and
chopped
salt and freshly ground black
pepper
2 pinches of sugar
½ tsp dried basil

Heat the oil in a saucepan and add the onion. Sauté for about 5 minutes, stirring occasionally to prevent the onion sticking. When the onion is soft and transparent, add the celery, and cook for a further 3 to 5 minutes. Then add the tomatoes, garlic, and salt, pepper, sugar and basil. Simmer gently for 35 to 40 minutes, with the saucepan

41

uncovered. Leave to cool a little and liquidize. If you are lucky enough to be using fresh basil, add it just before liquidizing. Reheat to serve. The sauce will keep in the refrigerator very well for 3 to 4 days.

Chicken liver and rice balls with tomato sauce

How I love this first course! In fact, I really prefer chicken liver and rice balls as a main course, with a green salad to accompany, for supper for just Godfrey and me.

Use Arborio rice if you can get it – it just makes the chicken liver and rice balls that little bit better than ordinary long grained white rice – or try using brown rice which should work just as well.

Serves 6–8   For a first course, allow 4 to 5 balls per person

---

2–3 pt/1.2–2 L chicken stock (or water plus 2 chicken stock cubes)

1 lb/500 g rice (Arborio if possible)

2 oz/50 g butter

2 medium onions, skinned and very finely chopped

1 lb/500 g chicken livers, picked over and any bitter green or yellow bits removed

salt and freshly ground black pepper

a pinch of fresh or dried thyme

2 eggs, well beaten

4 tbsp grated Parmesan (fresh if possible)

1 tbsp finely chopped parsley

5–6 tbsp breadcrumbs

oil for deep frying (I like to use sunflower)

Tomato sauce (see above)

Put the chicken stock into a saucepan and bring to the boil. When it is boiling, reduce the heat to simmer and add the rice, stirring for a minute. Simmer gently until the rice

42

is just tender. Drain the rice and leave to cool. Melt the butter in a frying pan and add the onions. Sauté for 5 to 7 minutes, stirring occasionally to prevent the onions burning. Chop the chicken livers and add when the onions are soft and transparent. Continue cooking, stirring from time to time, for a further 4 to 5 minutes. Season with the salt, freshly ground black pepper and thyme. Stir first the liver and onion mixture into the rice, and then half the beaten egg mixture. Stir in the grated Parmesan and parsley. With wet fingers, shape the mixture into evenly sized balls. Roll each ball first in the breadcrumbs, then in the remaining beaten egg, and finally in breadcrumbs again.

Arrange the breadcrumbed balls on a baking tray, and chill in the refrigerator. Just before your guests arrive, take the chicken liver and rice balls out of the refrigerator, and heat oil for deep frying in a saucepan to a depth of about 3 in/7.5 cm. Deep fry the balls until they are golden brown. Keep them warm in an ovenproof dish lined with two or three thicknesses of kitchen paper in a low oven.

Smoked haddock gougère

You can make this dish with any fish (or ham or chicken), but I like it best with smoked haddock. We are great fish eaters in our family, and we are lucky enough to get really good fish from our fish merchant in Mallaig. His haddock is undyed – undyed smoked fish is well worth hunting out in preference to the garish, vivid yellow dyed smoked fish so widely marketed. Large stores are becoming aware of the harm the chemicals used in dyeing can do to us, and many now sell smoked undyed fish.

The gougère bit of this recipe is simply a cheesy choux pastry – I say 'simply' because some people have a hang-up about making choux pastry, although it is extremely easy. This dish is very convenient and won't come to any harm if it is frozen before it is cooked.

FOR THE CHEESE CHOUX
PASTRY
4 oz/100 g butter, cut into pieces
½ pt/300 ml water
6 oz/175 g strong plain flour
1 heaped tsp dry mustard powder
salt and freshly ground black
pepper
freshly grated nutmeg
4 large eggs
4 oz/100 g strong Cheddar,
grated

FOR THE SMOKED
HADDOCK SAUCE
2 lb/1 kg smoked haddock
2 pt/1.2 L milk
1 onion, skinned and cut in half
1 celery stick
2 oz/50 g butter
2 oz/50 g flour
freshly grated nutmeg
freshly ground black pepper

Melt the butter in the water over a moderate heat. Sieve the flour and mustard powder together. When the butter is completely melted bring the liquid to boiling point. As the first bubbles appear, add the flour and mustard powder all at once. Draw off the heat and beat hard until the mixture comes away from the sides of the pan. Beat in the seasonings and leave to cool for about 10 minutes. Then beat in the eggs, one by one, and lastly beat in the grated cheese, reserving 2 tablespoons for the top of the gougère. Butter an ovenproof dish and spoon in the cheesy mixture, heaping it up round the sides, and putting a thin layer over the bottom of the dish.

Put the haddock in a large saucepan with the milk, onion and celery. Bring slowly to simmering point and simmer gently for 5 minutes. Leave the fish to cool in the milk. When it is cool, strain off 1½ pt/1 L of the cooking liquor.

To make the sauce melt the butter in a saucepan and stir in the flour. Cook for a couple of minutes, then gradually add the strained milk from the fish, stirring all the time until the sauce boils. Let it boil for one minute, then draw the pan off the heat, and stir in the grated nutmeg and freshly ground black pepper (no salt is needed because the fish is usually salty enough). Flake the fish from the skin, removing any bones, and stir the flaked fish into the sauce. Pour the sauce into the middle of the dish of cheesy pastry, and sprinkle it with the remaining grated cheese. If you want to freeze it, do so at this point. If not, keep it in the refrigerator until you are ready to bake it. It takes about 35 minutes in a hot oven – 425°F/220°C/ Gas 7/ top right oven in a 4 door Aga – until the pastry is puffed up and golden brown. Serve immediately.

Bacon, potato and cheese pie

This rather stodgy sounding dish is a top favourite with our children, and makes a perfect lunch in the chilly winter months. It is so easy to make, consisting as it does of a good cheesy sauce containing fried onions and crispy bacon poured over boiled, chunky cut potatoes. I like to serve it with one of the green vegetables, such as cabbage, which are so good in February.

Serves 6–8

---

2 lb/1 kg potatoes, scrubbed and boiled until just cooked, and drained
2 oz/50 g butter
2 tbsp oil (I use sunflower)
3 medium onions, skinned and thinly sliced
2 oz/50 g flour
1½ pt/1 L milk

4 oz/100 g Cheddar or Lancashire cheese, grated
freshly ground black pepper and a little salt if you think it needs it
6 rashers of smoked bacon, grilled until crisp and crumbled

45

Heat the butter and oil together in a saucepan and add the onions. Sauté for 5 to 7 minutes, stirring occasionally to make sure that the onions cook evenly and don't stick to the bottom of the pan. Then stir in the flour, and cook for a couple of minutes stirring all the time. Gradually add the milk, stirring all the time until the sauce boils. Take the pan off the heat, and stir in the grated cheese (reserving 2 tablespoons for the top of the pie) and the pepper. Stir the broken bits of bacon into the sauce. (The bacon should provide enough salt for the dish.) Cut the potatoes roughly into 1 in/2.5 cm cubes, and put them in an even layer in an ovenproof dish. Pour the sauce over the potatoes, and gently mix it in. Sprinkle the remaining cheese on top. Put the pie into a hot oven – 400°F/200°C/ Gas 6/top right oven in a 4 door Aga – for 15 to 20 minutes, or until the cheese on top is golden brown. Serve immediately. You can make this dish in advance, and reheat it to serve, in which case reheat it in a slightly cooler oven – 350°F/180°C/Gas 4/bottom right oven in a 4 door Aga – for about 30 minutes.

Marinated pigeon breasts with celery and walnuts

I think pigeon breasts are delicious, so good in fact that for me they rate as delicacies. It does depend, however, on how they are prepared and cooked. I marinate them for as long as possible, two or three days ideally, but I have marinated them for a week and they were better than ever! The celery and walnuts in this recipe act as a garnish and provide a good crunchy contrasting texture. Their flavours complement each other as well as the pigeon. I like to serve creamy mashed potatoes with this dish, and perhaps a mixture of carrots and parsnips. Root vegetables go well with pigeon, as with all game dishes.

6 pigeons, with the breasts cut
off the carcasses
FOR THE MARINADE
3 tbsp oil (olive oil ideally)
2 onions, skinned and sliced
1 celery stick, sliced
½ pt/300 ml red wine
6 juniper berries, crushed
a handful of parsley
2 garlic cloves, chopped
FOR THE SAUCE
2 tbsp oil (I like to use
sunflower)

1 tbsp flour
reserved pigeon marinade
¼ pt/150 ml chicken stock
1 tbsp redcurrant or blackcurrant
jelly
salt and freshly ground black
pepper
FOR THE GARNISH
2 oz/50 g butter
6 celery sticks, wiped and fairly
thinly sliced
3 oz/75 g shelled walnuts
salt

Heat the oil in a saucepan and add the onion and celery. Sauté for 5 minutes, then pour in the wine and add the juniper berries, parsley and garlic. Simmer for 5 minutes, then take the pan off the heat and leave to cool completely. When the marinade is cold, pour over the pigeon breasts in a dish, and leave for at least 2 hours – longer if possible – turning the pigeon breasts over once or twice during the marinating time. Drain the pigeon breasts (reserving the marinade), and pat them dry with absorbent kitchen paper. Heat the oil in a frying pan, and cook the pigeon breasts for about 2 minutes on each side, if you like them pink in the middle. If you like them better cooked, give them another 2 minutes each side. Take them out of the pan and put them on a dish in a warm oven. Dust the flour into the frying pan to take up any surplus fat. Strain the marinade and add to the pan, together with the chicken stock and the redcurrant jelly. Cook until the sauce boils and the jelly has melted. Season with salt and pepper.

Melt the butter in a pan and add the celery and walnuts. Season with a little salt. Cook for 10 minutes, stirring to prevent the celery and walnuts burning and to make sure they cook evenly.

To serve, slice the pigeon breasts in half horizontally and lay them in a serving dish. Pour the sauce over the pigeon and arrange the walnut and celery garnish down the centre.

This dish really can't be prepared ahead of time, but it doesn't take very long to cook. It will keep warm in a low temperature oven for about 20 minutes without spoiling.

Toad in the hole with onion gravy

When I wrote my first cookery book, a great friend of ours said to me, 'But you haven't got a recipe for Toad in the hole, and I can't find it in any cook book!' He was quite right – I searched and I couldn't find it either. Perhaps it's because people have their own versions of this dish. It's quick to make, loved by child and adult alike, and deserves to be on record, so here is how I make Toad in the hole! It is perfect February food.

If you can get tiny chipolatas so much the better, but if not, just cut the sausages in half. I like to use pork sausages, but use beef instead of pork if you prefer. I find *Toad in the hole* on its own rather dry, so I make an *Onion gravy* to go with it.

Serves 6–8

---

1 lb/500 g pork sausages, grilled and halved (if you don't grill the sausages before cooking, the ones which stay submerged in the 'hole' don't have that appetizing brownness)
6 oz/175 g flour, sieved
a pinch of salt

freshly ground black pepper
3 large eggs
½ pt/300 ml milk and water mixed
2 tbsp dripping or 3 tbsp oil (preferably sunflower)
Onion gravy *(see below)*

Sieve the flour and salt into a bowl, and make a well in the middle. Break the eggs into the well, and with a hand whisk gradually incorporate the eggs into the flour, adding the milk and water mixture as you go. Beat well, cover with a tea towel and leave to stand for 30 minutes. Put the dripping or oil into an ovenproof dish or a roasting tin and put the dish in a hot oven – 425°F/220°C/Gas 7/top right oven in a 4 door Aga – to melt the dripping. When it has melted pour the batter into the hot fat and arrange the sausages in the batter. Bake in a hot oven – 425°F/220°C/Gas 7/top right oven in a 4 door Aga. It will take about 35 minutes to become puffed up and golden brown.

Onion gravy

---

2 tbsp dripping or 3 tbsp
   sunflower oil (but the gravy is
   so much nicer if made with
   dripping)
3 onions, skinned and thinly
   sliced

1 rounded tbsp flour
1 pt/600 ml chicken or vegetable
   stock
a few drops of gravy browning if
   you like

Melt the dripping or heat the oil in a saucepan, and add the onions. Sauté for 5 to 7 minutes, until they are soft and transparent. Stir in the flour and cook for a further couple of minutes. Then, stirring all the time, gradually add the stock. Stir until the gravy boils. Stir in the gravy browning if you are adding it. Serve with *Toad in the hole* (see above).

Sautéed kidneys with port and grainy mustard sauce

I find that people either love or loathe kidneys – the same with sweetbreads, brains and liver. Godfrey and I love them, and, judging by their popularity when they appear on the menu here at Kinloch, so do a large proportion of our guests! The great thing to remember when cooking kidneys – and liver, too, for that matter – is not to overcook them. Overcooking makes them tough. This doesn't apply to ox kidney, which is used in steak and kidney pies and puddings, but it certainly does to lamb and calf kidneys. In this recipe the kidneys are sautéed in butter, and served with a delicious sauce of finely chopped onion simmered in port, with grainy mustard and cream stirred in at the end. It's a very easy dish and so good! I like to serve it with creamy mashed potatoes and a green vegetable, such as Brussels sprouts.

Serves 6   I allow 2 to 3 kidneys per person

---

18 lamb or calf kidneys, skinned, halved and cored (I find a pair of sharp scissors the best tool for this job)

2 medium onions, skinned and very finely chopped

½ pt/300 ml port

2 tbsp grainy mustard

½ pt/300 ml double cream

salt and freshly ground black pepper

2 oz/50 g butter

Put the onions and port in a saucepan, and simmer, with the pan uncovered, for 25 to 30 minutes, until the port is reduced by about two-thirds and the onions are soft. Stir in the mustard, cream and seasoning, and simmer all together. Meanwhile melt the butter in a frying pan and sauté the kidney halves until the juices just stop running pink. Serve the kidneys with the sauce poured over them and, if you like, sprinkled with finely chopped parsley.

Vanilla meringues
with hot fudge sauce

This pudding is Godfrey's favourite pud of all time. The children seem to fall about in ecstasy whenever it is mentioned, and the guests fairly lap it up too. It is one of the most convenient of all puddings to prepare, so plan it for a dinner or lunch party when you may be pushed for time – the meringues can be made up several days in advance and kept in an airtight tin, and the fudge sauce can be made the day before and kept in the refrigerator, needing only reheating to serve. The cream for filling the meringues can be whipped in the morning, so all you need to do about an hour before dinner is to sandwich together the meringues with the cream, and have a jug warming ready to put the sauce into.

Serves 6 (with 3 over)

---

6 large egg whites　　　　　　　　*1 tsp vanilla essence*
12 oz/350 g caster sugar

Line 2 baking trays with siliconized greaseproof paper (essential for making meringues, because they just can't stick to it). Have ready a piping bag with a fluted nozzle if you have one or 2 dessertspoons to scoop the meringue on to the paper. (I find a piping bag much easier to use, and the meringues end up looking much the same in shape and size!)

Whisk the egg whites until they are fairly stiff, then continue whisking, adding the caster sugar gradually. Whisk until the sugar is all incorporated. Whisk in the vanilla essence. Pipe or spoon the mixture into meringues about 2 in/5 cm in diameter on the paper. Bake in a cool oven – 250°F/130°C/Gas 1/top left oven in a 4 door Aga –

for 2 to 3 hours, or until they are hard to the touch. Leave to cool and store until required in an airtight tin.

To assemble the meringues

½ pt/300 ml double cream

Whip the cream until stiff. Sandwich together the meringues with the whipped cream, and pile them on to a large serving plate. I think they look much more attractive piled up rather than laid out in a single layer. If you have a dish on a stem or an old cake stand, meringues will look lovely heaped onto it. Serve the *Hot fudge sauce* separately in a jug.

Hot fudge sauce

¼ pt/150 ml double cream   *4 oz/100 g soft brown sugar*
4 oz/100 g butter   *1 tsp vanilla essence*

Put all the ingredients together in a saucepan to melt and dissolve over a low heat. When the butter has melted completely and the sugar dissolved, boil for 7 to 10 minutes. Then leave to cool, and keep in the refrigerator until needed. Reheat to serve.

Marron glacé iced cream

I need hardly say that this is a very rich pud, and therefore right up my street. You can, if you like, gild the lily and serve it with the *Hot fudge sauce* (see opposite), but it is very good with no sauce at all.

Serves 6–8

---

4 large eggs, separated
4 oz/100 g icing sugar
½ pt/300 ml double cream

1 tsp vanilla essence
4 oz/100 g marrons glacés, chopped

Whisk the egg whites until they are fairly stiff. Sieve the icing sugar and whisk it in, a spoonful at a time. Continue whisking until all the icing sugar is incorporated and the meringue is stiff.

Whip the cream and the egg yolks together until fairly stiff, and add the vanilla essence. Fold together the two mixtures and add the chopped marrons glacés. Spoon the cream into a polythene tub, seal and put in the freezer. Remove from the freezer just before you start dinner and it should be ready to serve for pudding.

Hot chocolate soufflé with vanilla sauce

This is a fairly rich pudding, so try to follow a light main and first course with it. It is quite delicious, combining as it does two of my most favourite flavours – chocolate and vanilla. Hot soufflés, whether sweet or savoury, are all the better for being served with an accompanying sauce like the *Vanilla sauce* below.

53

---

8 oz/250 g bitter chocolate
a little butter for greasing
6 large egg yolks
4 oz/100 g caster sugar

8 large egg whites
sieved icing sugar for dusting
Vanilla sauce *(see below)*

Butter a 2 pt/1.2 L soufflé dish. Break the chocolate into smallish pieces and put them to melt in a bowl resting over a saucepan of gently simmering water. Beat the egg yolks, gradually incorporating the caster sugar, until the mixture is pale and thick. Stir in the melted chocolate.

Whisk the egg whites until very stiff. With a large metal spoon, carefully and quickly fold the whisked whites into the chocolate mixture. Pour the mixture into the buttered soufflé dish and bake for 20 to 25 minutes in a fairly hot oven – 400°F/200°C/Gas 6/top right oven in a 4 door Aga. Have ready a tablespoon of sieved icing sugar to dust the soufflé as it emerges from the oven. Serve immediately with *Vanilla sauce* (see below).

Vanilla sauce

Makes ½ pt/300 ml

½ pt/300 ml double cream
3 large egg yolks
1 l tsp sieved cornflour

2 oz/50 g caster sugar
½ tsp vanilla essence

Put the cream in a saucepan over a low to moderate heat. Don't let it boil. Beat the egg yolks in a bowl together with the sieved cornflour, gradually adding the sugar. Continue beating until pale. Pour on some of the hot cream, mix well and pour on the rest of the hot cream. Return the mixture to the saucepan and stir over a low heat until the sauce coats the back of a wooden spoon.

The cornflour should prevent the sauce curdling, but if it does seem about to curdle, take the pan off the heat and beat the sauce with a wire whisk. If the heat is low, the sauce shouldn't curdle in the first place!

When the sauce is the consistency of thick pouring cream take the pan off the heat and stir in the vanilla essence. If you are making the sauce ahead of time, cover the surface of the sauce with a piece of greaseproof paper wrung out in cold water to prevent a skin forming. Reheat gently and serve.

Pineapple tart

A deliciously fresh tasting tart with a creamy texture, good whether eaten cold or warm. It can be made in the morning for dinner the same evening.

Serves 6–8

FOR THE PASTRY	FOR THE FILLING
4 oz/100 g butter, hard from the refrigerator, cut in pieces	*1 medium pineapple*
5 oz/150 g flour	*4 oz/100 g butter*
1 oz/25 g icing sugar	*4 oz/100 g caster or granulated sugar*
	5 large eggs, beaten

If you have a food processor, put all the pastry ingredients into the bowl and process until the mixture resembles fine breadcrumbs. If you haven't got a food processor (yet!), mix the flour and icing sugar together in a bowl. Rub in the butter with the tips of your fingers until you have a fine crumb-like texture. Pat evenly round the bottom and sides

55

of an 8 in/20 cm flan dish, and put in the refrigerator for at least half an hour, longer if possible, before baking in a moderate oven – 350°F/180°C/Gas 4/bottom right oven in a 4 door Aga – for 20 minutes, or until the pastry is golden brown.

To make the filling put the butter, sugar and beaten eggs into a bowl. (I beat the eggs and then sieve them into the bowl with the butter and sugar. This isn't really necessary, but it does produce a very smooth filling.) Rest the bowl over a saucepan of gently simmering water, making sure the bowl is free of the water, and stir occasionally until the sugar has dissolved and the butter melted, then take off the heat. Meanwhile cut the skin off the pineapple, and chop the flesh into chunks, removing the hard central core if it is very hard (sometimes this bit can be positively wooden). Put the pineapple flesh into a food processor or liquidizer and blend to a smooth purée. Stir the pineapple purée into the butter, sugar and egg mixture, and pour into the baked pastry. Carefully transport the flan back to the oven, and bake at 350°F/180°C/ Gas 4/bottom right oven in a 4 door Aga for 20 to 25 minutes, or until the filling is firm to the touch. Remove from the oven and serve either cold or warm. It is easier to cut when cold, but the filling is only slightly softer when warm, so don't let me put you off! It is delicious either way.

Pavlova with Seville orange curd

For meringue addicts – and it will come as no surprise to you to learn that I am one – this pud is heaven. It is also extremely easy, almost rating as a panic pudding, providing you have a jar of *Seville orange curd* (see below) stored away in the refrigerator.

4 large egg whites	*½ tsp wine vinegar*
8 oz/250 g caster sugar	*½ pt/300 ml double cream*
1 tsp vanilla essence	*1 lb/500 g Seville orange curd*
1 l tsp sieved cornflour	*(see below)*

Line a 12 × 14 in/30 × 35 cm baking tray with siliconized greaseproof paper. Whisk the egg whites until stiff. Whisking all the time, gradually incorporate the caster sugar, until the meringue is very stiff. Whisk in the vanilla essence. With a metal spoon fold in the cornflour and the wine vinegar. Spoon the meringue on to the lined baking tray, and smooth into a square or oval shape, whichever you prefer. Bake for 5 minutes in a moderate oven – 350°F/180°C/Gas 4/bottom right oven in a 4 door Aga – and then bake for a further 50 minutes in a cool oven – 250°F/130°C/Gas 1/top left oven in a 4 door Aga. At the end of the cooking time, take the pavlova out of the oven and leave to cool completely. Turn it on to a serving dish (or a pretty tray, if you have a square pavlova which doesn't fit a dish) and peel the paper off the back. Whip the double cream until fairly stiff. Fold together the whipped cream and orange curd, and spoon over the cold pavlova. You can make this pudding in the morning, leaving the spooning of the cream and curd until just before your guests arrive.

Seville orange curd

Orange or lemon curd is wonderfully useful – folded into whipped cream as a filling for meringues or light sponge cakes, quite apart from spreading on warm brown toast or hot scones! I've tried making curd with sweet oranges, but it lacks the necessary sharp tang and isn't very pleasant at all. When it's made with Seville oranges, on the other hand, you get the full orange flavour with the citrus sharpness – quite delicious. A jar of orange or lemon curd makes a good little present, too.

Makes about 12 oz/350 g

---

2 large whole eggs plus 2 large egg yolks	*4 oz/100 g caster sugar*
4 oz/100 g butter	*grated rind and juice of 2 Seville oranges*

In a jug beat together the 2 whole eggs and the 2 yolks, then sieve them into a bowl. Cut up the butter into the bowl, and add the sugar and orange rinds and juice. Put the bowl over a saucepan of gently simmering water, and stir occasionally (there's no need to stir continuously) until the curd is really thick. Take the bowl off the heat, and spoon the curd into jars or a bowl. Leave to cool. Store in the refrigerator.

March

Kinloch reopens on 1 March, so this is the time when we get into gear for the coming ten months of work. Not that we haven't been busy during January and February, what with all that marmalade-making! But life is so different when the house is empty of hotel guests, and March is the month when we get used to sharing our house again with our visitors. We are always very ready to start again – we love the contrasts in our life here on Skye.

Weather-wise March is a pretty bleak month, with any fine and sunny days being a bonus. As the days grow noticeably longer, I get impatient for the warmer weather. Shrove Tuesday always falls sometime in March, depending on the date of Easter, and I find myself inspired to make pancakes and *crêpes* galore – plain simple pancakes with lemon and sugar for the children, and slightly more elaborate savoury and sweet *crêpes* for the guests.

First Courses

Jerusalem artichoke timbales with sauce Bercy
Chicken liver and mushroom crêpes
Nettle soup
Prawn roulade
Spiced spinach strudel

Main Courses

Casseroled lamb with tomato and pesto
Chicken with grapes and paprika
Crab tart
Monkfish medallions with vermouth and mushrooms
Seafood lasagne

Puddings

Baked rhubarb and orange pudding
*Rhubarb and orange suédoise with ginger cream and
ginger meringues*

Rhubarb and ginger sorbet
Chocolate and cinnamon cream pie
Coffee crêpes with Tia Maria cream and grated chocolate

Jerusalem artichoke timbales with sauce Bercy

Jerusalem artichokes have one of the most delicious tastes I know. They also have two drawbacks, one is that they are undeniably a fiddle to prepare – they are so knobbly there really is no quick way to peel them (personally I don't begrudge a moment spent in the peeling because they are so good to eat). Their other drawback comes after they are eaten – they are one of the most wind-provoking of all vegetables, even more so than cabbage, onions and beans, and that is really quite something! But they are well worth a little discomfort afterwards. These timbales served with *Sauce Bercy* are very easy to make and are a really good first course for a dinner party.

Serves 8

---

2 lb/1 kg Jerusalem artichokes
2 pt/1.2 L chicken stock
4 large egg yolks and 2 whites
salt and freshly ground pepper

freshly grated nutmeg
⅓ pt/200 ml double cream,
*   whipped*
Sauce Bercy *(see below)*

Peel the artichokes (leaving you with about 1½ lb/750 g) and cook them in the chicken stock until tender. Drain the chicken stock into a bowl, and put the artichokes into a food processor or liquidizer. Process or blend the artichokes to a smooth purée, then add the 4 egg yolks, one by one. Turn the purée into a bowl, season with salt, pepper and nutmeg, and fold in the whipped cream. Whisk the 2 egg whites and fold them into the purée with a metal spoon. Divide the mixture among 8 buttered rame-kins. Stand the ramekins in a roasting tin, and pour boiling water into the tin around them. Bake in a moderate oven – 350°F/180°C/Gas 4/bottom right oven in a 4 door Aga – for about 25 minutes, until the mixture is firm to the touch. Take them out of the oven and leave to stand for 5 to 10 minutes. Turn the timbales out of the ramekins on to serving plates. Pour a spoonful of *Sauce Bercy* (see below) over each timbale and serve.

Sauce Bercy

This delicious sauce can be liquidized if you prefer. It is good with all grilled fish, meat and chicken or steamed vegetables.

---

1 onion, skinned and finely chopped
4 tbsp dry white wine
2 fl oz/50 ml chicken stock (if you are making the Jerusalem artichoke timbales *(see above) use the stock that the Jerusalem artichokes were cooked in)*

2 oz/50 g butter, cut into pieces
juice of half a lemon
1 tbsp finely chopped parsley

Put the onion into a saucepan together with the white wine and chicken stock. Bring to a gentle simmering point and simmer, with the saucepan uncovered, until the liquid has reduced by half and the onion is soft. Whisk in the butter a piece at a time, then whisk in the lemon juice, making sure that the liquid doesn't boil at all after the butter is added. Just before serving, whisk in the finely chopped parsley.

Chicken liver and mushroom crêpes

Pancakes or crêpes can be made a day in advance – or even longer, and frozen – providing they are going to be served hot. If pancakes have been frozen and are served cold, they do tend to be rather leathery. In this recipe the crêpes (the word 'crêpe' has more panache than 'pancake'!) are filled with a mushroom and chicken liver mixture, and smothered in a creamy cheese sauce. They make a very good first course or a simple main course for lunch or supper.

Serves 6 allowing 2 per person, with 4 over

FOR THE CRÊPES
8 oz/250 g flour
a pinch of salt
2 whole eggs plus 2 yolks
1 pt/600 ml milk
1 oz/25 g melted butter
FOR THE FILLING
1 lb/500 g chicken livers
2 oz/50 g butter
1 onion, skinned and finely chopped
8 oz/250 g mushrooms, wiped and thinly sliced

1 l tbsp flour
salt and freshly ground black pepper
½ pt/300 ml chicken stock
FOR THE SAUCE
2 oz/50 g butter
2 oz/50 g flour
1 pt/600 ml milk or milk and water mixed
salt and freshly ground black pepper
4 oz/100 g Cheddar, grated

Sieve the flour and salt into a bowl, and make a well in the middle. Add the whole eggs and the 2 yolks to the well, and a little of the milk. Using a wire whisk, beat together the eggs, gradually mixing in the flour from around the well. Add more milk as more flour is incorporated into the batter. Finally add the melted butter, and beat thoroughly. Leave the batter to sit for half an hour before making up the crêpes. This amount of batter should make about 16 medium sized crêpes.

Pick over and chop the livers, removing any bitter greenish bits. Melt the butter in a saucepan or frying pan and add the onion. Sauté for 5 minutes, stirring occasionally so that the onion cooks evenly. Then add the chicken livers, and cook for a couple of minutes before adding the mushrooms. You may need to add more butter at this stage, or a tablespoon of oil (I use sunflower oil). Continue cooking, stirring from time to time, for 4 to 5 minutes, until the chicken livers are just tinged pink inside. Sprinkle over the flour, season with salt and freshly ground black pepper, and stir in the stock. Continue stirring until the mixture boils, then draw the pan off the heat and leave to cool. Melt the butter over a moderate heat. Stir in the flour, mix to a paste and cook for 2 minutes, stirring all the time. Gradually add the liquid, still stirring, until the sauce thickens. Boil gently for a couple of minutes and draw off the heat. Season to taste and stir in half the Cheddar, reserving the other half for the top. Continue stirring until the cheese is melted and the sauce is smooth.

TO ASSEMBLE THE DISH

Spoon some chicken liver and mushroom filling on each crêpe, and roll it up. Butter a wide, shallow ovenproof dish and pack the rolled crêpes into it. Pour the sauce over the crêpes and sprinkle the remaining grated cheese over the top. Reheat in a moderate oven – 350°F/180°C/Gas 4/ bottom right oven in a 4 door Aga – for 20 minutes, or until the sauce is bubbling and the cheese on top is melted. Alternatively you can finish the dish under a hot grill to brown and melt the cheese.

Nettle soup

Nettles are traditionally eaten in some parts of Europe in the spring as a means of cleansing the body! I don't think you need an excuse to eat nettles – they are fresh-tasting and make a very good soup and they are delicious if they are picked when they are very tiny – about 5–6 in/12–15 cm high. If you wait until they are quite tall, they tend to have a bitter taste. As with all soups, *Nettle soup* will be as good as the stock used in the making. Wear gloves to pick the nettles.

---

4 good handfuls of freshly picked young nettles	*2 pt/1.2 L chicken stock*
2 oz/50 g butter	*salt and freshly ground black pepper*
2 medium onions, skinned and chopped	*freshly grated nutmeg*
2 medium potatoes, scraped and chopped	*6–8 slices of lemon to garnish*

Melt the butter in a saucepan and add the onions. Sauté for about 5 minutes, stirring occasionally, until the onions are soft and transparent. Add the potatoes, and sauté for a further few minutes. Pour on the chicken stock and bring to the boil. Simmer for 20 minutes, then add the nettles, pushing them down into the soup. Simmer for a further 15 to 20 minutes. Allow to cool and then liquidize. Sieve the liquidized soup into a clean saucepan and reheat to serve. Taste and season with salt, pepper and nutmeg. Before serving, float a thin slice of lemon in each plateful of nettle soup.

Prawn roulade

This roulade is made from milk flavoured with onion, celery, peppercorns and mace, and made into a very soft and lightly textured casing for a creamy prawn filling. The prawns (you can use little brownish pink shrimps if you can get them) are folded into soured cream with parsley and just a hint of garlic. It makes a delicious first course for a dinner party that can conveniently be made in the morning for dinner the same evening, or it makes a very good main course for lunch, accompanied by a green salad and brown rolls.

Serves 8

FOR THE ROULADE
1 pt/600 ml milk
1 onion, cut in half
2 celery sticks, broken in half
about 12 peppercorns
a blade of mace
½ tsp sea salt
2 oz/50 g butter
2 oz/50 g flour

freshly grated nutmeg
5 large egg yolks and 4 whites
FOR THE FILLING
½ pt/300 ml double cream
juice of half a lemon
1 garlic clove, crushed
8 oz/250 g shelled prawns
2 tbsp finely chopped parsley

Put the milk into a saucepan with the onion, celery, peppercorns, mace and salt. Bring to simmering point, then take the saucepan off the heat and leave to sit for an hour or so. Strain the flavoured milk into a jug.

Melt the butter in a saucepan and stir in the flour. Cook for a couple of minutes, stirring occasionally, then gradually add the milk, stirring all the time until the sauce boils. Season with freshly grated nutmeg and beat in the egg yolks, one by one.

Whisk the egg whites until they are very stiff. Using a large metal spoon, fold them quickly and thoroughly into the sauce.

Line a baking tray approximately 12 × 14 in/30 × 35 cm with a piece of siliconized greaseproof paper and pour the mixture on to it. Bake in a moderate oven – 350°F/180°C/Gas 4/bottom right oven in a 4 door Aga – for 20 minutes, or until the roulade is just firm to touch. Then take it out of the oven, cover first with a fresh piece of greaseproof paper and then with a damp tea towel, and leave to cool completely.

Meanwhile whip the cream for the filling together with

the lemon juice and garlic. Fold in the prawns and the parsley.

When the roulade is quite cold, lay a fresh piece of greaseproof paper on a work surface, and turn the roulade on to it. Carefully peel the paper off the back of the roulade, tearing it in parallel strips so that there is less likelihood of the roulade tearing too!

Spread the prawn filling evenly over the roulade. Roll the roulade up lengthwise, and place it on a serving dish. Dust with more finely chopped parsley to serve or, if you prefer, decorate with very thinly sliced cucumber.

Spiced spinach strudel

This spinach strudel is made with filo pastry, which is widely available ready-made from delicatessens. If you have to buy more than you need, just wrap up any unused leaves of filo pastry and freeze them.

The spinach filling for the strudel is quite spicy, and I like to serve it with a tomato sauce. The sauce is purely optional, however, an embellishment rather than an integral part of the dish!

Serves 8

---

2 lb/1 kg chopped frozen
    spinach, thawed and pressed
    to extract the surplus water
2 oz/50 g butter
1 onion, skinned and very finely
    chopped
1 large garlic clove skinned and
    finely chopped

1 tsp cumin
salt and freshly ground black
    pepper
12 sheets of filo pastry
4 oz/100 g melted butter or 6–8
    tbsp olive oil

Melt the butter in a saucepan and add the onion. Sauté for 5 minutes, stirring occasionally, then add the garlic and cook for a further couple of minutes. Stir in the well-drained spinach, the cumin, the salt and pepper. Cook for about 5 minutes, then take the saucepan off the heat, and cool the spinach mixture. You can make this the day before you want to serve the strudel if it is more convenient, and keep it in a covered container in the refrigerator.

Lay the sheets of filo pastry out, brush each with melted butter or with olive oil and put them in twos, so you have 6 sheets of double thickness. Divide the spinach mixture among the 6 sheets, spreading it over the pastry. Roll up each sheet, like a Swiss roll, and lay the rolls on a buttered baking sheet. Brush the rolls with melted butter or olive oil, and bake in a hot oven – 400°F/200°C/Gas 6/top right oven in a 4 door Aga – for 15 to 20 minutes, until the pastry is golden brown. To serve, cut each strudel into 4, allowing 3 pieces per person. Serve with *Tomato sauce* (see page 41) if you like.

Casseroled lamb with tomato and pesto

Pesto is a paste made from basil, pine nuts, olive oil and cheese and is sold ready-made in jars. When basil is growing in the garden you can make your own pesto, but not in March! – during the winter months I buy it ready-made. It enhances tomato dishes tremendously. I like to serve this casserole with tagliatelle (or any noodles) tossed in cream and freshly grated Parmesan cheese, and a green salad.

3 lb/1.5 kg lamb, cut roughly
into 1 in/2.5 cm chunks and
trimmed of excessive fat
2 tbsp flour
salt and freshly ground black
pepper
3 tbsp olive oil

2 medium onions, skinned and
finely sliced
2 garlic cloves, skinned and finely
chopped
2 × 15 oz/450 g tins of tomatoes
½ pt/300 ml dry white wine
a pinch of sugar
2 tbsp pesto

Season the flour with salt and pepper. Coat the pieces of lamb with the seasoned flour.

Heat the olive oil in a heavy casserole, and brown the pieces of lamb all over, a few at a time. Keep the browned lamb warm in a low oven. Add the onions to the oil and meat juices in the casserole and sauté for about 5 minutes, until they are soft and transparent. Then add the garlic and the tomatoes, breaking the tomatoes up against the sides of the casserole with your wooden spoon. Stir in the white wine, sugar and pesto, season and bring to the boil. Return the browned lamb to the casserole, cover with a lid, and cook for 1 hour in a moderate oven – 350°F/180°C/ Gas 4/bottom right oven in a 4 door Aga. Like so many casseroles, this one tastes even better if made a day in advance, allowing the flavours to mingle and fuse, and then reheated to serve.

Chicken with grapes and paprika

This recipe is easy, quick and delicious. It can be made in advance and reheated, with the soured cream added just before serving. I like to accompany it with boiled brown rice and a green vegetable. It makes an ideal main course for a dinner party.

Serves 6

---

6 chicken breasts
1 oz/25 g flour
salt and freshly ground black
   pepper
2 oz/50 g butter
1 tbsp oil (I use sunflower)
1 onion, skinned and finely
   chopped

4 tbsp paprika
1 pt/600 ml dry cider
¼ pt/150 ml soured cream
8 oz/250 g grapes, seedless if
   possible, if not, halved and
   seeded

Season the flour with salt and pepper. Coat the chicken breasts with the seasoned flour. Heat the butter and oil together in a casserole, and brown the chicken breasts all over. Transfer them to an ovenproof dish and keep them warm in a low oven while you make the sauce. Add the onion to the fat in the casserole. Sauté for about 5 minutes, until the onion is soft and transparent. Stir in the paprika and pour in the cider, stirring until the sauce boils. Return the chicken pieces to the casserole, and cover with a lid. Simmer gently on top of the stove for 25 to 30 minutes. Just before serving, stir in the soured cream and grapes. Don't let the sauce boil again once the cream has been added. Garnish with finely chopped parsley if you like.

Crab tart

Crab tart makes a very rich and delicious main course for a lunch or dinner party, providing all your guests can eat shellfish! Here at Kinloch we always mix together the white and brown crab meats. All sorts of ingredients really enhance and bring out the flavour of crab – nutmeg, mustard, cheese, sherry – and they are all here in this recipe. I would accompany the *Crab tart* with hot brown bread or rolls and a good salad.

Serves 6–8

FOR THE PASTRY
4 oz/100 g butter, hard from the
   refrigerator, cut in pieces
6 oz/175 g flour
½ oz/15 g icing sugar
a pinch of salt
FOR THE CRAB FILLING
1 lb/500 g crab meat, white and
   brown mixed

5 large eggs
3 oz/75 g Cheddar, grated
1 rounded tsp dry mustard
   powder
a dash of Tabasco
2 fl oz/50 ml dry sherry
salt and freshly ground black
   pepper
freshly grated nutmeg

If you have a food processor, put all the pastry ingredients in together and process until the mixture resembles fine breadcrumbs. If you are making the pastry by hand, sieve the flour, sugar and salt into a bowl. Rub in the pieces of butter with the tips of your fingers until the mixture is like fine breadcrumbs.

Pat the pastry round the sides and bottom of a 9 in/22 cm flan dish. Put the dish in the refrigerator for at least 30 minutes, before baking it blind in a moderate oven – 350°F/180°C/Gas 4/bottom right oven in a 4 door Aga – for 20 minutes, or until the pastry is pale golden.

Put the crab meat into a food processor and blend together with 2 whole eggs plus 3 yolks (reserve the 3 whites in a bowl), the grated cheese, mustard powder, Tabasco, sherry, salt, pepper and nutmeg. Process until all the ingredients are well incorporated. Alternatively put all the ingredients in a bowl and whisk thoroughly with a fork.

Whisk the 3 remaining egg whites until very stiff. With a large metal spoon, fold the whisked whites into the crab mixture. Pour this into the baked pastry case, and bake in a moderate oven – 350°F/180°C/Gas 4/bottom right oven in a 4 door Aga – for 35 to 40 minutes, until the filling is risen and firm. Serve immediately.

Monkfish medallions with vermouth and mushrooms

Monkfish is one of my favourite fish. The flesh is firm and has a wonderful flavour. In this recipe the fish is cut across, so that each medallion has the gristle-like bone in the centre. The fish is then cooked in butter with sliced mushrooms and served with a vermouth sauce, the recipe for which was given to me by Betty Allen, a great friend of ours who, with her husband Eric, runs Airds Hotel in Port Appin, Argyllshire.

Serves 6

---

about 2½ lb/1.25 kg monkfish, trimmed of its rather slimy membrane and cut in pieces through the bone about 1 in/2.5 cm thick. As the tail narrows, make the slices a bit thicker. I allow 2 medallions per person
1 lb/500 g mushrooms, wiped and sliced
3 oz/75 g butter

1 tbsp oil (sunflower, preferably)
FOR THE SAUCE
4 tbsp dry vermouth
half a small onion, very finely chopped
4 fl oz/100 ml fish stock
¼ pt/150 ml double cream
2 oz/50 g butter, cut into 6 pieces
salt and freshly ground black pepper

Make the sauce first. Put the onion, vermouth and fish stock together in a saucepan and bring to the boil. Simmer until the liquid has reduced by half. Add the cream and boil again to reduce, until the sauce is the consistency of pouring cream. Whisk in the butter, a piece at a time, until it is all incorporated into the sauce. Season to taste.

Heat the butter and oil for cooking the fish together in a frying pan. Add the medallions of monkfish and fry until the fish is cooked through – about 5 to 7 minutes. Add the sliced mushrooms and continue frying for 2 to 3 minutes. Arrange the monkfish medallions on a serving dish, surround with the mushrooms and pour the sauce over. Sprinkle with finely chopped parsley if you like and serve.

Seafood lasagne

You can vary the seafood contents for this creamy lasagne according to what you can get – it's a dream of a dish for fish lovers like me. Ready-to-bake lasagne is a real help in making this – it saves all that pre-cooking of the sheets of lasagne.

Serves 6–8

---

about 8 oz/250 g ready-to-bake lasagne verde
3 oz/75 g butter
1 small onion, skinned and very finely chopped
2 oz/50 g flour
1¾–2 pt/1 L milk
2 tsp tomato purée
salt and freshly ground black pepper
freshly grated nutmeg

4 oz/100 g cheese, grated (Lancashire for preference, but Cheddar will do)
1 lb/500 g crab meat
4 oz/100 g shelled cooked prawns
6–8 scallops, cooked and cut in chunks
8 oz/250 g cooked, flaked white fish (a firm fish such as cod, turbot or hake)
2 tbsp chopped parsley

Melt the butter in a saucepan and add the onion. Sauté for 5 minutes, stirring occasionally to make sure that the onion cooks evenly. Stir in the flour and cook for a further couple of minutes, stirring from time to time. Add the milk gradually, stirring all the time, until the sauce boils (it will be quite runny), then whisk in the tomato purée, the salt, pepper and nutmeg, and 2 oz/50 g of the cheese. Stir in the crab meat, prawns, scallops and white fish, mixing all together thoroughly. Spoon some of the sauce into the bottom of a shallow ovenproof dish. Cover with a layer of lasagne. Spoon on another layer of shellfish sauce, and so on, until all the lasagne and sauce are used up, ending with a layer of sauce. Mix together the remaining 2 oz/50 g grated cheese and the parsley and sprinkle over the surface. Bake in a moderate oven – 350°F/180°C/Gas 4/bottom right oven in a 4 door Aga – for 30 to 35 minutes, until the lasagne is tender when you pierce it with a knife, and the cheese on top is bubbling and golden brown. Serve with a tomato salad and garlic bread.

Baked rhubarb and orange pudding

This pudding combines a layer of baked rhubarb in an orangy sauce with a very light spongy top layer. It is very simple to make, can be made ahead of time and reheated to serve, and I have successfully frozen a whole pudding which happened to be left over, so it freezes too.

Serves 6–8

1½ lb/750 g rhubarb	*grated rind of 2 oranges*
3 oz/75 g soft brown sugar	*5 eggs, separated*
3 oz/75 g softened butter	*2 oz/50 g flour*
8 oz/250 g caster sugar	*½ pt/300 ml milk*
grated rind and juice of 1 lemon	

Wash and roughly chop the rhubarb. Put in an ovenproof dish with the soft brown sugar and bake in a moderate oven – 350°F/180°C/Gas 4/bottom right oven in a 4 door Aga – for 20 minutes or until tender. Leave in the ovenproof dish and set aside to cool. Beat the butter in a bowl, gradually adding the caster sugar. Beat until the mixture is pale and fluffy. Beat in the grated lemon and orange rinds, and then the lemon juice. Beat the 5 yolks into the butter and sugar mixture one by one. Don't worry if the mixture curdles at this stage, it won't affect the end result. Sieve the flour and beat it in, and lastly add the milk. Whisk the egg whites until they are very stiff. With a metal spoon, fold the whisked whites quickly and thoroughly into the pudding mixture. Pour over the rhubarb in the ovenproof dish. Stand the dish in a roasting tin half-filled with hot water. Bake in a moderate oven – 350°F/180°C/Gas 4/bottom right oven in a 4 door Aga – for 40 to 45 minutes, until the pudding is golden brown and firm to the touch. You can serve this pudding cold, but I much prefer it served warm.

Rhubarb and orange suédoise with ginger cream and ginger meringues

A combination of the complementary flavours of orange and ginger with rhubarb in a delicious and convenient dessert for a dinner party. The suédoise can be made two or three days in advance and kept in the refrigerator. The meringues can be made several days in advance, too, and stored in an airtight container.

FOR THE SUÉDOISE
2 lb/1 kg rhubarb
pared rind of 1 orange (I use a
  potato peeler to get peel
  without pith)
5–6 oz/150–175 g granulated
  sugar
3 sachets of gelatine (1½ oz/
  40 g)
juice of 1 orange

FOR THE GINGER CREAM
½ pt/300 ml double cream
6 pieces of preserved ginger,
  drained of their syrup and
  chopped
FOR THE GINGER
  MERINGUES
2 egg whites
4 oz/100 g caster sugar
1 rounded tsp powdered ginger,
  sieved

Wash and trim the rhubarb and cut it into 1 in/2.5 cm chunks. Put the rhubarb, orange rind and sugar in a saucepan, cover and cook over a gentle heat until the rhubarb is tender. Take the pan off the heat and leave to cool. Sprinkle the gelatine on to the orange juice, and pour on ½ pt/300 ml boiling water. Stir until completely dissolved, then liquidize together with the rhubarb. Pour the purée into a bowl and put in the refrigerator to set. This is really best made the day before you want to serve it.

Whip the cream for the ginger cream until stiff and stir in the chopped ginger.

Line 2 baking trays with siliconized greaseproof paper. Whisk the egg whites until stiff, then gradually add the sugar, whisking until it is all incorporated. Fold in the ginger with a metal spoon and pipe small meringues about 1 in/2.5 cm across on to the lined baking trays. Bake in a cool oven – 250°F/130°C/Gas 1/top left oven in a 4 door Aga – for about 2½ hours.

To assemble the dessert, dip the bowl of rhubarb suédoise into a sink or bowl of very hot water for a few seconds, then invert it on to a serving plate. Shake the bowl a bit (I jump up and down) and the rhubarb jelly should come out of the bowl easily. Spread the ginger whipped cream over the rhubarb until it is completely covered, and then cover the cream with the ginger meringues.

Rhubarb and ginger sorbet

Rhubarb is such a good fruit that I like to make the very most of it when it's in season. The younger the rhubarb the better – as with most things. There are two flavours which I associate with rhubarb – one is orange and the other ginger. Both complement rhubarb beautifully. In this recipe I combine rhubarb with ginger to make a refreshing sorbet.

Serves 6

---

4 oz/100 g granulated sugar
½ pt/300 ml water
juice of half a lemon
1 lb/500 g rhubarb, washed and
  trimmed into roughly 1 in/2.5
  cm chunks

4 oz/100 g soft brown sugar
2 rounded tsp powdered ginger
6 pieces of preserved ginger,
  drained of their syrup and
  chopped

Heat the granulated sugar and the water together in a saucepan until the sugar has dissolved completely. Then boil fast for 5 minutes. Stir the lemon juice into the sugar syrup and take the pan off the heat.

Put the prepared rhubarb into another saucepan together with the soft brown sugar and the powdered ginger. Cover the pan and cook the rhubarb over a moderate heat until tender – the rhubarb will make enough juice of its own without you needing to add any water. Allow to cool a little and then liquidize. Sieve the rhubarb purée and stir into the syrup. Stir in the preserved ginger. When it is quite cold pour into a polythene container and freeze. After about 2 hours of freezing take it out of the freezer and beat well with an electric whisk. Return it to the freezer, and repeat the beating process after another 2 or so hours of freezing. About half an hour before you want to serve the sorbet, transfer the container from the freezer to the refrigerator. This sorbet is very good served with ginger or vanilla biscuits or almond tuiles.

Chocolate and cinnamon cream pie

This creamy chocolate pie combines the flavours of cinnamon and chocolate, which go together so well. It can be made in advance and frozen, but not for too long, 2 to 3 weeks at the most. It is a most popular pudding with children and adults alike.

Serves 6–8

FOR THE PASTRY
4 oz/100 g butter, hard from the
  refrigerator and cut in pieces
5 oz/150 g flour
1 oz/25 g icing sugar
a few drops of vanilla essence
FOR THE FILLING
6 oz/175 g dark chocolate – the
  better the chocolate you use,
  the better the end result!

½ pt/300 ml milk
3 large egg yolks
4 oz/100 g caster sugar
1 rounded tsp cornflour, sieved
2 rounded tsp powdered
  cinnamon
1 l dstsp gelatine sprinkled over
  3 tbsp cold water
½ pt/300 ml double cream

If you have a food processor, put all the ingredients for the pastry in together and process until the mixture resembles breadcrumbs in texture. If you are making the pastry by hand, sieve the flour and sugar into a bowl. Rub in the pieces of butter with the tips of your fingers until the mixture is like fine breadcrumbs. Add the vanilla essence and stir in with your fingers. Pat this mixture around the sides and bottom of a 8–9 in/22 cm flan dish. Chill the dish in the refrigerator for at least 30 minutes, before baking in a moderate oven – 350°F/180°C/Gas 4/bottom right oven in a 4 door Aga – for 20 to 25 minutes, until the pastry is golden brown. Leave to cool.

Break the chocolate into the milk in a saucepan. Put over a gentle heat until the chocolate has melted. Meanwhile beat together the egg yolks, gradually adding the caster sugar, cornflour and cinnamon. Pour a little of the hot milk into the yolk mixture, mix well, and return to the rest of the milk and chocolate in the saucepan. Stir this custard mixture over a gentle to moderate heat until it is thick enough to coat the back of a wooden spoon and leave a path when you draw your finger down it. It should be the consistency of unwhipped double cream. Take the saucepan off the heat, and immediately stir the gelatine and water mixture into the hot custard, stirring until the granules of gelatine are completely dissolved. Leave the custard to cool completely, stirring it occasionally to prevent a skin from forming.

Whip the double cream. When the chocolate custard is quite cold, fold the whipped cream into it. Pour the filling into the cooled baked pastry shell and leave to set. You can gild the lily by decorating the pie with more whipped cream and grated chocolate or serve it just as it is. If you have put it to set in the refrigerator, remember to take it out an hour or two before serving, so that it will be at room temperature.

Coffee crêpes with Tia Maria cream and grated chocolate

Because Shrove Tuesday always falls during March, I thought it would be a good idea to include a toothsome pancake pudding. These coffee-flavoured crêpes are filled with whipped cream flavoured with Tia Maria, my favourite liqueur for all coffee and chocolate puddings. They are extremely good.

Serves 6

FOR THE PANCAKE
   BATTER (MAKES
   ABOUT 26 CRÊPES)
8 oz/250 g plain flour
2 oz/50 g caster sugar
2 whole eggs plus 2 yolks
¾ pt/450 ml milk
¼ pt/150 ml strong coffee
1 oz/25 g butter, melted

FOR THE FILLING
1 pt/600 ml double cream
3 fl oz/75 ml Tia Maria
4 oz/100 g dark chocolate, grated
1 oz/25 g icing sugar
½ oz/15 g cocoa powder

Sieve the flour and caster sugar for the pancake batter together into a bowl, and make a well in the middle. Break the 2 whole eggs into the well and add the 2 yolks. Pour in a little of the milk, and mix with a wire whisk, gradually incorporating the flour, gradually adding more milk, and finally the coffee, until everything is well mixed together. Beat in the melted butter, and leave the batter to stand for half an hour before making it up into pancakes.

Whip the cream for the filling, whipping in the liqueur, until fairly stiff. Fold the grated chocolate into the cream. Spoon some of the cream on to each crêpe and roll it up. Arrange the rolled crêpes in an ovenproof dish. Sieve the icing sugar and cocoa powder together over the crêpes, and put the dish under a very hot grill until the icing sugar just begins to caramelize. Serve at once! You can fill the crêpes in the morning and get them all ready to pop under the grill for dinner the same evening.

April

When April comes I feel that spring is at last a distinct possibility. Up here on Skye new growth is a couple of weeks behind central and southern Britain, so it isn't until mid or late April that we notice any real greening up of our hedges and trees. The wild flowers on Skye in April and May must be among the most beautiful anywhere in the world – great clumps of primroses, and a particularly strong variety of violets which grow in profusion around us here at Kinloch. We generally get some hot weather sometime during April, which is a treat because the midges which plague us later in the year are not around in April.

Easter usually falls somewhere during April which, from a culinary point of view, brings to mind chickens and eggs – and chocolate! April is also the first month when I feel able to stop feeding my family, friends and guests with hot, sustaining casserole-type dishes, and I begin to think of the new young vegetables just coming into season.

First Courses

Creamy carrot and turnip soup
Grilled goat's cheese with sautéed leeks and walnuts
Marinated prawns with spring onions
Smoked venison with melon
Stuffed mushrooms

Main Courses

Fish cakes with lemon and parsley cream sauce
Garlic, mushroom and red pepper risotto
Livi's liver
Roast loin of pork with prune and red wine sauce
Ragoût of lamb with lemon and saffron

Puddings

Coffee cream bavarois with Tia Maria
Hot cross buns
Orange and caramel profiteroles
Vanilla and coconut cream cake

Creamy carrot and turnip soup

For a chilly day in April there is nothing to beat a soup which clings to the root vegetables of the winter months. This carrot and turnip soup makes a warming and tasty first course for lunch or dinner. As with all soups, it is really only as good as the stock used in its making. If I haven't got any chicken stock on the go (my favourite for most soups), I make vegetable stock, which is very easy and quick to throw together and so very much better than any stock cube! Just put into a large saucepan any vegetables (with the two exceptions of potatoes and turnips, which both seem to make stock bitter), mushroom stalks, carrot peelings, the outer leaves of cauliflowers, onions, celery, anything, as much water as will comfortably fit in the pan and boil gently for 30 to 40 minutes. Strain, discard the vegetable debris, and there you are.

Serves 6–8

---

2 oz/50 g butter

1 tbsp oil (I use sunflower)

2 medium onions, skinned and chopped

1 lb/500 g carrots, peeled and chopped

half a small turnip, weighing 8–12 oz/250–350 g, peeled and chopped

2 pt/1.2 L chicken or vegetable stock

salt and freshly ground black pepper

freshly grated nutmeg

tiny croûtons, fried in butter and ½ tsp curry powder, to garnish

2 tbsp finely chopped parsley

Heat the butter and oil together in a saucepan. Add the onions and sauté for 5 minutes, stirring occasionally to prevent them sticking. Add the carrots and turnip, and sauté for a further 5 minutes. Pour on the stock, and season with salt, freshly ground black pepper and nutmeg. Bring the stock to the boil, cover the pan and simmer gently for 35 to 40 minutes, until the carrot and turnip are tender. Take the pan off the heat, leave to cool a little and then liquidize. Sieve the liquidized soup into a clean saucepan.

Reheat the soup to serve. Fry the croûtons in butter with half a teaspoon of curry powder. Stir the finely chopped parsley through the soup just before serving (so that the parsley keeps its bright, fresh colour). Hand the croûtons separately.

Grilled goat's cheese with sautéed leeks and walnuts

There is a great affinity between goat's cheese and walnuts, and in this simple but delicious first course the two flavours come together with leeks to produce a very good start to a dinner party.

Serves 6

---

8 oz/250 g goat's cheese
(log-shaped if possible)
a baguette, the wider sort rather
than the very narrow French
bread sticks
2 tbsp walnut oil plus 1 tbsp for
the toast
6 medium leeks, washed,
trimmed and diagonally sliced
in roughly 1 in/2.5 cm chunks

3 oz/75 g walnuts, roughly
chopped
salt and freshly ground black
pepper
1 garlic clove, skinned
1 tbsp finely chopped parsley to
garnish

Slice the goat's cheese into 6 evenly sized pieces. Cut 6 slices from the baguette, each about 1 in/2.5 cm thick.

Heat the oil in a wide shallow saucepan or a frying pan.

85

Add the prepared leeks and sauté gently for 5 minutes, turning them from time to time so that they cook evenly. Cook the leeks on a low heat so that they retain their greenness – the end result is so much more attractive. Then add the walnuts, season with salt and pepper, and cook for a further 5 minutes. Meanwhile brush the slices of bread for toasting with walnut oil and rub with the cut garlic clove. Toast the slices of bread on both sides. Put a slice of goat's cheese on each slice of toasted bread, and toast until golden brown and puffy – 1½ mins. Put a slice of toast and cheese on each serving plate, arrange a spoonful of sautéed leeks and walnuts beside it, sprinkle with finely chopped parsley to garnish and serve.

Marinated prawns with spring onions

This easy first course is one of those ideal dishes which is both delicious and low in calories. It can be made ahead of time, leaving only the arrangement on a serving dish for the last minute. I like to serve the prawns on a bed of shredded lettuce, but you could serve them in individual ramekins, with or without the lettuce. Wholemeal or, better still, granary bread accompanies them best.

Serves 6

1 lb/500 g shelled prawns
a bunch of spring onions
4 tbsp olive oil
4 tbsp dry white wine
½ tsp salt
½ tsp sugar
1 garlic clove, skinned and finely chopped

a dash of Tabasco
several grinds of the black pepper mill
finely shredded lettuce for serving
lemon wedges and 2 tbsp finely chopped parsley to garnish

Trim the spring onions and slice them thinly. Put them together with all the other ingredients except the prawns into a saucepan. Bring to the boil and simmer gently for 5 minutes. Take the saucepan off the heat, and mix the prawns into the hot dressing, combining them thoroughly. Leave to cool, then arrange on a serving plate on a bed of finely shredded lettuce, with chopped parsley sprinkled over and lemon wedges around the edge.

Smoked venison with melon

Smoked venison may sound a rather unlikely item to be found in homes outside Scotland, but in fact it is fairly widely available now throughout Britain. I urge those of you who haven't yet tried it to do so – it's delicious. I like it best served like Parma ham, with slices of melon.

Serves 6

2 ripe juicy melons – Ogen, if in season, or Galia	*12 oz/350 g smoked venison, thinly sliced*

Slice the melons in half and scoop out the seeds. Slice into segments about 1 in/2.5 cm thick and cut off the skin. Arrange the slices of smoked venison across the melon segments on each serving plate.

Stuffed mushrooms

These mushrooms are for garlic lovers like me. They can be prepared in the morning, just ready to cook before serving for dinner the same evening. The stuffing consists of cream cheese, almonds and garlic, and I like to serve them with warm brown rolls to mop up the juices.

---

1 lb/500 g large mushrooms, wiped and with their stalks removed

6 oz/175 g cream cheese (you can substitute quark if you are calorie counting)

2 garlic cloves, skinned and chopped

Salt and freshly ground black pepper

1 oz/25 g ground almonds

2 oz/50 g fresh breadcrumbs

juice of 1 lemon

1 tbsp finely chopped parsley

Butter a baking tray and arrange the mushrooms on it. Process the cream cheese until smooth in a food processor or beat by hand. Add the garlic, black pepper, ground almonds, breadcrumbs, lemon juice and parsley to the processor and blend into a thick paste. Beat all the ingredients into the cream cheese by hand if you are not using a processor – you will get a coarser stuffing with this method. With a teaspoon and a wet finger, spoon the mixture into each mushroom, pressing it down well.

Put the baking tray of mushrooms into a fairly hot oven – 400°F/200°C/Gas 6/top right oven in a 4 door Aga – for 10 minutes, or until the stuffing is crisp on top and the mushrooms are soft. Alternatively you can grill the mushrooms if you are using the oven for something else. Keep them warm until you are ready to serve.

Fish cakes
with lemon and parsley cream sauce

These fish cakes are made with a mixture of cod and smoked haddock. I like the taste of smoked fish in fish cakes (and fish pie too, for that matter) and I like the large flakes of fish which are typical of cod. You can serve a

Tomato sauce (see page 41) with these fish cakes, but I love the creamy lemony sauce which accompanies them here – it does make for a more luxurious dish altogether. Fish cakes can be made ahead of time, only needing to be shallow fried before serving, and they freeze well too.

Serves 6

1½ lb/750 g fish – roughly ¾ lb/375 g cooked smoked haddock and ¾ lb/375 g cooked cod

1½ lb/750 g creamy well mashed potatoes (about 2½ lb/1.25 kg weighed before cooking)

2 rounded tbsp finely chopped parsley

2 eggs, beaten in a shallow dish

2–3 oz/50–75 g fresh breadcrumbs, dried and toasted

oil for frying (I use sunflower)

Lemon and parsley cream sauce *(see below)*

Flake the cooked fish and remove any skin and bones. Mix together well the fish, the mashed potatoes and the parsley. Form into balls of even size and flatten into cake shapes. Line a baking tray with siliconized greaseproof paper. Coat each cake in the beaten egg, drain it a little, and dip it into the breadcrumbs. Lay the breadcrumbed cakes on the lined baking tray. Put them in the refrigerator until you are ready to cook them. If you want to freeze them, do so at this stage. Give them a couple of hours to thaw. When you are ready to cook the fish cakes, pour oil to a depth of about ½ in/1 cm into a frying pan and heat it gently. Cook the fish cakes for 2 to 3 minutes on each side, until they are golden brown. Keep them warm on an ovenproof dish lined with 2 or 3 thicknesses of kitchen paper to absorb excess grease. Serve with *Lemon and parsley cream sauce* (see next page).

Lemon and parsley cream sauce

Makes ½ pt/300 ml

---

2 oz/50 g butter
1 rounded tsp flour
3 egg yolks
½ pt/300 ml single cream

grated rind and juice of 2 lemons
salt and freshly ground black
   pepper
2 tbsp finely chopped parsley

Put the butter, flour, egg yolks, cream, lemon rind (but not the juice), salt and pepper into a food processor or liquidizer and blend until smooth. Alternatively you can whisk them by hand. Pour into a heatproof bowl, and stand the bowl in a roasting tin filled with water, so that the water comes halfway up the sides of the bowl. Bring the water to a gentle boil on top of the stove. Stir from time to time until the sauce thickens to the consistency of thick pouring cream – this will take between 30 and 40 minutes. When the sauce is the right consistency and you are ready to serve, stir in the lemon juice and the chopped parsley. You can leave the sauce standing in the water with the heat turned off for ages – up to an hour, but don't add the parsley until you are about to serve or it loses its bright, fresh green colour, which is one of its reasons for being in the sauce!

Garlic, mushroom and red pepper risotto

A good risotto is a treat to eat. A real risotto can only be made with an Italian rice, such as Arborio rice, which can absorb lots of liquid without going mushy. It also has an excellent flavour. A risotto is one of those useful dishes which can contain a variety of ingredients – diced ham or chicken, for example, or a selection of vegetables. In this recipe I use garlic, mushrooms and red peppers, and top the risotto with lots of freshly grated Parmesan. It is one of my favourite dishes and if you use vegetable rather than chicken stock, it makes an ideal vegetarian main course.

Serves 6

---

4 tbsp olive oil
1 medium onion, skinned and
   finely chopped
2 red peppers, halved, de-seeded
   and fairly finely chopped
1 lb/500 g mushrooms, wiped
   and chopped
10 oz/300 g Arborio rice
½ pt/300 ml dry white wine

1 pt/600 ml chicken or vegetable
   stock
2 garlic cloves, skinned and
   chopped
salt and freshly ground black
   pepper
2 oz/50 g freshly grated
   Parmesan
1 tbsp finely chopped parsley

Heat the oil in a casserole or large frying pan. Add the onion and sauté for 5 minutes, stirring occasionally so that it cooks evenly. Add the red peppers and cook for a further 5 minutes, then add the mushrooms and the rice. Stir until the rice is thoroughly coated with oil. Cook for 3 to 4 minutes, stirring occasionally, before pouring on the wine and stock. Stir in the garlic, salt and freshly ground black pepper. Simmer very gently for about 25 minutes stirring from time to time. Just before serving, stir in the Parmesan and the parsley.

Livi's liver

It sounds corny I know, and too good (or bad) to be true, but my sister Livi is one of the best cooks I know. She has a winning way with liver, and this is her recipe. You can use either lamb's or calf's liver – calf's liver is that bit more delicious, but lamb's liver is nearly as good. We can't buy calf's liver locally anyway, and there must be many people in Britain in the same boat. I like to serve this dish with creamy mashed potatoes and spinach.

Serves 6

---

2 lb/1 kg lamb's or calf's liver
2 oz/50 g butter
1 tbsp oil (I use sunflower)
1 rounded tbsp flour
¾ pt/450 ml chicken or vegetable stock
3 fl oz/75 ml medium dry sherry

3 tsp redcurrant jelly
salt and freshly ground black pepper
3 fl oz/75 ml soured cream
2 tbsp finely chopped parsley to garnish

Slice the liver very thinly, trimming away any bits of tube. Heat the butter and oil together in a frying pan. When it is frothy hot but before it turns brown, toss in the liver and cook for just long enough on each side to turn the liver golden brown – about half a minute each side. Do the liver in relays, so that the heat in the frying pan stays high. (If you try to cook all the liver at once, the heat in the frying pan is reduced and the liver stews rather than seals.) Keep the cooked liver warm in an ovenproof serving dish in a low oven.

Stir the flour into the remaining fat in the frying pan and cook for a minute or two. Then stir in the stock, sherry and redcurrant jelly. Stir until the sauce boils and the jelly melts. Season with salt and pepper, return the liver to the sauce and cook for 2 to 3 minutes. Just before serving, stir in the soured cream and sprinkle with the parsley.

Roast loin of pork with prune and red wine sauce

I love pork and, judging by its popularity when it is on the menu here, I am not alone. I love pork served cold as well as hot, and any leftover pork becomes a meal in itself served with salad, baked potatoes and chutney. For this main course dish I roast pork loin, and accompany it with a red wine and chopped prune sauce. The sauce doesn't take a minute to make, and its sharpness and sweetness go so very well with the rich pork meat.

Serves 6–8

---

a piece of loin of pork weighing about 4 lb/2 kg
FOR THE SAUCE
fat and juices from roasting the pork
1 medium onion, skinned and finely chopped
1 rounded tbsp flour

½ pt/300 ml red wine
½ pt/300 ml vegetable stock
salt and freshly ground black pepper
1 tbsp lemon juice
about 8 cooked prunes, stoned and quartered

Roast the pork in a hot oven – 425°F/220°C/Gas 7/top right oven in a 4 door Aga – for 40 minutes or so, then lower the temperature to 350°F/180°C/Gas 4/bottom right oven in a 4 door Aga and roast for a further hour. If the loin has crackling on top (sometimes they are sold without the crackling) rub it with salt before roasting.

To make the sauce, drain some of the fat and juices from the pork into a saucepan while the pork is cooking (there is no need to wait until the last minute to make the sauce). Add the onion to the saucepan. Cook over a moderate heat for 5 to 7 minutes, stirring occasionally, then stir in the flour. Cook for a further couple of minutes, then gradually add the red wine and vegetable stock, stirring

93

continuously until the sauce boils. Season with salt and pepper, and stir in the lemon juice. Finally add the prunes. Keep it warm until you are ready to serve and then pour it into a bowl or sauce boat.

When you are ready to carve the pork, first cut off the crackling to make carving easier. With a very sharp knife, cut the meat off the bone and then carve it into slices. I take the meat off the bone and carve it into thickish slices in the kitchen, arranging them on a warm serving dish. It speeds up the serving of the main course so that the food is hotter when your guests start to eat.

Ragoût of lamb with lemon and saffron

You can substitute turmeric for the saffron in this recipe if you like, but it makes the dish much more ordinary. Saffron is the ultimate spice, and in this very simple yet delicious ragoût it is combined with cinnamon and lemon to produce an exquisite flavour. I like to serve it with brown rice, with grated lemon rind and chopped parsley stirred through the rice, and puréed spinach, with a garnish of toasted pine kernels.

Serves 6

2½ lb/1.25 kg lamb, cut from the top of the leg, trimmed of fat and cut into 1 in/2.5 cm cubes
2 tbsp flour
4 tbsp oil (I use sunflower)
1 lemon
½ tsp powdered cinnamon

1 garlic clove, skinned and finely chopped
2 large pinches of saffron (or 2 rounded tsp turmeric)
salt and freshly ground black pepper
1 pt/600 ml chicken or vegetable stock

Toss the cubes of lamb in the flour so that they are evenly coated. Heat the oil in a frying pan and brown the lamb, a few pieces at a time. Keep the browned lamb warm in the oven as you go. Transfer the lamb to a casserole or ovenproof dish. Slice the lemon very thinly and lay the slices over the meat. Stir the cinnamon, garlic, saffron or turmeric, salt and pepper into the stock, and pour it over the meat. Cover the casserole or dish tightly with a lid and bake in a moderate oven – 350°F/180°C/Gas 4/bottom right oven in a 4 door Aga – for 1 hour. Like most casseroles, this tastes even better made a day in advance and reheated. To serve, bring the liquid just up to simmering point and simmer very gently for 15 minutes. If you are serving the casserole immediately after making, give it another 15 minutes' cooking time.

Coffee cream bavarois with Tia Maria

This creamy pud really is a dream. Any pudding which involves coffee or chocolate almost *has* to include coffee liqueur in its ingredients because it enhances the flavours so well. If coffee liqueur doesn't feature in your drinks cupboard I strongly advise you to invest in a bottle for cooking purposes.

Serves 6

½ pt/300 ml milk	½ oz/15 g gelatine powder
3 tbsp good instant coffee	¼ pt/150 ml Tia Maria
4 large egg yolks	½ pt/300 ml double cream
4 oz/100 g caster sugar	grated chocolate to finish

Put the milk in a saucepan and sprinkle on the coffee. Heat to scalding point. Beat the egg yolks in a bowl, gradually adding the caster sugar. Beat well, then pour some of the hot coffee milk on to the yolk mixture. Mix well and pour the yolk mixture into the saucepan with the rest of the coffee milk. Cook over a gentle heat, stirring all the time, until the coffee custard is thick enough to coat the back of a wooden spoon and leave a path when you draw your finger across it. Sprinkle the gelatine on the coffee liqueur (Tia Maria), let it soak up and then pour it into the hot custard, stirring until the gelatine has completely dissolved. Leave to cool completely, giving it an occasional stir to prevent a skin forming.

Whip the double cream. When the custard is quite cold, fold in the cream and pour the mixture into a glass or china serving bowl or individual dishes. Decorate with the grated chocolate.

Hot cross buns

Easter generally falls sometime during April. How I wish 'they' would peg the date of Easter once and for all! Home-made hot cross buns are just that little bit nicer than bought ones, and really require no great effort.

Makes about 2 dozen buns

FOR THE BUNS
2 tsp plus 3 oz/75 g caster sugar
½ pt/300 ml warm water
1 oz/25 g dried yeast
1 lb/500 g plain flour
1 lb/500 g wholemeal flour
2 tsp powdered mixed spice
1 tsp powdered cinnamon
1 tsp freshly grated nutmeg
1 tsp salt
½ pt/300 ml warm milk
2 large eggs, beaten

4 oz/100 g melted butter
4 oz/100 g mixed peel
4 oz/100 g raisins or currants
(I prefer raisins)
FOR THE CROSSES
2 oz/50 g flour mixed to a paste
of piping consistency with cold
water
FOR THE GLAZE
2 oz/50 g granulated sugar
2 tbsp water

Stir the 2 teaspoons of caster sugar into the warm water, and then stir in the yeast. Leave in a warm place until it has trebled in volume and is frothy. Sieve together the flours, 3 oz/75 g caster sugar and the spices and salt, into a large bowl and stand in a warm place. (The warmer all your ingredients are the quicker everything will rise.) When the yeast is well risen, stir it into the sieved dry ingredients together with the milk, the beaten eggs, the melted butter, and the mixed peel and raisins or currants. Mix thoroughly, turn on to a floured surface and knead well for 7 to 10 minutes. Put the dough back into the bowl, cover with a cloth and leave in a warm place for 45 minutes to 1 hour, or until the dough has doubled in size.

When the dough is about twice its original size, turn it on to the floured surface once more and knead again for about 5 minutes. Divide the dough into 24 evenly sized pieces, and knead each one into a bun shape. Arrange the buns well-spaced on greased baking trays, cover with a cloth and leave until the buns have doubled in size. When they are well risen, carefully pipe the shape of a cross on each bun with the flour and water paste. Take care just to rest the cross on top of the bun and not press the piping nozzle down into the dough. Bake in a hot oven – 425°F/220°C/Gas 7/top right oven in a 4 door Aga – for about 15 minutes, or until the buns are golden brown.

When the buns are cooked, transfer them to wire racks to cool. Make the glaze by dissolving the sugar in the water over a gentle heat, and then boiling fast for 1 minute. Brush the top of each bun with the glaze. To freeze the buns, put them uncovered on baking trays in the freezer. When frozen, pack in polythene bags. Thaw for 1–2 hours and reheat in a cool oven – 200°F/100°C/Gas ¼/top left oven in a 4 door Aga.

Orange and caramel profiteroles

The profiteroles in this recipe have a caramel glaze and are filled with a rich orange-flavoured crème pâtissière. If you prefer, you can fill them with whipped cream flavoured with grated orange rind and orange liqueur, but crème pâtissière does go so well with the crisp-topped profiteroles. Both the profiteroles and the crème pâtissière can be made· in the morning and assembled late in the afternoon for dinner the same evening. If you assemble them in the morning, they tend to be rather soggy by the evening.

Serves 6–8

FOR THE PROFITEROLES
4 oz/100 g butter, cut into pieces
½ pt/300 ml water
4 oz/100 g flour
1 tsp caster sugar
3–4 eggs
FOR THE CARAMEL
  COATING
3 oz/75 g granulated sugar

FOR THE ORANGE CRÈME
  PÂTISSIÈRE
½ pt/300 ml milk
3 egg yolks
1 l tsp cornflour, sieved
2 oz/50 g caster sugar
½ pt/300 ml double cream
3 fl oz/75 ml orange liqueur
grated rind of 2 oranges

Put the butter and water into a saucepan. Melt the butter over a low heat. Meanwhile sieve the flour and caster sugar. When the butter is all melted, bring the liquid just up to boiling point. Add the sieved flour and sugar all at once to the liquid, take the saucepan off the heat, and beat the flour into the butter and water until the paste which forms comes away from the sides of the saucepan. Leave to cool for 15 to 20 minutes, and then beat in the eggs, one by one. The mixture should be smooth and glossy but not too runny. If the eggs are large, 3 will probably be enough. Rinse a baking sheet with water, and then pipe blobs of choux pastry about 1 in/2.5 cm across onto it. Bake the profiteroles in a hot oven – 400°F/200°C/Gas 6/top right oven in a 4 door Aga – for 15 to 20 minutes, until the profiteroles are puffed up and golden brown, and quite firm to the touch. Remove the profiteroles from the baking sheet with a palette knife, and leave them to cool on a wire rack.

Melt the sugar for the caramel coating in a saucepan over a moderate heat, shaking the pan so that the sugar melts evenly (it will tend to burn in patches if it is left unwatched). When it is all melted, remove the pan from the heat. Dip the top of each profiterole in the hot caramel, being careful not to let any caramel drip on to your skin. Leave the coated profiteroles on the wire rack until you are ready to fill them with the orange crème pâtissière.

Put the milk for the crème pâtissière in a saucepan and heat to scalding point. Beat the egg yolks together with the sieved cornflour in a bowl. Gradually add the caster sugar. Beat well, then pour a little of the hot milk on to the yolk mixture. Mix well and pour back into the saucepan with the rest of the hot milk. Stir over a gentle heat until the custard thickens enough to coat the back of your wooden spoon fairly thickly – the consistency of double cream. Take the pan off the heat, and let the custard cool, stirring it from time to time to prevent a skin forming. Meanwhile whip the cream together with the orange liqueur and the grated orange rind. When the custard is quite cold, fold together the cream and the custard.

To assemble the profiteroles, slice each one in half, fill with a teaspoonful of orange crème pâtissière and put the two halves back together. Arrange on a serving dish.

Vanilla and coconut cream cake

Most people love cakes, but sadly we are all so calorie- and cholesterol-conscious that a good cake at tea time is a rare treat. You can get away with it by serving a particularly luxurious cake as a dinner party pudding, and this one fills the bill. It is a light and fluffy sponge cake, flavoured with vanilla and filled and covered with whipped cream. Toasted coconut is sprinkled and pressed all over the top and sides of the cake. Toasting enhances the flavour of coconut enormously.

Serves 6–8

FOR THE SPONGE CAKE	FOR THE FILLING AND
3 large eggs	TOPPING
3 oz/75 g caster sugar	*¾ pt/450 ml double cream*
1 tsp vanilla essence	*1 oz/25 g caster sugar*
3 oz/75 g self raising flour	*1 tsp vanilla essence*
	4 oz/100 g desiccated coconut,
	toasted and cooled

Butter and flour 2 × 7 in/18 cm sandwich tins. Line each tin with a disc of siliconized greaseproof paper. Break the eggs into a bowl and whisk, gradually adding the caster sugar. Whisk until the mixture is very thick, so thick that it will form peaks. This will take about 10 minutes of whisking. Whisk in the vanilla essence and sieve in the flour, folding it quickly and thoroughly into the egg mixture with a large metal spoon. Divide the mixture between the 2 cake tins, and bake in a moderate oven – 350°F/180°C/Gas 4/bottom right oven in a 4 door Aga – for 20 minutes, or until each cake is golden brown and just beginning to come away from the sides of the tin. Take them out of the oven, leave to cool for a minute in their tins, and then turn out onto a wire rack to cool.

Whip the cream for the filling until fairly stiff, adding the caster sugar and vanilla essence. Put one half of the cake on a serving plate, spread with cream and sprinkle with coconut. Sandwich with the top half of the cake. Spread the top and sides of the cake with the rest of the whipped cream. Sprinkle the cream with the coconut. Leave to stand until you are ready to serve it. A serrated knife will cut an egg sponge like this much more easily than a straight-bladed knife.

May

May is one of the prettiest months of the year, at least it is on Skye where we have wonderful wild flowers growing in abundance, and the trees and bushes are bright with their fresh new greenery. The bluebells carpet great chunks of ground for much of the month, and towards the middle of May the rhododendrons and azaleas start to come out too. Our rather dangerous single-track roads are covered with lambs and their suicidal mothers, who always cross roads on corners, never on straight bits of road where they can be seen by motorists.

Looking to the larder, May brings us the first salmon (although occasionally we get them in April) which seems to be more delicious than salmon at any other time – I can never work out whether this is because it is several months since we last tasted salmon, or whether it really does have a better taste at the start of the season. I think it probably *is* better fish.

The delicious early vegetables become more widely available as the month goes on, including the most delectable of all – asparagus. Several of the recipes in this chapter use asparagus.

First Courses

Asparagus soup
Asparagus timbales with hollandaise sauce
Cheese and tomato ring with crab
Marinated mushrooms and spring onions
Onion and cheese tart

Main Courses

Asparagus tart with cheese pastry
Monkfish baked with lime
Pork fillets with ginger and cream
Roast rack of lamb with minty hollandaise sauce
Sautéed chicken livers with green peppercorns

Puddings

Apple cake with cream cheese buttercream
Cherry fudge crumble
Cherry upside-down cake
Coffee and almond meringue cake

Asparagus soup

This soup makes a small amount of asparagus go a long and delicious way. It is very simple to make and velvety smooth in texture. I steam the asparagus tips and float them in each plateful of soup, along with a swirl of cream and a dusting of finely chopped parsley. You really only do justice to the asparagus if you use good chicken stock – don't be tempted to take a short cut via a stock cube!

Serves 6–8

---

1 lb/500 g asparagus, tips cut off and set aside, woody ends cut off and discarded

2 oz/50 g butter

2 medium onions, skinned and chopped

2 medium potatoes, peeled and chopped

2 pt/1.2 L chicken stock

salt and freshly ground black pepper

freshly grated nutmeg

cream and finely chopped parsley to garnish

Melt the butter and add the onions. Sauté for about 5 minutes, stirring occasionally so that the onion cooks evenly. Add the potatoes and cook for a further 7 to 10 minutes, stirring from time to time to prevent the onions and potatoes sticking. Chop the stalks of asparagus and add them to the pan. Pour on the chicken stock. Season with salt, pepper and grated nutmeg. Half-cover the saucepan with a lid, and bring the stock to simmering point. Simmer gently for half an hour, or until the pieces of asparagus and potato are tender. Meanwhile steam the asparagus tips until they are just tender.

When the soup is cooked, leave it to cool a little. Liquidize the soup and sieve it into a clean saucepan. Taste and adjust the seasoning. Reheat to serve. Garnish each plateful with a swirl of cream, a few asparagus tips and a sprinkling of finely chopped parsley.

Asparagus timbales
with hollandaise sauce

If you grow your own asparagus or have access to a plentiful supply (what bliss!), you may find yourself looking for different ways of cooking it. These timbales are an unusual dish, but easy to make.

Serves 8

---

1 lb/500 g asparagus
4 large eggs, beaten
½ pt/300 ml single cream
salt and freshly ground black
 pepper

freshly grated nutmeg
Hollandaise sauce *(see below)*

Butter 8 large ramekins. Steam the asparagus until it is tender, then blend it to a purée in either a food processor or a liquidizer. Sieve the purée (I know this sounds a fiddle, but it really doesn't take a second and is worth doing for a smooth and velvety textured purée). Return the purée to the food processor or liquidizer, and blend in first the beaten eggs and then the cream. Season with the salt, pepper and nutmeg. Spoon this mixture into the buttered ramekins, and stand the ramekins in a roasting tin. Pour hot water into the tin so that it comes halfway up the sides of the ramekins. Bake in a moderate oven – 350°F/180°C/Gas 4/bottom right oven in a 4 door Aga – for 25 minutes, or until the asparagus mixture feels quite firm to the touch. Take the tin out of the oven and take the ramekins out of the tin. Let them sit for 10 minutes before turning them out onto serving plates. To turn them out, run the tip of a knife round the edge of the timbale, cover the ramekin with a plate, invert both plate and ramekin and the timbale should come out easily and in one piece. Serve with *Hollandaise sauce* (see below).

105

Hollandaise sauce

4 tbsp white wine vinegar	*4 oz/100 g butter, cut in pieces*
5–6 peppercorns	*2 large egg yolks*
1 bayleaf	*a pinch of salt*
a slice of onion	

Put the wine vinegar, peppercorns, bayleaf and onion into a small saucepan and boil fast until the liquid has reduced to about a tablespoonful.

Strain the reduced liquid into a heatproof bowl and add a piece of butter about half the size of a walnut. Beat the yolks into the vinegar, one by one, and stand the bowl in a roasting tin of simmering water or rest it over a saucepan of simmering water. Whisking the mixture continuously, add the butter a piece at a time.

If the sauce looks as though it is about to curdle, take the bowl off the heat and whisk vigorously, adding a spoonful or two of the hot water over which the sauce has been thickening. This usually does the trick.

Once the sauce is made, serve it as soon as possible. Curdling is most likely to happen while the sauce is keeping warm waiting to be served.

Cheese and tomato ring with crab

This makes a good buffet dish as well as a convenient first course, because it is very decorative. It is also a good main course for lunch – in fact, a most versatile dish! The ring mould is made of tomatoes and cream cheese, flavoured with garlic and flecked with chopped parsley. The parsley provides a good colour contrast. The centre of the ring is filled with a mixture of fresh crab and rice, bound together with a little mayonnaise. The ring mould can be made a day in advance.

Serves 6–8

FOR THE RING MOULD
6 tomatoes, liquidized and
*   sieved, to give roughly ¾*
*   pt/450 ml purée*
1 oz/25 g powdered gelatine
½ pt/300 ml freshly-squeezed
*   orange juice*
salt and freshly ground black
*   pepper*
1 tbsp Worcestershire sauce
1 large garlic clove, skinned and
*   chopped*

2 tbsp finely chopped parsley
8 oz/250 g cream cheese (you can
*   substitute quark if you prefer)*
FOR THE FILLING
4 oz/100 g cooked brown rice
8 oz/250 g crab meat, white and
*   brown meats mixed*
2 tbsp mayonnaise
salt and freshly ground black
*   pepper*

Put the puréed tomatoes into a food processor or large bowl. Sprinkle the gelatine onto the orange juice in a saucepan and heat until the gelatine has dissolved completely, taking care not to let the orange juice boil. Add the seasonings, Worcestershire sauce, garlic, parsley and cream cheese to the puréed tomatoes. Blend or whisk, gradually pouring in the orange gelatine mixture, until you have a smooth mixture. Pour into a 9 in/22 cm ring mould, and leave in the refrigerator to set overnight. To turn out, dip the ring mould into a bowl of hot water for a few seconds. Cover with a plate, invert giving a gentle shake, and the cream cheese and tomato mould should come easily out of the tin.

Mix all the ingredients for the filling together well, and pile into the centre of the cream cheese and tomato ring mould. Leave in a cool place until you are ready to serve.

Marinated mushrooms and spring onions

This first course is both good and easy on the conscience for those who are counting calories. I like to serve it with warm brown bread or rolls, to mop up the marinade. You can also serve this as an accompanying salad for a main course. It has to be made at least 12 hours in advance.

Serves 6

---

1 lb/500 g button mushrooms, wiped and with their stalks cut level with the caps
2 tbsp olive oil
½ pt/300 ml dry white wine
1 bunch of spring onions, trimmed and finely sliced
½ tsp cumin
freshly ground black pepper (I like lots)
2 pinches of salt
a dash of Tabasco
1 tbsp finely chopped parsley

Put the olive oil, white wine, spring onions, cumin, pepper, salt and Tabasco into a saucepan. Bring to the boil and simmer gently, with the saucepan uncovered, until the liquid has reduced by about a quarter. Add the mushrooms to the saucepan, cover with a lid and simmer for 5 minutes, shaking the pan from time to time. Then, with a slotted spoon, remove the mushrooms from the liquid and put them into a serving dish. Boil the liquid fast in the saucepan, uncovered, for a further 3 to 5 minutes. Pour the marinade over the mushrooms, and mix in the chopped parsley. Leave to cool completely before serving. You can make this a day in advance and keep it in the refrigerator, but take it out a couple of hours before serving to allow it to come to room temperature.

Onion and cheese tart

This tart makes a perfect first course or a light main course for lunch or supper and is lovely to take on a picnic. Onions and cheese are meant for each other – simple but delicious!

Serves 6–8

FOR THE PASTRY
4 oz/100 g butter, hard from the refrigerator and cut into pieces
6 oz/175 g flour
½ oz/15 g icing sugar
salt and pepper
FOR THE FILLING
4 medium to large onions, skinned and very thinly sliced
3 tbsp oil (I use sunflower)

2 large eggs plus 2 large egg yolks
¾ pt/450 ml milk or milk and cream mixed
salt and freshly ground black pepper
freshly grated nutmeg
4 oz/100 g mature Cheddar, grated
finely chopped parsley to garnish

If you have a food processor, process all the ingredients until the mixture is like fine breadcrumbs. If not, sieve the flour, sugar and salt into a bowl. Rub in the pieces of butter with your fingertips until the mixture resembles fine breadcrumbs. Pat the mixture round the sides and base of a 9 in/22 cm flan dish. Put the dish into the refrigerator for at least half an hour before baking blind in a moderate oven – 350°F/180°C/Gas 4/bottom right oven in a 4 door Aga. Bake for 20 to 25 minutes, until the pastry is golden brown. Take out of the oven.

Alternatively make a conventional shortcrust pastry flan shell and bake blind until golden brown.

Heat the oil and add the onions. Sauté gently for 25 minutes, stirring occasionally to prevent the onions sticking and to make sure they cook evenly. When they are cooked, spread them over the base of the pastry shell. Beat together the eggs, egg yolks, milk or milk and cream, salt, pepper, nutmeg and cheese. Pour this mixture over the onions in the flan case, and bake in a moderate oven – 350°F/180°C/Gas 4/bottom right oven in a 4 door Aga – for 15 to 20 minutes, until the filling is just set. Allow to cool a little, and dust with finely chopped parsley if you like before serving.

Asparagus tart with cheese pastry

This makes a good vegetarian main course and is also ideal for a picnic. The cheesy pastry complements the delicate taste of the asparagus filling, without overpowering it.

Serves 6

FOR THE PASTRY
3 oz/75 g butter, hard from the
   refrigerator, cut into pieces
3 oz/75 g mature Cheddar,
   grated
1 rounded tsp dry mustard
   powder
5 oz/150 g flour
salt and pepper
a dash of Tabasco

FOR THE FILLING
1 lb/500 g fresh asparagus,
   unchewable ends trimmed off
   and stalks steamed until just
   tender
2 large eggs plus 3 large egg
   yolks
¾ pt/450 ml single cream (you
   can use milk if you prefer, but
   it doesn't really do justice to
   the dish)
salt and freshly ground black
   pepper
freshly grated nutmeg

If you have a food processor, process all the ingredients together until the mixture resembles breadcrumbs. If not, sieve the flour, mustard and salt into a bowl. Mix in the cheese, pepper and Tabasco. Rub in the pieces of butter with your fingertips until the mixture resembles fine breadcrumbs. Pat the mixture round the sides and base of a 9 in/22 cm flan dish, and put the dish into the refrigerator for at least half an hour before baking in a moderate oven – 350°F/180°C/Gas 4/bottom right oven in a 4 door Aga – for 20 to 25 minutes, until the pastry is golden brown.

Arrange the steamed asparagus in the flan, with the tips pointing towards the centre.

In a bowl, beat together the eggs, egg yolks, cream or milk, salt, pepper and nutmeg. Pour this over the asparagus, and bake in a moderate oven – 350°F/180°C/Gas 4/bottom right oven in a 4 door Aga – for 15 to 20 minutes, until the filling is just set. Serve warm or cold.

Monkfish baked with lime

I like to serve this baked monkfish with spicy brown rice – boiled rice flavoured with cumin and cardamom – and peppers sautéed in olive oil and garlic. I love the combination of flavours. Monkfish is an excellent fish, although rather expensive these days. Its white dense texture and total absence of big bones make very good eating.

Serves 6

2 lb/1 kg monkfish tail, weighed when cut off the central cartilage-like bone	1 celery stick
	10 peppercorns
	1 tsp salt
shredded rind and juice of 2 limes	1 pt/600 ml water
2 onions, skinned and halved	wedges of lime to serve

Trim the membrane off the outside of the monkfish. Put the shredded lime rind into a saucepan and cover with water. Bring to the boil and simmer for 5 minutes. Drain and put to one side for a garnish.

Put the onions, celery, peppercorns, salt and water into a saucepan, cover with a lid, and boil for 5 minutes.

Arrange the monkfish in an ovenproof dish, pour over the lime juice and the hot, strained vegetable stock. Cover the dish with either a lid or foil, and bake in a moderate oven – 350°F/180°C/Gas 4/bottom right oven in a 4 door Aga – for 35 minutes, or until the fish is cooked through. Test after 25 minutes – if your piece comes from a bigger fish, it will need longer cooking time than smaller fillets. When it is cooked drain it well and arrange it on a bed of cooked rice which has a teaspoon each of cumin and crushed cardamom stirred through it. Sprinkle the shredded lime rind over the surface. Serve with wedges of lime and with a juicy vegetable, such as the *Three-pepper salad* (see page 145), which complement it so well.

Pork fillets with ginger and cream

This simple but delicious dish makes a perfect main course. It is rather rich, so precede it with something fairly plain – the *Marinated mushrooms with spring onions* (see page 108) would be ideal. I like to serve it with creamy mashed potatoes and a green vegetable, such as spinach.

Serves 6

---

3 large pork fillets	2 tbsp lemon juice
2 tbsp flour, seasoned with salt and freshly ground black pepper	2 fl oz/50 ml water
	1/4 pt/150 ml soured cream
2 oz/50 g butter	3 pieces of preserved ginger, drained of their syrup and chopped
1 tbsp oil (I use sunflower)	
1/4 pt/150 ml green ginger wine	

Slice each of the fillets lengthwise but not right through. Flatten them out and beat them into escalopes. Cut each escalope in half across the centre, making 6 escalopes. Coat the escalopes with seasoned flour.

Heat the butter and oil in a frying pan. Sauté the escalopes until they are browned on each side and cooked through, about 4 to 5 minutes. Remove them from the pan and keep them warm on a serving dish in a low oven. Pour into the frying pan the ginger wine, lemon juice and water, and stir well. Let it boil away until the liquid has reduced by half, then stir in the soured cream and the chopped ginger. Boil again until the sauce has thickened, then pour it over the cooked escalopes and serve. It will keep warm satisfactorily for about half an hour before serving.

Roast rack of lamb with minty hollandaise sauce

A luxurious main course which combines the spring flavours of lamb and fresh young mint in a simple way. I like to serve with it a dish of baked sliced potatoes and onions and a green vegetable – perhaps very small new courgettes about finger size. If you like, you can buy some paper frills for dressing up the lamb after cooking.

Serves 6

2 racks of lamb, prepared by your butcher, chined, and with the top 1½ in/3.5 cm meat cut away from the bones
MINTY HOLLANDAISE SAUCE
5 tablespoons white wine vinegar
6 peppercorns

a slice of onion
1 bayleaf
4 egg yolks (from large eggs)
8 oz/250 g butter, cut in small pieces
a couple of pinches of salt
2 tbsp chopped mint, preferably applemint

113

Make sure that the outer skin is trimmed off the racks, leaving the fat exposed. If your butcher hasn't done this, do so yourself. An easy method is to put the racks of lamb into the deep freezer for half an hour, then strip off the papery skin – it will come away easily without you having to cut it off – inevitably some of the fat will come with it.

Roast the lamb for 20 minutes in a hot oven – 400°F/200°C/Gas 6/top right oven in a 4 door Aga – then lower the temperature to 350°F/180°C/Gas 4/bottom right oven in a 4 door Aga, and cook for a further 20 minutes. Keep warm.

Make the *Minty hollandaise sauce* as you would the classic hollandaise sauce on page 106, stirring in the chopped mint and salt to taste when all the butter has been added. Serve, in a sauceboat or bowl, with the rack of lamb.

Sautéed chicken livers with green peppercorns

The combination of green peppercorns and chicken livers is so good. I serve it on a bed of plain boiled brown rice, with either a green vegetable or a salad to accompany it.

Serves 6

1½ lb/750 g chicken livers
2 oz/50 g butter
1 tbsp oil (I use sunflower)
3 onions, skinned and very thinly sliced

1 garlic clove, skinned and finely chopped
¼ pt/150 ml medium dry sherry
2 tsp green peppercorns, drained of their brine
salt

Pick over the chicken livers, throwing out any green bits – these taste bitter when cooked. Chop them roughly. Heat

114

the butter and oil together in a frying pan. Add the onion and sauté for 5 to 7 minutes, stirring occasionally so that it cooks evenly. Add the chopped garlic and pour on the sherry. Let it bubble away for about 3 minutes, by which time the liquid will have virtually evaporated. Over a fairly high heat, add the chicken livers to the frying pan. Add the peppercorns and cook, stirring from time to time, until the livers are just pink in the middle, about 5 to 7 minutes. Season to taste with salt. Serve on a bed of boiled brown rice, topped with a dusting of parsley.

Apple cake with cream cheese buttercream

This rather gooey cake definitely falls into the category of pudding rather than cake, because it really is too messy to eat with your fingers – surely a good advertisement in itself!

Serves 6–8

FOR THE APPLE CAKE
½ pt/300 ml apple purée
6 oz/175 g soft brown sugar
¼ pt/150 ml sunflower oil
2 eggs, beaten
8 oz/250 g self-raising flour
1 rounded tsp cinnamon

1 rounded tsp ground ginger
3 oz/75 g raisins
FOR THE BUTTERCREAM
4 oz/100 g cream cheese
4 oz/100 g butter
8 oz/250 g icing sugar, sieved
1 tsp vanilla essence

You can make the apple purée simply by simmering 1 lb/500 g chopped cooking apples with a very little water and sugar until soft, and then liquidizing and sieving them to a smooth purée.

Mix the purée together with the soft brown sugar, the

sunflower oil and the beaten eggs. Sieve in the self-raising flour, the cinnamon and the ginger, and mix well. Add the raisins and mix again.

Butter and lightly flour a 9 in/22 cm cake tin. Line the base with siliconized greaseproof paper. Pour in the mixture. Bake in a moderate oven – 350°F/180°C/Gas 4/ bottom right oven in a 4 door Aga – for 35 to 40 minutes. Allow to cool in the tin for 10 minutes, then turn out on to a serving dish to cool completely.

For the buttercream, beat together the cream cheese, butter and icing sugar, and add the vanilla essence. Spread over the top and sides of the cooked apple cake.

Cherry fudge crumble

The only fiddle with cooking cherries is removing their stones, but it really is worth the effort. This easy pudding is greatly enjoyed by child and adult alike. The crumble is made not of flour, but of porridge oats mixed with butter and demerara sugar. It gives a rather flapjack-like crumble – quite delicious.

Serves 6

1½ lb/750 g cherries, stoned	5 oz/150 g demerara sugar
5 oz/150 g butter	5 oz/150 g porridge oats

Arrange the cherries in an ovenproof dish. Melt the butter in a saucepan and stir in the sugar and the porridge oats. Spread this mixture over the cherries. Bake in a moderate oven – 350°F/180°C/Gas 4/bottom right oven in a 4 door Aga – for 30 minutes, then either raise the oven temperature or put the dish under a heated grill just to toast the top of the pudding, for 4 to 5 minutes – watch that it doesn't

burn. Serve warm, with cream if you like, which I don't
but Godfrey most certainly does!

Cherry upside-down cake

Cherries have such a short season that it seems a pity not
to make the most of them. I think perhaps that cherries are
nicest of all eaten just as they are, but they are also very
good cooked, either as a filling for pies or tarts or in
puddings. This pudding is also delicious served cold as a
cake.

Serves 6–8

---

1 lb/500 g cherries, stoned
5 oz/150 g soft brown sugar
3 oz/75 g softened butter
3 large eggs

5 oz/150 g self-raising flour,
  sieved
a few drops of vanilla essence

Butter and flour an 8 in/20 cm cake tin. Line the base with
siliconized greaseproof paper. Arrange the cherries over
the bottom of the prepared tin, and sprinkle 2 oz/50 g of
the soft brown sugar over them. Beat the butter in a bowl,
gradually adding the rest of the soft brown sugar, until the
mixture is pale and fluffy. Beat in the eggs, one by one,
alternately with the flour. Finally beat in the vanilla
essence. Pour the cake mixture over the cherries in the
cake tin. Bake in a moderate oven – 350°F/180°C/Gas
4/bottom right oven in a 4 door Aga – for 25 to 30 minutes,
or until the cake is risen and golden brown, and just
beginning to come away from the sides of the tin. Leave to
cool for a minute in the tin, then turn it out onto a serving
dish, and serve warm as a pudding. Accompany it with a
mixture of whipped cream, yoghurt and brown sugar, if
you like, or just with whipped cream.

117

Coffee and almond meringue cake

Now this is a *very* sweet and luscious pudding, a grand finale for a dinner party, and right up my street. The nuts in the meringue provide a good contrasting crunch. The coffee icing on top may be too sweet for some – if you don't like the sound of it, just don't do it, but it is awfully good.

Serves 6–8

FOR THE MERINGUE
4 egg whites
8 oz/250 g caster sugar
3 oz/75 g flaked almonds, toasted and cooled
FOR THE FILLING
½ pt/300 ml double cream, whipped

FOR THE COFFEE ICING
2–3 oz/50–75 g sieved icing sugar
2 tbsp strong black coffee
2 oz/50 g flaked almonds, toasted and cooled

Line 2 baking trays with siliconized greaseproof paper, and draw a 8–9 in/20–22 cm circle on each sheet of paper.

Whisk the egg whites until stiff, then gradually add the caster sugar, whisking all the time until the sugar is all incorporated. Fold in the flaked almonds. Divide the meringue mixture between the 2 drawn circles on the lined trays, and smooth the meringue tidily into circles. Bake in a moderate oven – 350°F/180°C/Gas 4/bottom right oven in a 4 door Aga – for 5 minutes, then lower the temperature to 200°F/110°C/Gas ½ and bake for 1½ to 2 hours, until quite firm. Cool on a wire rack.

Whip the cream for the filling 2 or 3 hours before dinner. Spread one half of the meringue cake with cream and sandwich the two halves together. Mix the icing sugar and coffee together thoroughly. Spread over the cake and sprinkle the flaked almonds around the edge of the icing. The cake is now ready to serve. Cut it with a serrated knife rather than a straight-bladed knife.

June

June on Skye is wonderful – providing the weather is good! When guests book they occasionally ask me which month can be counted on for fine weather. I can guarantee anything except the weather. There is no month in the year here on Skye when you can safely predict fine weather, but the compensation in this part of Scotland is that the weather can change dramatically fast. You can wake up to a day where the rain is falling in sheets and the mist is so low it is hanging around shoulder level, but by lunchtime the sun will be blazing in a cloudless blue sky. It does, of course, work the other way too! If we have fine weather in June – and there's a 50-50 chance! – we also have very short hours of darkness. We have photographs taken by guests outside our front door at midnight and it is really twilight, and with the bright moon slanting down across the water it is just so beautiful. June sees the rhododendrons and azaleas in full bloom in this part of the world, and it is one of the most beautiful months in the year.

New vegetables are in full spate in the kitchen, and Pete and I are full of inspiration for summery food for the menus. Strawberries are in their prime – we are lucky, and have ours grown organically for us nearby – and feature regularly on the daily menu.

First Courses

Baked courgettes with red pepper purée
Gazpacho
Smoked mackerel and walnut pâté
Avocado terrine
Tomato and garlic cheesecake

Main Courses

Cold roast duck in orange, grapefruit and honey jelly
Collops of pork fillet with cream, brandy and apple sauce
Smoked chicken and mango salad with curried mayonnaise
Salmon kedgeree with hollandaise sauce
Stuffed peppers

Puddings

Brown sugar meringues with lemon and elderflower curd
Fresh lime sorbet
Strawberry and orange tart
Strawberries in orange jelly
Strawberries in elderflower syrup

Baked courgettes with red pepper purée

This first course combines some of the best of the savoury summer flavours – courgettes, red peppers, olive oil and garlic. It can be eaten hot or cold, and I like to serve brown rolls or bread with it, to mop up the red pepper purée. It also makes a good accompanying vegetable for a main course.

Serves 6–8

FOR THE COURGETTES
2 lb/1 kg courgettes, as tiny as
   possible
2 tbsp olive oil
1 garlic clove, skinned and very
   finely chopped
salt and freshly ground black
   pepper
a sprig of thyme

FOR THE RED PEPPER
   PURÉE
3 tbsp olive oil
1 onion, skinned and chopped
4 red peppers, halved, deseeded
   and chopped
1 garlic clove, skinned and
   chopped
salt and freshly ground black
   pepper
chopped parsley to garnish

Trim the courgettes. If they are very tiny, just cut their ends off. If they are a bit larger, halve them lengthways. If they are large, slice them diagonally into pieces. Pour the olive oil into an ovenproof dish, add the courgettes and stir them around so that they are coated in oil. Add the chopped garlic, salt, pepper and thyme, and mix well. Cover the dish with a lid or a piece of foil and bake in a hot oven – 400°F/200°C/Gas 6/top right oven in a 4 door Aga – for 25 minutes, or until the courgettes are tender when pierced with the point of a knife.

To make the purée, heat the olive oil in a saucepan and add the onion, red peppers, garlic, salt and pepper. Cook, stirring occasionally, for 30 minutes, or until the red pepper is really soft. Liquidize, and pour the thick purée over the cooked courgettes. Dust with chopped parsley and serve hot or cold.

Gazpacho

Gazpacho is one of my most favourite cold soups. It is so refreshing on a hot summer evening, and it is such a convenient first course because it can be made entirely on the previous day and kept in a covered bowl in the refrigerator. Everybody who makes gazpacho has their own variation on the same theme. For those of you who haven't made it, this is how I do it, but you can adjust the quantities to suit your own taste. Basically, it is a combination of any or all of tomatoes, cucumber, onion and garlic and peppers, blended with olive oil, wine vinegar and breadcrumbs.

Serves 6–8

1½ lb/750 g tomatoes, skinned, deseeded and chopped (2 tomatoes extra finely chopped and reserved for garnish)

3 slices of white bread, crusts cut off

¼ pt/150 ml olive oil

3 tbsp red wine vinegar

1 cucumber, peeled, deseeded and chopped (a 2 in/5 cm chunk finely diced and reserved for garnish)

2 red peppers and 1 green pepper, deseeded and chopped (2 tbsp mixed, chopped peppers reserved for garnish)

1 garlic clove, skinned and chopped

1 small onion, skinned and chopped

½–¾ pt/300–450 ml cold water

salt and freshly ground black pepper

a handful of parsley, a few basil leaves, and 2 tsp finely chopped chives to garnish

---

Liquidize the tomatoes. Put the bread into a bowl and pour over it the olive oil and vinegar, and liquidized tomatoes. Leave until the bread is soggy, and then liquidize together with all the rest of the ingredients, except those which have been kept on one side for garnishing. Blend until smooth, adding cold water until the soup is the consistency of pouring cream. Pour the soup into a bowl, cover and put in the refrigerator for several hours or overnight.

Mix the reserved tomatoes, cucumber, peppers, and the parsley, basil leaves and chives together thoroughly and add a spoonful to each serving of gazpacho.

Smoked mackerel and walnut pâté

The toasted walnuts provide a good texture in this pâté, and their flavour goes very well with the rich smoked mackerel. The pâté is improved by a lot of lemon. Although I'm suggesting it here as a first course, which is where you usually find pâtés, I also like to serve it with granary bread or toast and a salad as a main course for lunch.

Serves 6–8

1½ lb/750 g smoked mackerel, skin and as many bones as you can find removed
1 garlic clove, skinned and chopped
juice of 2 lemons and grated rind of 1 lemon

1 tbsp Worcestershire sauce
freshly ground black pepper
10 oz/300 g cream cheese
2 oz/50 g walnuts, toasted for 5–10 minutes, cooled and broken into bits

---

Put the smoked mackerel into a blender or food processor, and add the chopped garlic, lemon juice, Worcestershire sauce and black pepper. Blend until smooth. Add the cream cheese and blend again until all is thoroughly incorporated. Turn the pâté into a bowl and fold in the cooled walnut bits. Don't add them to the pâté at the blending stage or they become ground to the same texture as the pâté.

This pâté keeps well in a covered bowl, in the refrigerator for 3 to 4 days.

Avocado terrine

This terrine is very easy to make, and it makes a wonderfully savoury and decorative first course for a dinner party. Or it could be a vegetarian main course, too, for a summer party, if you replace the chicken stock with vegetable stock. Through the middle of the terrine are avocado halves, which look very attractive as the terrine is sliced. Serve with a tomato and basil salad – it contrasts well with the pale green of the terrine and the flavours are excellent together – and warm brown rolls.

Serves 8

---

6 medium avocados
1/4 pt/150 ml dry white wine
1/2 pt/300 ml chicken stock
3 sachets gelatine (1 1/2 oz/40 g)
1 large garlic clove, skinned and chopped
3 tbsp lemon juice, plus some to brush the avocado halves with

a dash of Tabasco
1 tbsp Worcestershire sauce
salt and freshly ground black pepper
1/2 pt/300 ml double cream, whipped or you can substitute mayonnaise, if you happen to be on a dairy-free diet

---

Line a 9 in/22 cm loaf or terrine tin with clingfilm, pressing it carefully into the corners with your fingertips. Cut each avocado in half, and carefully remove the skin from the back of the 3 most perfect halves – if they are properly ripe it should come away easily. Cut the tops off the three halves and set aside with the unpeeled halves. Brush the 3 perfect halves with lemon juice to prevent the flesh turning brown. Scoop the flesh out of the other avocado halves into a liquidizer or food processor, taking care not to miss the brightest green and most nutritious flesh, which lies next to the skin. Put the white wine and chicken stock together in a saucepan and sprinkle on the gelatine. Heat gently until the gelatine is completely dissolved. Add this to the avocado flesh in the blender or processor, and add the chopped garlic, lemon juice, Tabasco, Worcestershire sauce, salt and pepper. Blend until you have a very smooth purée. Then add the whipped cream to the mixture and blend again until the cream is thoroughly incorporated. Pour half the purée into the prepared loaf or terrine tin. Arrange the avocado halves nose to tail along the centre of the tin, and pour the rest of the purée on top. Cover with clingfilm, and put the tin into the refrigerator for several hours to set.

Just before serving, take the tin out of the refrigerator, dip it into a bowl of hot water for a very few seconds and turn it out on to a serving plate. Peel the clingfilm off the terrine. Cut it into slices about ½ in/1 cm thick. Serve with a tomato salad which has plenty of torn-up fresh basil leaves mixed in. If you can't get fresh basil, mix 2 teaspoons of pesto (see page 68) into the vinaigrette dressing for the salad.

Tomato and garlic cheesecake

A cheesecake is usually associated with the pudding course of lunch or dinner, but this savoury version makes a delicious first course – or indeed a main course for a vegetarian meal if you replace the chicken stock with vegetable stock. In this recipe, the filling is tomato and garlic, flavoured with basil – that herb which must have been created specially to enhance the flavour of tomato. You can use any savoury biscuits for the base – I like to use wholemeal bran biscuits, because they provide a good and crunchy contrast to the smooth filling. Some savoury biscuits will go soft once the filling is poured on.

Serves 6–8

FOR THE BASE
12 oz/350 g wholemeal bran biscuits
3 oz/75 g butter, melted
1 garlic clove, very finely chopped
FOR THE FILLING
2 sachets gelatine (1 oz/25 g)
½ pt/300 ml chicken or vegetable stock

8 tomatoes, skinned, liquidized and sieved (their purée should measure about 1 pt/600 ml)
8 oz/250 g cream cheese (you can substitute quark if you like)
1 garlic clove, skinned and chopped
a few leaves of fresh basil
salt and freshly ground black pepper
finely chopped parsley and chives

Mash the biscuits to crumbs either in a food processor or with a rolling pin. Mix with the butter and garlic. Press round the sides and base of an 8 in/20 cm flan dish. Bake in a moderate oven – 350°F/180°C/Gas 4/bottom right oven in a 4 door Aga – for 15 minutes. Take out of the oven and set aside to cool.

Sprinkle the gelatine on the stock in a saucepan. Dissolve the gelatine granules in the stock over a gentle heat, taking care that the liquid does not boil. Put the tomato pureé into a blender or food processor together with the cream cheese, garlic, basil, salt and pepper, and blend until smooth. Pour in the gelatine and chicken stock, and blend again. Pour into the baked flan case. Leave to set. Garnish before serving with finely chopped parsley and chives, sprinkled in the middle or around the edges of the cheesecake.

Cold roast duck in orange, grapefruit and honey jelly

I like all meats just as much cold as hot, or even more. Cold roast duck is delicious, with the cooked meat stripped off the carcass and set in this soft jelly. The sharp taste of the jelly contrasts well with the richness of the duck, with just enough sweetness from the honey to take the edge off the citrus fruits. This is an ideal dish for a summer buffet.

Serves 6

---

3 ducks, each weighing 4–5 lb/2–2.5 kg
FOR THE JELLY
2 oranges
1 grapefruit
½ pt/300 ml red wine vinegar
2 tbsp thick honey
¾ pt/450 ml chicken or giblet stock

3 l tbsp arrowroot (if you have difficulty finding arrowroot, it is always available in chemist's shops)
salt and freshly ground black pepper
2 tbsp chopped chives for garnish

Put the ducks in a roasting tin and roast in a hot oven – 400°F/200°C/Gas 6/top right oven in a 4 door Aga – for 1½ hours. Then take them out of the oven and allow to cool, before stripping the meat from the carcasses. Leave the legs whole.

Pare the rind from the oranges and the grapefruit with a potato peeler, and shred the rind finely. Cut into evenly sized pieces and put into a saucepan. Cover with cold water. Bring the water to the boil and simmer gently for 10 minutes. Drain, and set the rinds on one side. With a serrated knife cut the pith off the oranges and the grapefruit, and, cutting towards the centre of each fruit, cut out the segments into a bowl. Set aside.

Put the wine vinegar and the honey into a saucepan and boil fast until well reduced to a caramel-like syrup. Add the stock and any juices which have collected in the bowl with the segmented fruit, and boil fast for 5 minutes. Slake the arrowroot with a little water in a bowl, then mix in a little of the hot sauce. Pour the arrowroot mixture into the saucepan and stir over a moderate heat until the sauce boils. Boil for a minute, then take the saucepan off the heat, season with the salt and pepper, and leave to cool. When it is cold, stir in the cooked, shredded rinds and the fruit segments, and mix together with the duck meat. Arrange on a serving dish, and sprinkle the chopped chives over the surface to serve.

Collops of pork fillet with cream, brandy and apple sauce

This rather rich dish is perfect for a dinner party in June – or at any other time of the year! Pork fillet is such a tender meat and the flavour of the cream and brandy, with the edge just taken off their richness by the apples, complements it very well. I like to serve this dish with new potatoes and fresh peas with applemint, or mangetout.

Serves 6

---

4 pork fillets, each trimmed and cut into 4, making 16 rounds, or collops, each about 1½ in/ 3.5 cm thick, flatten them with a rolling pin
2 eating apples
juice of a lemon

1 tbsp oil (I use sunflower)
2 oz/50 g butter
3 fl oz/75 ml brandy
½ pt/300 ml double cream
salt and freshly ground black pepper
finely chopped parsley

Peel, core and slice the apples, and cover them with the lemon juice to prevent them going brown.

Heat the oil and butter together in a large shallow pan, such as a frying pan. Brown and cook the collops of pork fillet in the pan, allowing about 4 to 5 minutes on each side, turning them fairly frequently to prevent them browning too much. Stick a knife into one to see if it is cooked. When they are cooked, pour over the brandy and ignite it with a match. After a few seconds, pour on the cream. Drain the apple slices and add them to the pork and cream, with the seasoning. Cook all together for about 3 minutes. Arrange the pieces of pork on a warmed serving dish, with the apple slices down the centre, and the creamy sauce poured over the top. Sprinkle with finely chopped parsley and serve.

The apple slices still have a crunch to them, giving a good contrast in texture as well as adding their flavour to the dish.

Smoked chicken and mango salad with curried mayonnaise

In this recipe the smoked chicken is chopped into bite-sized pieces along with the mango flesh. The delicious mango taste is accentuated by the addition of lime juice, and then combined with the chicken and the curried mayonnaise. It makes an easy, delicious and slightly unusual chicken salad – a perfect main course for a summer party. I like to serve it with a rice salad – perhaps brown rice mixed with fresh peas and toasted flaked almonds.

2 smoked chickens, each weighing about 3–3½ lb/1.5–1.75 kg	1 tsp honey or sugar
	1 garlic clove, skinned and chopped
4 mangoes, skinned	1 rounded tsp curry powder
juice of 1 lime	freshly ground pepper
FOR THE CURRIED MAYONNAISE	¼–½ pt/150–300 ml oil (I use sunflower or a mixture of olive and sunflower)
1 egg plus 1 egg yolk	
1 l tsp mustard powder	3 tbsp wine vinegar
½ tsp salt	2 tbsp boiling water

Put the egg, the yolk, mustard powder, salt, honey, garlic, curry powder and pepper into a food processor or blender and liquidize. Then gradually add the oil, a drop at a time to start with. When all the oil is incorporated, add the wine vinegar – use more or less to suit your taste. Finally blend in the boiling water, which makes the mayonnaise thinner and helps it to coat the chicken and mangoes.

Strip the chicken meat off the carcasses, chopping it into bite-sized pieces. Cut the mango flesh off the stones, chop it and mix with the lime juice. Combine the chopped chicken and mango flesh. Fold the curried mayonnaise into the mixture and arrange the chicken salad on a serving plate, perhaps with shredded lettuce around the sides and chopped parsley and chives scattered over.

Salmon kedgeree with hollandaise sauce

It was my sister Livi's brilliant idea to serve kedgeree with *Hollandaise sauce*. If you have access to fresh salmon during the summer you may have some left over. Salmon kedgeree is a delicious way of using up leftover salmon, but when it is served with *Hollandaise sauce* (see below) it becomes a dish worthy of any dinner party.

Serves 6–8

10–12 oz/300–350 g salmon, flaked, with any skin and bones removed
2 oz/50 g butter
1 medium onion, skinned and finely chopped
1 rounded tsp curry powder
¼ pt/150 ml single cream

8 oz/250 g cooked brown rice
3 hard-boiled eggs, chopped
salt and freshly ground black pepper
freshly grated nutmeg
2 rounded tbsp finely chopped parsley
Hollandaise sauce *(see below)*

Melt the butter in a frying pan and add the finely chopped onion. Sauté, stirring, for about 5 minutes, then stir in the curry powder. Cook for another couple of minutes, then stir in the cream. Mix together the cream mixture, the salmon, rice, hard-boiled eggs, and season with salt and freshly ground black pepper.

Reheat the kedgeree. Fork the finely chopped parsley through the kedgeree and serve.

Hollandaise sauce

---

5 tbsp wine vinegar
6 peppercorns
a slice of onion
1 bayleaf

3 large egg yolks
6 oz/175 g butter, cut in small bits

Put the wine vinegar, peppercorns, slice of onion and bayleaf together in a saucepan and reduce by half. Strain into an ovenproof bowl – a pyrex bowl is fine. Add 1 piece

131

of butter, and beat in the egg yolks. Put the bowl over a saucepan of simmering water, and whisk in the butter, a piece at a time, whisking until the sauce is thick. Serve immediately.

Stuffed peppers

I allow two peppers per person for this dish, preferably one red and one yellow – I find red and yellow peppers so much nicer than green. In this recipe the peppers are simmered in boiling water and stuffed with a mixture of finely chopped vegetables sautéed in olive oil and then combined with aduki beans, tomato purée, thyme and garlic. The stuffed peppers are then baked. They taste delicious either hot or cold.

Serves 6

12 peppers (6 red and 6 yellow if possible)

12 oz/350 g aduki beans, soaked for several hours or overnight

3 tbsp olive oil

2 medium onions, skinned and finely chopped

2 celery sticks, trimmed and thinly sliced

1 garlic clove, skinned and finely chopped

2 courgettes, wiped, ends cut off and finely diced

4 tsp tomato purée

1 sprig of thyme, chopped or 2 pinches of dried thyme

salt and freshly ground black pepper

Drain the aduki beans, put them into a saucepan and cover with fresh water. Bring to the boil and simmer for 1 hour.

Meanwhile cut the tops off the peppers and dice. Scoop out and discard the seeds. Cut a thin slice from the base of each pepper so they will stand up. Put the peppers in a large saucepan with cold water to cover them. Bring to the boil and simmer gently for 15 minutes. Drain. Grease an ovenproof dish with a tablespoon of olive oil and arrange the peppers in it.

Heat the olive oil and sauté the onions for 5 minutes, stirring from time to time. Add the celery, garlic, diced pepper tops and courgettes. Sauté for about 10 minutes, stirring occasionally so that the vegetables cook evenly. Stir in the tomato purée, the thyme and the salt and pepper. Drain the cooked aduki beans, reserving half the cooking liquid. Stir the beans and liquid into the vegetables and simmer until most of the water has evaporated.

Divide the stuffing among the peppers. Bake the peppers in a moderate oven – 350°F/180°C/Gas 4/bottom right oven in a 4 door Aga – for 20 to 25 minutes. Serve hot or cold – they are equally good either way.

Brown sugar meringues with lemon and elderflower curd

I've tried recipes for meringues with soft brown sugar, but I've never been able to make them work – they go sticky and never seem to harden properly. I love brown sugar meringues, however, and these, made with a mixture of demerara sugar and granulated sugar, are foolproof. They keep in a tin as well as white sugar meringues. They are particularly good filled with *Lemon and elderflower curd* and whipped cream.

Serves 6

4 large egg whites	*½ pt/300 ml double cream,*
4 oz/100 g demerara sugar	*whipped*
4 oz/100 g granulated sugar	Lemon and elderflower curd
	(see below)

Line a baking tray with siliconized greaseproof paper (without which I, for one, certainly could not make meringues).

Whisk the egg whites until stiff then, still whisking, add the demerara and granulated sugars mixed together, a spoonful at a time, until all the sugar is incorporated. Pipe or spoon the meringue onto the lined baking tray – I find you get more evenly shaped meringues if they are piped. Aim for meringues about 2 in/5 cm in diameter. Bake in a cool oven – 200°F/110°C/Gas ½/top left oven in a 4 door Aga – for 2 to 2½ hours. Cool on a wire rack, and store in an airtight tin or container until you are ready to fill them.

Either fold the whipped cream and curd carefully together or use them separately. Sandwich the meringues together with a spoonful of curd and a spoonful of whipped cream. Pile them high on a serving dish so that they are a decoration in themselves.

Lemon and elderflower curd

Elderflower is a wonderful taste and enhances lemon curd tremendously. This lemon curd makes a good little present, potted in a pretty jar, and keeps in the refrigerator for 3 to 4 weeks.

Makes 8 oz/250 g

---

3 oz/75 g butter
1 whole egg plus 2 egg yolks
3 oz/75 g caster or granulated
  sugar

grated rind of 2 lemons and juice
  of 1½ lemons
a handful of elderflower heads

Cut the butter in pieces into a heatproof bowl. Beat together the egg and yolks, and sieve them into the bowl with the butter – sieving removes any stringy bits of egg and makes for a smoother curd. Add the sugar, grated lemon rind and lemon juice to the bowl, and rest the bowl over a saucepan of gently simmering water. Stir occasionally as the butter and sugar melt and dissolve, but there is no need to stir continuously. Pluck the tiny elderflower heads off the stem. When the curd has thickened, take the bowl off the heat and stir in the elderflower heads. Leave to cool. Store in an airtight jar in the refrigerator.

Fresh lime sorbet

This sorbet is a convenient and most refreshing pud. It is good served just as it is, or with a plate of crisp vanilla biscuits or with a bowl of seasonal fruit, such as strawberries. Limes now feature as part of the Kinloch twice-weekly fruit and vegetable order – they have such a wonderful smell and taste and are good in so many ways, with fish, chicken and vegetables, and, as in this recipe, in sweet things too.

Serves 6

pared rind and juice of 4 limes	*6 oz/175 g granulated sugar*
1 pt/600 ml water	*2 egg whites*

Put the pared lime rinds and water into a saucepan together with the sugar. Dissolve the sugar in the water over a moderate heat, then boil fast for 5 minutes. Take the saucepan off the heat, stir in the lime juice and leave to cool. When it is quite cold, fish out and discard the lime rinds, and pour the liquid into a polythene container. Cover with a lid and put into the deep freeze for about 2 hours.

Take the container out of the freezer. Scoop the freezing lime syrup from round the edges of the container and whisk the slush into the liquid, using an electric whisk. Clean the whisk and whisk the 2 egg whites until they are stiff. Using a metal spoon, fold the whites into the slush. Cover the container and freeze again.

After another 2 hours, take the container out of the freezer again, whisk again, and refreeze. If possible, repeat the operation once more – the sorbet will be much lighter in texture for it. Take the sorbet out of the freezer about half an hour before serving.

Strawberry and orange tart

In this recipe the strawberries are arranged on an orange-flavoured crème pâtissière on a crisp shortbread-like pastry flan.

Serves 6–8

FOR THE PASTRY
4 oz/100 g butter, hard from the refrigerator
6 oz/175 g flour
1 oz/25 g icing sugar
a few drops of vanilla essence
FOR THE CRÈME PÂTISSIÈRE
½ pt/300 ml milk
3 egg yolks

1 tsp cornflour, sieved
2 oz/50 g caster sugar
grated rind of 2 oranges
2 tbsp orange liqueur
¼ pt/150 ml double cream, whipped
FOR THE STRAWBERRY FILLING
3 tbsp redcurrant jelly
1–1½ lb/500–750 g strawberries

If you have a food processor, cut the butter for the pastry into it and add the flour, icing sugar and vanilla essence. Process until the mixture resembles fine breadcrumbs. To make the pastry by hand, sieve the flour and sugar into a bowl. Cut the butter into the flour and sugar and rub with your fingertips until you have a mixture like fine bread-crumbs. Add the vanilla essence.

Pat the pastry mixture round the sides and base of an 8 in/20 cm flan dish, and put the dish in the refrigerator for at least an hour. Bake blind in a moderate oven – 350°F/180°C/Gas 4/bottom right oven in a 4 door Aga – for about 25 minutes, or until the pastry is golden brown. Take it out of the oven and set aside to cool.

Put the milk for the crème pâtissière into a saucepan and heat to scalding point. Beat the egg yolks in a bowl together with the sieved cornflour, and gradually add the caster sugar. Beat well. Pour a little of the hot milk on to the yolk and sugar mixture and beat again. Pour this mixture into the saucepan with the rest of the milk. Stir over a gentle heat until the custard is sufficiently thick so that when you draw a path down the back of your wooden spoon with your fingertip it stays. Take the saucepan off the heat, and leave the custard to cool. When it is quite cold, stir in the orange rind and liqueur, and fold in the whipped cream. Pour the crème into the baked pastry case.

Melt the redcurrant jelly in a saucepan and leave to cool slightly. Arrange the strawberries attractively over the crème pâtissière. If you haven't got many strawberries, cut them in half. Arrange the larger ones round the outside and work inwards with the smaller ones. When they are all in place, brush with the slightly cooled redcurrant jelly – this glaze gives a most gratifyingly professional look to the end result!

Strawberries in orange jelly

The sharpness of fresh orange brings out the true flavour of strawberries in a way that no cream does. This light and refreshing pud tastes good and looks very attractive, too.

1½ lb/750 g strawberries, hulled, with the larger ones cut in half so that they are more or less the same size
½ pt/300 ml water
2 oz/50 g caster or granulated sugar
pared rind of 1 orange

pared rind and juice of 1 lemon
3 sachets gelatine – approximately 1½ oz/40 g
4 tbsp cold water
1 pt/600 ml freshly squeezed orange juice (6–8 large oranges will be enough)

Put the ½ pt/300 ml water, the sugar and the pared rinds of the orange and lemon into a saucepan over a moderate heat. Dissolve the sugar in the water, then boil fast for 5 to 7 minutes.

Meanwhile sprinkle the gelatine over the cold water. Remove the syrup from the heat and stir the gelatine into it, stirring until the gelatine has dissolved. Pour the orange and lemon juices into the syrup. Strain through a fine sieve into a serving bowl to set, or into a jelly mould to set and turn out. Push the strawberries into the jelly to set. If you like, you can arrange the strawberries in a pattern by first allowing some of the liquid orange jelly to set round the sides of the mould, then putting in a layer of strawberries and pouring more liquid jelly in, letting it set, and so on. I don't think it's worth the effort, frankly – to me the strawberries look beautiful in disarray in the glistening orange jelly.

Strawberries in elderflower syrup

The flavour of elderflower enhances lots of fruits, such as lemons and gooseberries, but perhaps more than any other it enhances strawberries. When you make this syrup, let the strawberries stand in the syrup for several hours before serving, so that they really absorb the elderflower flavour.

Serves 6–8

---

2 lb/1 kg strawberries, hulled
1 pt/600 ml water
6 oz/175 g granulated sugar

pared rind and juice of 2 lemons
3 handfuls of elderflower

Put the water, sugar and lemon rind (but not the juice, yet) into a saucepan and let the sugar dissolve in the water over a gentle heat. Then boil fast for 5 minutes. Draw the pan off the heat and add the lemon juice and elderflower. (There is no need to pluck the tiny flowers from the stalks as the syrup is strained.) Allow the syrup to cool completely and then strain it through a sieve. Put the strawberries in a serving bowl and pour the syrup over them. Leave for several hours before serving.

July

July heralds the start of the school holidays. I love it when all the children are at home – our two eldest are away at boarding school – and the summer holidays are an extremely hectic few weeks. I am always trying to work out a way of making the summer holidays fun without leaving me feeling like a limp rag when September arrives, but so far I haven't succeeded. Working parents, like me, sometimes bear a burden of guilt during the holidays, feeling that we should be doing more with the children and the steady stream of their friends who come to stay. But we are very lucky to live in such a particularly beautiful place where there is so much to do, what with making dens in the bushes and fishing and swimming in the sea or river – always assuming the weather is good!

The kitchen abounds with soft fruits during July and August, and informality is the keynote of entertaining during these months, with barbecues and picnics whenever possible. This is the sort of meal preparation with which the children can help.

Skye is at its busiest in July and August, and Godfrey and I just hang on the words of the weather forecaster each day. There isn't anything we can do of course, but we do feel somehow responsible for the weather. This is such a beautiful place, and it is so sad when visitors come and stay for a few days but never actually see the mountains surrounding us because of an enshrouding mist! Luckily we have some fine, sunny and hot weather at some point in July – hopefully!

First Courses

Avocado cheesecake
Chilled courgette and rosemary soup
Red pepper bavarois with three-pepper salad
Smoked trout and horseradish mousse
Tomato, chive and basil mousse

Main Courses

Aubergine salad
Chilled prawn curry
Cold poached monkfish in avocado sauce
Lime-baked chicken with tarragon sauce
Smoked haddock cream

Puddings

Almond and nectarine pavlova
Apricot roulade with lemon and apricot cream
Blackcurrant and mint mousse
Gooseberry and elderflower iced cream
Raspberry sorbet with raspberry sauce

Avocado cheesecake

This cheesecake has a base of crushed wholemeal bran biscuits, and a smooth filling of puréed avocado mixed with cream cheese and flavoured with garlic. It looks extremely decorative, especially with a garnish of sliced tomatoes around the edge.

Serves 6–8

FOR THE BASE
*12 oz/350 g wholemeal bran
    biscuits*
3 oz/75 g melted butter
*1 garlic clove, skinned and very
    finely chopped*
FOR THE FILLING
3 avocados
*1 sachet gelatine – approximately
    ½ oz/15 g*
¼ pt/150 ml chicken stock

*8 oz/250 g cream cheese (or
    quark if you prefer a low-fat
    cheese)*
2 tbsp lemon juice
*1 garlic clove, skinned and
    chopped*
a dash of Tabasco
salt and freshly ground pepper
*4–5 tomatoes, skinned and
    sliced, to garnish*
*finely chopped parsley and chives
    to garnish*

First prepare the base. Break the bran biscuits into the food processor and process until fine – the noise is horrendous, but it only takes a minute – or crush them by hand with a rolling pin. Mix together well the crushed biscuits, melted butter and garlic. Press around the sides and base of an 8–9 in/20–22 cm flan dish. Bake blind in a moderate oven – 350°F/180°C/Gas 4/bottom right oven in a 4 door Aga – for 15 minutes. Leave to cool.

Cut each avocado in half, flick out the stone, and scoop out the flesh into a bowl or food processor, taking care to scrape the flesh from the inside of the skin, where the colour is a slightly darker shade of green. Sprinkle the gelatine on the chicken stock, and heat gently until the gelatine has dissolved completely – don't let the stock boil.

Pour the chicken stock and gelatine onto the avocado flesh, and add the cream cheese, lemon juice, garlic, Tabasco, salt and pepper, and mix or process until you have a smooth pale green purée. The purée will be coarser if you mix it by hand. Pour onto the cooled biscuit crust. Leave for 3 to 4 hours to set. Just before you are ready to serve the cheesecake, arrange the sliced tomatoes around the edge. Sprinkle the finely chopped parsley and chives either in the middle of the cheesecake or over the sliced tomatoes, whichever you prefer.

Chilled courgette and rosemary soup

If you have a glut of courgettes, which can happen if you grow your own, this is a quick and simple soup flavoured with rosemary which will use some up. I usually serve it cold, but if the weather should happen to be foul it is equally good served hot.

Serves 6–8

---

2 oz/50 g butter
2 medium onions, skinned and chopped
1½ lb/750 g courgettes, wiped, with their ends trimmed off and sliced
1 garlic clove, skinned and chopped (optional)

2 tsp fresh rosemary leaves
2 pt/1.2 L chicken stock
salt and freshly ground black pepper
5 fl oz/150 ml natural yoghurt to garnish
2 tbsp chopped chives to garnish

Melt the butter in a saucepan and add the chopped onions. Sauté for about 5 minutes, stirring occasionally, then add the sliced courgettes. Cook for a further 5

143

minutes, then add the garlic (if you are using it), rosemary, chicken stock, salt and pepper. Simmer for about 25 minutes. Allow to cool a little. Liquidize and, for an extra smooth soup, sieve the liquidized soup into a bowl.

Chill thoroughly in the refrigerator for several hours. Swirl a spoonful of yoghurt into each plateful, sprinkle some chopped chives over the yoghurt and serve. This soup is a boon to calorie counters (of whom I'm one) – it really is very low in the dreaded calories.

Red pepper bavarois with three-pepper salad

If you don't have dariole moulds, you can make these *Red pepper bavarois* in ramekins. They look and taste delicious, and can be made in advance.

Serves 6

---

3 red peppers, halved, deseeded and chopped
2 sachets of gelatine – approximately 1 oz/25 g
1 pt/600 ml chicken stock
3 tbsp olive oil

1 large juicy garlic clove, skinned and chopped
salt and freshly ground black pepper
3 oz/75 g cream cheese
Three-pepper salad *(see opposite page)*

Sprinkle the gelatine over the chicken stock in a saucepan. Heat gently until the gelatine has dissolved completely – don't allow the stock to boil. Heat the olive oil in a saucepan or frying pan, add the chopped red peppers, and sauté for 10 minutes, stirring occasionally to make sure that the peppers cook evenly. Add the chopped garlic and cook for a further 5 to 10 minutes, until the pieces of red pepper are really soft. Season with salt and freshly ground black pepper. Put the cooked pepper and garlic mixture into a liquidizer or food processor and blend until smooth. Add the gelatine and chicken stock, and blend again. Finally add the cream cheese and blend until the mixture is really smooth. Divide the bavarois among 6 large dariole moulds or ramekins. Put them in the refrigerator to set.

To serve, dip each mould in hot water for a few seconds, and then turn out the bavarois on to a serving plate. Arrange the *Three-pepper salad* (see below) around the bavarois.

Three-pepper salad

This isn't so much a salad as a cold cooked vegetable – the strips of red, yellow and green pepper are sautéed in olive oil and garlic, then cooled and can be arranged around the turned-out *Red pepper bavarois* (see above).

Serves 6

2 red peppers	*2–3 tbsp olive oil*
2 yellow peppers	*1 garlic clove, skinned and finely*
1 green pepper (you can use more	*chopped*
green pepper if you like, but	*salt and freshly ground black*
some people find them rather	*pepper*
indigestible)	

Halve and deseed the peppers, and slice them into thin, evenly sized strips. Heat the oil in a saucepan and add the strips of pepper, and the garlic. Sauté over a fairly gentle heat for 20 to 25 minutes, until the peppers are soft. Take the pan off the heat, and leave to cool. Store in a cool place until serving.

Smoked trout and horseradish mousse

I do love all smoked foods, and smoked trout is a particular favourite. In this creamy smooth mousse the flavour of the trout is enhanced by the horseradish. You can either set it in a large dish, or in individual ramekins and turn them out onto a bed of shredded lettuce on each serving plate. Serve with hot brown toast.

Serves 6

2 smoked trout, skin and bones removed, flesh flaked

3 tsp grated horseradish (available in jars from most good delicatessens)

4 tbsp lemon juice

2 tbsp water

1 sachet of gelatine – approximately ½ oz/15 g

¾ pt/450 ml double cream, lightly whipped

freshly ground black pepper

slices of lemon and finely chopped parsley to garnish

Oil the ramekins or bowl. Put the flaked smoked trout into a liquidizer or food processor and blend. Add the horseradish and blend again. Put the lemon juice and water in a saucepan, sprinkle on the gelatine and heat until the gelatine has dissolved completely. Add this mixture to the trout, and blend until smooth. Add the lightly whipped cream and blend again until all is well mixed. Season with black pepper, blend, then divide the mousse mixture among the ramekins, or pour it into a bowl. Leave to set in the refrigerator for 2–3 hours or overnight. Turn it out to serve, and garnish with lemon slices and chopped parsley.

Tomato, chive and basil mousse

Savoury mousses are so easy to make and generally don't lose any flavour by being made the previous day. This fresh-tasting mousse combines the summery flavours of tomato, basil and chives, and is delicious served with warm brown rolls or garlic bread.

Serves 6

---

6 tomatoes, skinned and
  quartered
2 sachets of gelatine –
  approximately 1 oz/25 g
¼ pt/150 ml chicken stock
6 good-sized basil leaves
about 12 chives

salt and freshly ground black
  pepper
½ pt/300 ml double cream,
  whipped
tomatoes and basil to garnish
  (see below)

Sprinkle the gelatine over the chicken stock and heat gently until the gelatine has dissolved completely – don't allow the stock to boil. Put the tomatoes in a liquidizer or food processor. Add the basil leaves and chives. Blend until thick, then pour this mixture through a sieve, so that you get a smooth purée. Stir the dissolved gelatine and chicken stock into the purée. Season with salt and black pepper, and leave until it begins to set. Fold the whipped cream into the purée, and pour the mousse into a bowl to set.

Decorate with skinned, chopped tomatoes and torn basil leaves, tossed in 2 tablespoons of vinaigrette dressing. Leave to set for 2–3 hours or overnight. This mousse makes a good main course, served with one or two accompanying salads.

Aubergine salad

I am always on the look-out for interesting and unusual salads, and this combination is one that I like very much. It consists of cooked aubergines, peppers, tomatoes, onion and garlic, dressed with olive oil and white wine. I like to serve it with warm French bread.

Serves 6

---

3 large aubergines
1 onion (a Spanish onion, if possible)
1 green and 1 red pepper
6 tomatoes
1 large garlic clove, skinned and chopped

6 tbsp olive oil
2 tbsp dry white wine
salt and freshly ground black pepper
fresh basil leaves
shredded lettuce to garnish

Bake the aubergines whole in a hot oven – 400°F/200°C/ Gas 6/top right oven in a 4 door Aga – until soft, about 15 to 20 minutes.

Skin and finely slice the onion. Halve and deseed the peppers, and slice them into fine shreds. Skin the tomatoes, and halve, deseed and chop them. When the aubergines are cool enough to handle, peel them and chop the aubergine flesh.

Heat 5 tablespoons olive oil in a frying pan. Add the onion, peppers, and garlic and sauté for 5 minutes, stirring occasionally. Then add the aubergine flesh and tomatoes and sauté for 10 to 15 minutes, stirring from time to time. Stir in the remaining tablespoon of olive oil and the dry white wine. Season with salt and freshly ground black pepper. Tear up the basil leaves and stir them in. Leave to cool. Arrange in a serving dish, with shredded lettuce around the edges.

Chilled prawn curry

This delicious cold prawn curry makes a wonderful main course dish for a summer party. The sauce can be made two or three days in advance, and then combined with the mayonnaise and prawns on the day of the party. Serve the prawns on a bed of cooked brown rice mixed with a handful of raisins and tossed in a little vinaigrette dressing.

Serves 6

1½ lb/750 g shelled prawns, fresh or frozen
FOR THE SAUCE
2 tbsp oil (I use sunflower)
1 onion, skinned and finely chopped
1 apple, cored and chopped
2 tsp flour
1 rounded tbsp curry powder
2 tbsp mango chutney

1 × 15 oz/450 g tin of tomatoes or 6 fresh tomatoes, liquidized and sieved
FOR THE MAYONNAISE
6 tbsp mayonnaise
juice of half a lemon
salt and freshly ground black pepper
a dash of Tabasco
chives and parsley to garnish

Heat the oil in a saucepan and sauté the onion for about 5 minutes, stirring occasionally. Add the apple (skin and all) and cook for another 2 to 3 minutes. Stir in the flour and curry powder, cook for another couple of minutes and then stir in the chutney and the tomatoes. Cover the saucepan and simmer gently for 30 minutes. Cool, liquidize and sieve the sauce.

Mix together the mayonnaise, lemon juice, seasoning and Tabasco, and stir this into the sieved sauce. Stir in the prawns, and put the bowl to chill in the refrigerator until you are ready to serve.

On a serving dish arrange brown rice mixed with raisins and tossed in vinaigrette dressing, and spoon the prawn curry over the rice. Dust with chopped parsley mixed with chopped chives and serve.

Cold poached monkfish in avocado sauce

This makes an unusual main course for lunch or dinner, and a very good buffet dish, being easy to serve and easy to eat if you are standing up with a plate in one hand, a fork in the other, and wishing you had a third hand to hold your glass! It can all be prepared a day in advance, and kept in the refrigerator or a cool larder.

Serves 6–8

2½ lb/1.25 kg monkfish tail, weighed when cut off the central bone
2 pt/1.2 L water
2 onions, skinned and halved
2 bayleaves
2 celery sticks, halved
1 lemon, quartered

about 12 peppercorns
½ tsp sea salt
Avocado sauce *(see below)*
1 tbsp finely chopped parsley to garnish
1 tbsp finely chopped chives to garnish

Trim the monkfish of its skin and membrane if this hasn't already been done, and put the fish in a roasting tin or heatproof casserole. Put the water, onions, bayleaves, celery, lemon wedges, peppercorns and salt – and the fish bones and skin if you have them – into a saucepan and bring to the boil. Boil, covered, for 20 minutes. Strain the vegetable stock and pour it over the monkfish in the roasting tin. Simmer very gently over a low flame until the fish is cooked. How long this takes will depend on the thickness of the monkfish – if the fillets are cut from huge

150

fish they will take longer – about 20 minutes' cooking time on average. Draw off the heat and leave the fish to cool in the liquid. When it is cold, take it out of the liquid and cut into 1 in/2.5 cm bite-sized bits.

Carefully fold the pieces of monkfish into the *Avocado sauce* (see below). Arrange the fish on a shallow serving plate, surround with brown rice or shredded lettuce, and sprinkle the chopped parsley and chives over the surface. Keep in a cool place until you are ready to serve.

Avocado sauce

This smooth, pale green sauce can be also used as a delicious dip for crudités.

Serves 6–8

1 medium avocado (if it is very small, use 2)	*freshly ground black pepper (about 15 grinds)*
1 egg plus 1 egg yolk	*½ pt/300 ml oil (I like to use a mixture of olive and sunflower)*
1 rounded tsp mustard powder	
1 l tsp sugar	
½ tsp salt (use more if you like a saltier taste)	*3 tbsp wine vinegar*
	2 tbsp lemon juice

Put the egg, egg yolk, mustard, sugar, salt and pepper into a liquidizer or food processor and blend. While the machine is still blending, very slowly add the oil a drop at a time, until it is all used up and you have a thick mayonnaise. Blend in the wine vinegar and lemon juice, taste and add more lemon or vinegar if necessary.

Cut the avocado in half, flick out the stone, and scoop out the flesh into a food processor or bowl and blend by machine or hand until all is well mixed and smooth. Fold in the mayonnaise.

151

Lime-baked chicken with tarragon sauce

This is one of my favourite main course dishes for a lunch or dinner party in the summer. The lime makes a refreshing change from the lemon which more usually goes with chicken.

The chicken joints for this dish can be prepared in their baking tray several hours in advance, all ready to pop into the oven before your guests arrive. Once the sauce is made, it will keep warm without spoiling for 30 to 45 minutes, but you can blend together the ingredients all ready to cook several hours ahead, too.

Serves 6

---

6 chicken joints
pared rind of 2 limes, finely
   shredded (save the juice for the
   sauce)
several sprigs of tarragon
salt and freshly ground pepper
3 oz/75 g butter

FOR THE SAUCE
½ pt/300 ml single cream
2 oz/50 g butter
1 tsp flour
3 egg yolks
salt and freshly ground pepper
several sprigs of tarragon
juice of 2 limes

Put the shredded lime rinds into a saucepan, cover with cold water and bring to the boil. Simmer gently for 10 minutes, then drain. Chop the tarragon finely and mix with the salt and pepper into the butter. Spread butter over each chicken joint. Bake the chicken joints in a moderate oven – 350°F/180°C/Gas 4/bottom right oven in a 4 door Aga – for 40 minutes, basting from time to time.

Meanwhile make the sauce. Into a liquidizer or food processor put the single cream, butter, flour, egg yolks, salt and pepper. Blend until smooth, then pour into a heatproof bowl. Stand the bowl in a saucepan of simmering water, with the water coming half-way up the sides of the bowl – this helps the sauce to cook faster. Stir the sauce with a wire whisk occasionally as it cooks. It will take 35 to 40 minutes to thicken.

Chop the tarragon. When the sauce has thickened, stir in the lime juice and the tarragon. Don't add the tarragon until just before serving – if it is kept hot for any length of time, it loses its fresh green colour and turns brown. The flavour is just as good, but the appearance suffers a bit!

To test if the chicken is cooked, pierce the flesh with a sharp knife – if the juices run clear, the chicken is done; if they run pink, it needs longer. Arrange the chicken pieces on a warmed serving dish. Pour over the sauce and sprinkle the cooked shreds of lime rind on top.

Smoked haddock cream

Served with brown rice and tomato salad, this set mousse of smoked haddock makes a very good main course for lunch or supper. Our children love it. It has to be made ahead to allow it to set. I set mine in a ring mould about 9 in/22 cm in diameter and then turn it out. Alternatively you can put it into a glass or china dish to set, and serve it from the dish.

Serves 6

2 lb/1 kg smoked haddock	freshly ground black pepper
2 pt/1.2 L milk and water mixed	freshly grated nutmeg
1 onion, halved	5 tbsp mayonnaise
1 celery stick	2 egg whites
1½ sachets of gelatine – approximately ¾ oz/20 g	

153

Put the smoked haddock into a saucepan together with the milk and water, onion and celery. Over a gentle to moderate heat bring the liquid to simmering point. Simmer for 5 minutes, then take the saucepan off the heat, and leave the fish to cool in the liquid. When it is cold, strain off and reserve the liquid. Remove and discard the skin and bones from the fish and flake the flesh. Measure ½ pt/300 ml of the cooking liquid into a saucepan and sprinkle the gelatine over it. Dissolve the gelatine completely over a gentle heat. Put the flaked fish into a liquidizer or food processor together with the gelatine liquid and blend. Season with the pepper and nutmeg, and add the mayonnaise. Blend until the mixture is smooth, then fold in the stiffly whisked egg whites and pour out into a serving dish or an oiled ring mould. Leave to set in the refrigerator for several hours or overnight.

Almond and nectarine pavlova

This pudding combines the vanilla marshmallow-like texture and taste of pavlova with the delicate flavours of toasted almonds and nectarines. It doesn't take a minute to prepare, apart from toasting and cooling the almonds, and yet it makes a very special pudding.

Serves 6–8

---

3 oz/75 g flaked almonds, toasted and cooled	8 oz/250 g caster sugar
	1½ tsp vanilla essence
6 nectarines, skinned and neatly sliced	1 tsp cornflour
	1 tsp wine vinegar
4 egg whites	½ pt/300 ml double cream

Whisk the egg whites until stiff. Continue whisking and gradually add the sugar, a spoonful at a time, until it is all incorporated into the egg white. Whisk in the vanilla essence. Sieve the cornflour and fold it into the meringue, together with the wine vinegar and the flaked almonds. Line a baking tray 8 × 10 in/20 × 25 cm with siliconized greaseproof paper, and spoon the almond meringue onto to it in a large, even circle. Bake in a moderate oven – 350°F/180°C/Gas 4/bottom right oven in a 4 door Aga – for 5 minutes, then lower the heat to 250°F/130°C/Gas 1/top left oven in a 4 door Aga and bake for a further 1¼ hours.

Take out of the oven, leave to cool and then turn upside down onto a serving dish or tray. Whip the cream fairly stiffly. Spread the cream and sliced nectarines over the pavlova. The nectarines tend to discolour (not too much, but a bit) once sliced, and you may prefer to fold the sliced nectarines into the whipped cream before spreading over the pavlova.

Apricot roulade with lemon and apricot cream

I love roulades because they involve no last-minute effort, they look good and they are easy to serve. The idea for this apricot roulade came to me earlier this year, and we have been making it regularly for our guests here at Kinloch ever since.

Serves 6–8

1 lb/500 g dried apricots, soaked for a few hours	*grated rind of 1 lemon*
2 strips of lemon peel	*½ pt/300 ml double cream, whipped*
4 oz/100 g caster sugar	*icing sugar to sieve over the finished roulade*
4 large eggs, separated	

155

Bring the soaked apricots to the boil in fresh water. Add the lemon peel to the water. Simmer for 35 to 40 minutes or until tender. Meanwhile line a Swiss roll tin 12 × 14 in/30 × 35 cm with siliconized greaseproof paper.

Drain the cooked apricots while they are still hot and put them into a liquidizer or food processor. Blend until smooth, gradually adding the caster sugar. Take out and reserve 3 tablespoons of the mixture. Add the egg yolks, one by one, to the remaining mixture and blend until pale and thick. Whisk the egg whites until they are very stiff, and, using a large metal spoon, fold them quickly and thoroughly into the apricot mixture. Pour into the lined Swiss roll tin and bake in a moderate oven – 350°F/180°C/ Gas 4/bottom right oven in a 4 door Aga – for 20 to 25 minutes, until pale golden brown and well risen. Take the roulade out of the oven, cover with a fresh piece of siliconized greaseproof paper, and cover that with a damp tea towel. Leave to cool for several hours.

Fold the grated lemon rind and the reserved apricot purée into the whipped cream. Next assemble the roulade – lay a sheet of siliconized greaseproof paper on a table or work surface, and dust it with sieved icing sugar. Turn the cooked roulade onto the sugared paper and carefully peel the paper off the back of the cooked roulade, peeling it in strips parallel to the roulade, so that you don't tear the roulade. Spread the roulade with the cream and apricot mixture, and then roll it up lengthways onto a serving dish. Dust with more icing sugar before serving.

Blackcurrant and mint mousse

The flavours of blackcurrant and mint go together very well. I use applemint if possible – it has a much better flavour than spearmint. Applemint is the mint with broad, rather furry leaves. Don't be afraid to use a good handful of mint leaves – it is surprising how the flavours blend and people are hard pressed to guess what it is with the blackcurrants.

Serves 6–8

---

1 lb/500 g blackcurrants
a good handful of mint leaves
3 large eggs, separated
6 oz/175 g caster sugar
juice of 1 lemon

1 sachet of gelatine –
  approximately ½ oz/15 g
½ pt/300 ml double cream,
  whipped, but not too stiffly

Put the blackcurrants into a saucepan. Cover the pan and cook over a gentle heat until the currants are soft – don't add any water to the blackcurrants, as they soften they will make their own juice. When they are cooked, take them off the heat and leave to cool a bit. Blend the blackcurrants together with the mint leaves in a food processor or liquidizer until they are smooth. Leave to cool completely.

Whisk the egg yolks in a bowl, gradually adding the caster sugar. Whisk until they are thick, pale and much increased in volume. Sprinkle the gelatine over the lemon juice in a saucepan, and heat gently until the granules of gelatine have dissolved completely. Whisk this into the yolk mixture, along with the blackcurrant and mint purée. Leave until it is beginning to set – at the point where the mixture thickly coats the back of a metal spoon – and then fold in the whipped cream. Whisk the egg whites until they are stiff, and, using a metal spoon, fold them quickly and thoroughly into the mousse. Pour into a serving bowl to set. You can make this mousse a day in advance and keep it in the refrigerator overnight. Remember to take it out of the refrigerator to allow it to come to room temperature for a couple of hours before serving.

Gooseberry and elderflower iced cream

Elderflower brings out the flavour of gooseberries beautifully – cooked without elderflower they somehow taste so
ordinary. This iced cream has an exquisite flavour.

Serves 6–8

---

*1 lb/500 g gooseberries (don't
bother to top and tail them, as
they are going to be made into
a purée anyway)*
*2 handfuls of elderflower (on the
stalk, for the same reason as
the gooseberries – I don't
believe in wasted effort!)*

3 oz/75 g granulated sugar
4 eggs, separated
4 oz/100 g icing sugar, sieved
*½ pt/300 ml double cream,
  whipped*

Put the gooseberries into a saucepan together with the
elderflowers and the granulated sugar. Cover the pan and
cook over a gentle heat. As the gooseberries cook, juice will
seep out of them. When they are quite soft, take the
saucepan off the heat and leave to cool a bit. Blend the
gooseberries and elderflowers in a food processor or liquidizer and then strain the purée through a sieve. Leave to
cool completely.

Whisk the egg yolks with half the icing sugar, until the
mixture is pale and thick. Whisk the egg whites until they
are stiff, whisking all the time; gradually add the remaining icing sugar. With a large metal spoon, fold together the
gooseberry and elderflower purée, the whipped cream and
the yolk mixture. Lastly fold the meringue mixture into
the gooseberry mixture. Put into a polythene container,
seal and freeze. Take the container out of the freezer about
½ an hour before serving the iced cream.

Raspberry sorbet with raspberry sauce

Scotland produces the best raspberries in the world. We grow them in abundance here and they are one of the few fruits which I use out of season. Once I've made jars and jars of raspberry jam, I just have to freeze the excess raspberries. There is a limit, too, to just how frequently raspberries can feature on the menu here at Kinloch – twice a week, I reckon, no more.

This recipe for raspberry sorbet with raspberry sauce has very few calories and is a particularly delicious and refreshing end to a dinner or lunch party.

Serves 8

FOR THE SORBET
2 lb/1 kg raspberries
1 pt/600 ml water
6 oz/175 g granulated sugar
pared rind and juice of 2 lemons

3 egg whites
FOR THE SAUCE
8–12 oz/250–350 g raspberries
4 oz/100 g icing sugar

Put the water into a saucepan together with the granulated sugar and pared lemon rind (not the lemon juice). Heat gently until the sugar has dissolved completely, then boil fast for 5 minutes. Take the syrup off the heat, and stir in the lemon juice. Leave to cool.

Put the raspberries in a liquidizer or food processor and blend. Sieve the raspberry purée and stir into the strained syrup.

Pour into a large polythene container, seal and freeze. After about 2 hours take the container out of the freezer, scrape the frozen syrup off the sides into the centre and whisk with an electric whisk. Clean the whisk and whisk the egg whites until they are stiff. With a metal spoon, fold the egg whites into the half-frozen raspberry sorbet. Put the container back into the freezer. After another

159

couple of hours, take it out and whisk again, then return to the freezer. If you can, repeat this procedure once more. Whisking 3 times during freezing gives the sorbet a much lighter texture, making it easier to serve and eat. Take the sorbet out of the freezer half an hour before you want to serve it.

To make the accompanying sauce, blend together the raspberries and icing sugar. Strain through a sieve to make a really smooth seedless purée.

August

August is an extremely hectic month – busy, because of the school holidays, and hectic, because we are full to the gunnels with hotel guests, not to mention occasional visits from friends of ours. August is also a very busy time for cooks because there is such an abundance of fruit and vegetables to be made the most of in various ways – by cooking, freezing or preserving. Soft fruits are in wonderful supply and we have no problems deciding what to put on the menu when it comes to puddings! Other food tends to be geared to picnics, barbecues or family entertaining. It is surely one of the best months in the year for really enjoying seasonal British foods at their best and most abundant.

First Courses

Chilled lime and watercress soup

*Tomato, watercress and avocado salad with
crispy bacon dressing*

Pea, apple and mint soup

Spaghetti courgettes with garlic

Stuffed tomatoes with avocado pâté

Main Courses

Cold barbecued fillet of beef with horseradish cream sauce

Green salad with green dressing

Chicken in parsley and white wine jelly

Ceviche of salmon with tomato and cucumber mayonnaise

Squid with tomato and black olives

Puddings

Blackcurrant and lemon suédoise

*Redcurrant and whitecurrant compote
with almond meringues and kirsch cream*

Peach and hazelnut tart

Iced orange and apricot mousse

Nectarines with fudge sauce

Chilled lime and watercress soup

Although this is just a variation on lemon and watercress soup, the end result is quite different because limes have such a distinctive flavour. If you are serving it on a cold evening, just heat it up – it loses nothing by being served hot rather than chilled, and your guests will prefer a warming dish if the weather does turn inclement! On a proper fine summer's day, this makes a convenient first course for a dinner or lunch party, which can be made a day or two ahead and kept in the refrigerator. As with all soups, it will only be as good as the stock it is made with – sorry to sound so schoolmarmy, but it is so true.

Serves 6–8

---

juice of 2 limes and finely pared rind of 1 lime
3 good handfuls of watercress
2 oz/50 g butter
2 medium onions, skinned and chopped
2 medium potatoes, peeled and chopped

2 pt/1.2 L chicken or vegetable stock
salt and freshly ground black pepper
freshly grated nutmeg
1 lime, thinly sliced, for garnish

Melt the butter in a saucepan and add the onions. Sauté for 5 minutes or so, stirring occasionally, until the onion is soft and transparent. Add the potatoes, and cook for a further 5 minutes, stirring occasionally to prevent them sticking. Pour in the stock, add the pared lime rind and season with salt, pepper and nutmeg. Cover the pan and simmer the soup very gently for 20 minutes, or until the potato pieces are soft. Draw the pan off the heat, and allow to cool. Liquidize the soup together with the watercress, and pour into a bowl. Stir in the lime juice and put the bowl into the refrigerator to chill the soup thoroughly.

Float a slice of lime in each plateful to serve. The watercress gives the soup a beautiful bright green colour because it hasn't been cooked. If you do heat the soup to serve it, the green colour will dull a little but it will still taste very good.

Tomato, watercress and avocado salad with crispy bacon dressing

This salad makes a delicious first course, but, padded out with shredded lettuce, it is the ace favourite choice for lunch during the summer holidays with all the members of our family. Whenever I am racking my brains and ask what shall we have for lunch, the unanimous answer is *Tomato, watercress and avocado salad*, with the bacon dressing. I really think they would eat it every day for a week if I let them! I like to serve it with warm brown rolls, or the granary bread which we make each day for our guests here at Kinloch.

Serves 6–8

FOR THE SALAD

6 good-sized tomatoes, skinned (if for guests, not if for family!) and cut into wedges

4 handfuls of watercress, the thicker stalks removed and the watercress torn

3 avocados, peeled and cut into ½ in/1 cm chunks

FOR THE DRESSING

2 tsp mustard powder

½ tsp salt

½ tsp caster sugar

4 tbsp olive oil

1 tbsp wine vinegar (or more – to taste)

6 rashers of bacon, cooked until crisp, cooled on absorbent kitchen towels, then broken into bits

In a bowl, mix together the tomato wedges, torn watercress and chunks of avocado. Mix together the ingredients for the dressing, adding wine vinegar until the dressing is sharp enough for your taste. Add the crumbled bacon. Pour the dressing over the salad and toss carefully. To serve, divide between 6 (or 8) serving plates.

If you are making this salad for family consumption, add the shredded lettuce before you mix in the dressing.

Pea, apple and mint soup

A simple recipe combining the best of summer flavours – peas, apples and mint. For any recipe which uses mint, I do prefer to use applemint, the rather hairy, broader-leaved type which I think has a far superior flavour to the more common spearmint. This is a good way of using up garden peas which are still good but on the large side to serve as a vegetable. The apples just add the touch of tartness and sweetness that this soup needs and the hint of curry powder isn't detectable as such but does add a certain something to the overall flavour. This soup freezes well and can be served hot or chilled.

Serves 6–8

---

2 oz/50 g butter	1 lb/500 g shelled peas
3 onions, skinned and chopped	2 pt/1.2 L good chicken or
2 eating apples, chopped (skin,	vegetable stock
core and all – the soup will be	salt and freshly ground pepper
liquidized and sieved)	2 handfuls of mint
1 rounded tsp curry powder	thinly sliced apples for garnish

Melt the butter in a saucepan and add the onions. Sauté for about 5 minutes, stirring occasionally, then add the chopped apples. Cook for a further minute or two, then stir in the curry powder. Add the peas and stock. Season with salt and pepper, and stir in half the mint. Cover the pan and simmer gently for 20 minutes. Draw the pan off the heat and leave to cool. Add the remaining mint to the cooled soup and liquidize. Pour the liquidized soup through a sieve for a really velvety texture. Either serve chilled or reheat to serve hot. Whether you are serving the soup cold or hot, thinly slice a couple of apples, brush them with lemon juice and garnish each plateful with 3 to 4 slices.

Spaghetti courgettes with garlic

This is so easy to make I'm almost embarrassed to put it down. However, one of the reasons for this book is to share discoveries and I really consider this recipe to be one of the finds of the past summer. It will be particularly useful if you grow your own courgettes, for that time when they are in super-abundance and people are endlessly racking their brains for ideas to use them up. In this recipe the courgettes are sliced on a mandoline (watch your fingers!) into fine matchsticks, really just like spaghetti, and cooked for a minute in olive oil with crushed garlic and salt and pepper. They are absolutely delicious, and even guests who say that they don't particularly like courgettes rave about this dish. We serve them as an accompanying vegetable to the main course (they are as good with fish as with meat) but I also like to serve them as a light first course for family and friends, with hot garlic bread or rolls. They are also good served as a cold salad, but I like them best served hot, straight from the frying pan. The one vital thing is to cook them in the best olive oil you can get.

---

2 lb/1 kg courgettes	*5–6 tbsp olive oil*
1 large juicy garlic clove, skinned and crushed	*salt and freshly ground black pepper*

Cut the ends off the courgettes, and slice them on the finest shredder on the mandoline – it's worth investing in a mandoline just for this recipe if you don't already have one.

Pour the olive oil into a large frying pan and add the crushed garlic. When the oil is hot, add the salt, plenty of freshly ground black pepper and the shredded courgettes. Sauté the courgettes for just a minute, stirring all the time, and serve.

Stuffed tomatoes with avocado pâté

This simple first course also makes a good main course for lunch or supper, served with accompanying salads. It looks so pretty, too – the red tomatoes contrasting with the pale green avocado filling and the black olives. I like to serve these on a bed of shredded lettuce or spinach.

Serves 6

---

12 good-sized tomatoes	*salt and freshly ground black pepper*
3 avocados	*pepper*
1 garlic clove, skinned and chopped	*3 tbsp lemon juice*
8 oz/250 g cream cheese (or quark if you prefer a low fat substitute)	*4 oz/100 g black olives*

Cut the tops off the tomatoes, and a tiny slice from the base of each tomato, so that they stand up. Carefully scoop out the seeds from each tomato. Wipe out the inside of each tomato with a piece of kitchen towel to absorb excess moisture, and leave the hollowed-out tomatoes upside down on a baking tray lined with kitchen paper while you prepare the avocado filling.

Cut each avocado in half and scoop the flesh into a bowl or food processor. Add the chopped garlic, cream cheese, salt and pepper, and mix or process until smooth. Add the lemon juice, tasting to get it to the right sharpness for you. The stuffing will be coarser if you mix it by hand. Stuff the tomatoes with the avocado mixture – the easiest way is to use a piping bag. Decorate each tomato with a black olive and the lid of the tomato, if you like.

If you stuff the tomatoes much more than 2 hours before serving, cover the dish or serving plate with a loose layer of clingfilm, to help prevent the avocado filling discolouring too much – the more lemon juice you put in, the less it will discolour anyway.

Cold barbecued fillet of beef with horseradish cream sauce

In Godfrey's opinion there is nothing so good as cold roast beef, unless it is cold barbecued fillet of beef. For a special celebration in the summer we barbecue fillets of beef and serve them, cold and thinly sliced, with two or three salads and horseradish cream sauce. If it is a very special event, I make shortcrust tartlets filled with the horseradish cream, just to dress up the dish.

We all like our beef rare, so the meat is really just sealed all over on the barbecue, the cooking time being about 20 minutes. If you barbecue fillets, there is meat cooked to everyone's taste – rare at the thicker end, well done at the thinner end. If ever I'm roasting a fillet, I tend to tuck the thinner end under so that there is approximately the same thickness of meat at both ends. For this method I don't bother.

I like to serve a tomato salad with the beef, full of chopped basil leaves, and a melon and mint salad, tossed at the last minute in vinaigrette dressing.

Serves 6

---

1 fillet of beef, weighing about 2 lb/1 kg, trimmed of gristle and excess fat

Horseradish cream sauce *(see below)*

Have the barbecue ready – with the charcoal white – and put the trimmed fillet on the grill. Cook on all sides for about 15 to 20 minutes. Take the fillet off the barbecue and leave to cool. The cooking can be done in advance if it is more convenient for you. When the beef is cold, carve it into ¼ in/6 mm thick slices and arrange on a serving dish. Surround, if you like, with watercress and serve the *Horseradish cream sauce* separately in a sauce boat or bowl.

Horseradish cream sauce

Freshly made horseradish sauce is much nicer than the bought variety. It goes just as well with hot roast beef.

---

juice of 1 lemon
1 heaped tbsp grated horseradish

½ pt/300 ml double cream, whipped

Fold the lemon juice and grated horseradish into the whipped cream.

Green salad with green dressing

I find that we, as a family, are eating less meat and more vegetable main courses. The green salad in this recipe is something that I threw together for lunch the day the Duke and Duchess of York were married, and it was so good that I made it again and again . . . It is very simple, and consists of as many green items as you can lay your hands on. Do make it even if you can only muster three or four of my suggested ingredients. I like to use herbs in quantity – chunks of parsley and whole leaves of basil and applemint. The rather more unusual salad items, such as rocket, which my mother has been growing for some time and which is delicious, are now more widely available. And sorrel grows wild here in abundance. The dressing is thick with puréed avocado, and you really need chunky slices of granary bread to mop up the juices.

Serves 6–8

FOR THE GREEN SALAD
A selection of the following:
crisp iceberg lettuce, torn into smallish pieces
fresh spinach, torn into smallish pieces
nasturtium leaves, torn into bits
sorrel, torn into bits
a handful of parsley, the heads torn from the stems
a small bunch of chives, snipped into roughly 1 in/2.5 cm lengths
a handful of basil leaves
a handful of mint leaves (applemint if possible)
2 handfuls of watercress, any tough stalks thrown away, the rest torn up

FOR THE GREEN DRESSING
2 avocados
2 tsp mustard powder
½ tsp sugar
½ tsp salt
lots of freshly ground black pepper
¼ pt/150 ml oil (olive or sunflower)
3–4 tbsp lemon juice

Cut each avocado in half and flick out the stone. Scoop the flesh into a bowl or food processor and add the mustard powder, sugar, salt and pepper. Beat or blend until smooth. Then add the oil in a very slow trickle, continuing to beat or blend. Lastly add the lemon juice. Taste, and if it isn't sharp enough for you, add more lemon juice. Bind together all the green salad ingredients with the dressing and put into a salad bowl. I have a pretty white bowl in which this looks most effective, but any china or wooden salad bowl will do just as well.

Chicken in parsley and white wine jelly

This jellied chicken looks as good as it tastes at any party. It's ideal for a buffet because it is easy to eat with just a fork. The jelly is made of dry white wine and chicken stock, and is flecked with bright green parsley.

Serves 6–8

FOR THE CHICKEN
2 small chickens, each weighing 2½–3 lb/1.25–1.5 kg
3 medium onions, skinned and halved
3 carrots, peeled and halved
2 celery sticks, leaves and all
2 leeks, chopped
2 bayleaves
½ tsp salt

12 black peppercorns
2 egg whites
FOR THE JELLY
1 pt/600 ml clarified stock from the chicken liquid
1 pt/600 ml dry white wine, such as a Loire white
2 oz/50 g powdered gelatine
salt to taste
4 tbsp finely chopped parsley

171

Put the chickens into a saucepan or casserole, cover with water and add the prepared vegetables, bayleaves, salt and peppercorns. Bring to the boil and simmer gently, half covered, for about 2 hours. Test the chickens by piercing a thigh with a sharp knife – if the juices run completely clear, they are cooked, if they run at all pink, the chickens need longer. Then take the pan off the heat, and leave the chickens to cool in their cooking liquid.

When the chickens are cold, strip the meat, cutting it into evenly sized 1 in/2.5 cm pieces. Return the bones – but not the skin – to the stock, and bring back to the boil. Simmer for another hour. Strain the stock, and put it back in the saucepan. To clarify the stock, first bring it to the boil. Whisk 2 egg whites until stiff and whisk them into the boiling stock. Let the stock simmer under the egg whites, which will collect all the bits in the stock, for 15 to 20 minutes. Then strain through a large sieve lined with 2 thicknesses of kitchen paper into a bowl.

Measure the wine into a saucepan and sprinkle in the gelatine. Let the wine sponge up the gelatine, then measure the chicken stock into the saucepan. Heat gently, just enough to dissolve the gelatine granules completely. Taste and add salt as necessary. Take the pan off the heat and allow to cool. When the liquid is beginning to gel, add the chopped chicken and parsley – don't be tempted to add the parsley when the liquid is at all warm or the parsley will lose some of its fresh bright colour. Pour into a bowl or mould (this jelly doesn't turn out well from an elaborate mould, because of the chunks of chicken in it, and the best thing is a plain oval mould). Put it in the refrigerator to set for 2–3 hours or overnight. When it is quite firm, dip the mould into hot water for a few seconds and turn out onto a serving plate. Decorate, if you like, with bunches of fresh crisp parsley.

Ceviche of salmon
with tomato and cucumber mayonnaise

Purists or foodies say that true ceviche is made with shark. Well, I find shark rather hard to come by and so, I should think, do most people who don't live within a stone's throw of Billingsgate! You can, in fact, use any white fish, although the firmer fleshed the better. In this recipe I use salmon, which is just as delicious as any white fish for ceviche. The small cubes of fish are 'cooked' not by any heat source but by marinating for several hours in an acid mixture of lemon juice and white wine vinegar. In this case, they are served with a tomato and cucumber mayonnaise, which not only tastes delicious but provides a contrasting crunchy texture. I serve it with brown rice and a salad – or the spaghetti courgettes (see page 166) are very good with this.

Serves 6–8

---

3 lb/1.5 kg salmon, filleted, skinned and cut into ½ in/1 cm cubes or strips	½ tsp salt and freshly ground black pepper
¼ pt/150 ml lime or lemon juice	2 rounded tbsp finely chopped parsley and coriander to garnish
¼ pt/150 ml white wine vinegar	Tomato and cucumber
grated rind of 1 lemon	mayonnaise (see below)

Mix well together the cubed salmon, the lime or lemon juice, wine vinegar, grated lemon rind, salt and pepper in a wide shallow dish. Leave in a cool place for at least 4 hours. From time to time stir the salmon around, so that it marinates as evenly as possible.

To serve, drain the salmon of its marinade, and arrange on a serving dish. Sprinkle over the mixed parsley and coriander. Serve the accompanying mayonnaise (see below) separately in a bowl or sauce boat.

Tomato and cucumber mayonnaise

A delicious summery mayonnaise with a crunchy texture.

Makes about ⅓ pt/200 ml

---

1 whole egg plus 1 yolk
1 rounded tsp mustard powder
½ tsp salt
1 tsp caster sugar
freshly ground black pepper
about ¼ pt/150 ml oil (I use olive oil or a mixture of olive and sunflower)

about 3 tbsp wine vinegar (taste after adding 2 tbsp, and add more if you like a sharper mayonnaise)
3 tomatoes, skinned, deseeded and chopped
half a cucumber, halved lengthways, deseeded and finely diced

---

Put the whole egg and the yolk into a liquidizer or food processor, and add the mustard powder, salt, sugar and pepper. Blend until smooth. Continue blending and add the oil, drop by drop at first. When the mayonnaise is thick and smooth add the rest of the oil in a slow trickle, still blending. Lastly add the wine vinegar. If the mayonnaise is too thick, add 2 tablespoons very hot water. Turn the mayonnaise into a serving bowl, and carefully fold into it the tomatoes and cucumber.

Squid with tomato and black olives

We both love squid, as do most of our friends and, judging by how popular squid is when we put it on the menu here, a great many of our guests. It is so easy and quick both to prepare and cook. This dish can be served either hot or cold, and is equally good either way. I am generally governed by the weather – serving it cold on a very hot evening and hot on one of those chilly summer evenings.

2 lb/1 kg squid	*juice of half a lemon*
5 tbsp olive oil	*5–6 tomatoes, skinned, halved,*
2 garlic cloves, skinned and finely	*deseeded and cut into wedges*
chopped	*12 black olives, stoned and*
½ tsp salt	*halved*
lots of freshly ground black	*1 tbsp finely chopped parsley*
pepper	

Clean the squid by pulling out the plastic-like quill and the innards – they should come out easily. Wash the squid and pat dry with kitchen paper. Cut the tentacles into 1 in/2.5 cm lengths and the bodies into rings about ¼ in/6 mm thick.

Heat the olive oil in a frying pan and add the finely chopped garlic. Add the squid, and sauté, stirring so that it cooks evenly, until the pieces of squid are cooked and have turned opaque, about 2–3 mins. Season with salt, freshly ground black pepper and the lemon juice. Stir in the tomato wedges and halved black olives, and cook for a minute or two more. Turn onto a serving dish to serve hot, or to leave to cool and serve cold. Either way sprinkle with the finely chopped parsley before serving.

Blackcurrant and lemon suédoise

This simple and delicious pud has the added bonus of being low in calories for those who might be counting them – depending, of course, on how much whipped cream you eat with it! It is very good served with Greek yoghurt, too. The taste of lemon does seem to bring out the flavour of all other fruits.

175

---

2 lb/1 kg blackcurrants	*1 pt/600 ml water*
pared rind and juice of 2 lemons	*4 sachets gelatine –*
6 oz/175 g granulated sugar	*approximately 2 oz/50 g*

Put the blackcurrants into a saucepan (no need to top and tail them in this recipe), together with the lemon rinds and juice. Simmer until the blackcurrants are soft, then add the sugar, letting it dissolve in the hot blackcurrant juice. Sprinkle the gelatine over the water. When it has soaked into the water, stir this into the hot blackcurrants over a gentle heat. When the gelatine granules have completely dissolved, take off the heat and leave to cool.

Rinse out a jelly mould with cold water. Liquidize the blackcurrants and sieve the purée into a bowl. Pour the purée into the jelly mould and leave in the refrigerator to set for 2–3 hours or overnight. To turn out, dip the mould in hot water for a few seconds and invert onto a serving dish. Give the dish and mould a good shake, and the jelly should unmould itself with no trouble. If it won't come out, dip it into the hot water again and repeat the process. Serve with whipped cream or Greek yoghurt.

Redcurrant and whitecurrant compote with almond meringues and kirsch cream

Redcurrants and whitecurrants sadly aren't very widely available. They are so worthwhile growing. The jewel-like colours of stewed currants make a beautiful dish, set off best served in glass. I love to accompany them with small almond meringues, sandwiched together with kirsch-flavoured cream. Of course if you prefer, you can leave out the kirsch and just use plain whipped cream – as with all recipes, just adapt the ingredients to suit your taste.

Serves 6–8

---

1 lb/500 g redcurrants and whitecurrants, stripped from their tiny stems
2–3 oz/50–75 g sugar
FOR THE MERINGUES
3 large egg whites
6 oz/175 g caster sugar

2 oz/50 g flaked almonds, toasted until golden brown and cooled
FOR THE MERINGUE FILLING
½ pt/300 ml double cream
2 tbsp kirsch

Put the currants and sugar into a saucepan and cook over a gentle heat. As the currants begin to cook, their juices seep out and the sugar dissolves, making their own juice. When the currants are soft, take them off the heat and leave to cool. When they are cold, pour into a serving dish.

Line a baking sheet with siliconized greaseproof paper. Whisk the egg whites until stiff. Still whisking, gradually add the sugar until it is all incorporated and you have a stiff meringue. Fold the toasted flaked almonds into the meringue, quickly and thoroughly, with a large metal spoon. With 2 teaspoons, scoop the almond meringue mixture onto the baking sheet in small, evenly sized heaps. Bake them in a cool oven – 200°F/110°C/Gas ½/ top left oven in a 4 door Aga – for 1½ hours, or until they are quite firm. Take out of the oven and leave to cool. Not too long before your guests arrive, whip the cream with the kirsch. Sandwich together the tiny meringues with the cream and pile on a serving dish. They look much prettier piled up rather than arranged in a single layer.

Peach and hazelnut tart

The combination of rich pastry, whipped cream and juicy peaches makes this a luxurious pudding. The pastry case can be made a day in advance and the cream whipped, but it's best not to arrange the sliced peaches too long before serving as they tend to discolour.

Serves 6–8

FOR THE PASTRY
3 oz/75 g ground hazelnuts
4 oz/100 g butter, hard from the refrigerator
4 oz/100 g flour
1 oz/25 g icing sugar

FOR THE FILLING
8 peaches
lemon juice
½ pt/300 ml double cream
1 oz/25 g caster sugar

If you have a food processor, cut the butter into the bowl and add the ground hazelnuts, flour and icing sugar. Process until the mixture resembles fine breadcrumbs. If you are making the pastry by hand, put the hazelnuts, flour and sugar into a bowl. Cut in the butter and rub it with your fingertips until you have a crumb-like mixture. Pat the mixture around the base and sides of an 8 in/20 cm flan dish. Put the dish into the refrigerator for about an hour. Bake in a moderate oven – 350°F/180°C/Gas 4/ bottom right oven in a 4 door Aga – for 20 to 25 minutes, or until the pastry is golden brown. Leave to cool.

Skin the peaches and slice each one towards the stone. Brush with lemon juice, which helps to prevent them discolouring too much. Whip the cream together with the sugar. Spread the cream over the cooled pastry case, and, shortly before your guests arrive, arrange the slices of peach in a cartwheel pattern over the cream – an outer and an inner circle, the inner one going the opposite way to the outer.

Iced orange and apricot mousse

This iced mousse is light and delicious and, like any frozen pudding, convenient to plan for a dinner or lunch party, when you are going to be a bit pushed for time on the actual day itself.

Serves 8

---

8 oz/250 g apricots
juice of 2 oranges and pared rind
    of 1 orange
3 eggs, separated

2 oz/50 g icing sugar, sieved
½ pt/300 ml double cream
3 tbsp orange liqueur

Put the apricots into a saucepan together with the orange juice and rind (use a potato peeler to pare the rind as thinly as possible). Simmer gently until the apricots are soft. Then rub the apricots through a sieve, to get a smooth purée. Leave to cool.

Whisk the egg yolks, until they are thicker and pale. Whisk the egg whites until stiff, then gradually whisk in the sieved icing sugar, a spoonful at a time, until you have a stiff meringue. Whip the cream and orange liqueur together. Fold the apricot purée into the whipped cream. Fold the stiff yolk mixture into the apricot cream. Using a large metal spoon, fold the meringue mixture into the apricot mixture, and pour the whole thing into a large polythene container, seal and put in the deep freeze. Take the container out of the freezer 20 to 25 minutes before serving and keep it at room temperature. Scoop out into a chilled serving bowl to serve.

Nectarines with fudge sauce

This simple pudding consists of skinned nectarines covered with fudge sauce. It is not the most sophisticated of puddings, but the taste is hard to beat. The sauce can be stored in a screw-top jar in the refrigerator.

Serves 6

---

9 nectarines, skinned, halved and stoned
½ pt/300 ml double cream
4 oz/100 g butter

6–7 oz/175–200 g soft dark or light brown sugar
a few drops of vanilla essence

Cut each nectarine half in 3 and arrange in a shallow ovenproof dish. Put the cream, butter, sugar and vanilla essence together in a saucepan. Over a gentle heat melt the butter and dissolve the sugar, then boil for 5 to 7 minutes. Pour the sauce over the nectarines, and keep warm until you are ready to serve. I know it sounds like gilding the lily, but you can serve this with vanilla ice cream to satisfy even the sweetest of teeth.

September

I do love the autumn. When September comes I get a sort of second wind work-wise, and somehow feel invigorated. Quite early in the month there is a definite change in the colour of the trees here on Skye, and the bracken begins to turn coppery, too. With the heather in full bloom, this must be one of the most beautiful times of year in Scotland. The beastly midges, with which we are cursed during the summer months, at last begin to die off and by the third week in September they have virtually gone. If the weather is fine, September can be one of the most fruitful months for wild and free food – blackberries grow in abundance and there are pounds and pounds of chanterelles to be gathered from the mossy ground around our beech trees. The rowanberries are a vivid orangy red and ready for making into rowanberry jelly. There are all sorts of edible fungi, as well as chanterelles, growing in the woods round here. Some years we have such a glut of ordinary field mushrooms that we just can't keep up with the quantity coming into the kitchen! Given just such an abundance, I slice them, sauté them in butter and freeze them for use in soups, stuffings, casseroles, sauces and soufflés throughout the year. September is the first of the months when I feel like making warming dishes which use root vegetables, in fact having a real change of diet from the lighter food of the summer months.

First Courses

Chanterelle and leek soup
Mushroom and cheese feuilleté
Mushroom and garlic roulade
Mushroom and walnut pâté
Spinach, tomato and garlic soup

Main Courses

Cod baked with leeks and fresh ginger
Marrow stuffed with curried rice and vegetables
Roast duck with raspberry sauce
Venison braised with beetroot
Pork fillets in mushroom and soured cream sauce

Puddings

Blackberry and lemon mousse
Brown sugar meringues with lemon and blackberry sauce
Damson roulade
Plum compote with almond sponge cake
Spicy butter apple tart

Chanterelle and leek soup

When chanterelles are available I use them in everything I can, and they are particularly good in this soup. I reckon that any recipe which contains mushrooms can have chanterelles substituted. This soup, which like all soups is only as good as the stock in it, is very low in calories and makes a good dinner or lunch first course before a rich main course or pudding.

Serves 6–8

---

1 lb/500 g chanterelles, wiped and any bits of moss picked off, and chopped
2 oz/50 g butter
1 medium onion, skinned and finely chopped

4 medium leeks, washed, trimmed and very thinly sliced
½ tsp curry powder
2 pt/1.2 L chicken or vegetable stock
salt and freshly ground black pepper

Melt the butter in a saucepan and add the finely chopped onion. Sauté for 5 minutes, then add the sliced leeks, and cook over a gentle heat for a further 3 to 4 minutes. Add the chanterelles and curry powder, and sauté for another couple of minutes before pouring on the stock. Simmer very gently for 20 minutes, season with salt and freshly ground pepper and serve. If you are making it ahead of time, keep in a cool place and reheat to serve. This soup really needs no garnishing, but if you like sprinkle some finely chopped parsley on each plateful.

Mushroom and cheese feuilleté

A very quick and simple first course, which is also quite delicious and rather rich. The puff pastry is baked in a hot

183

oven, then split in half lengthways, cut in slices and sandwiched together with the cheesy mushroom filling.

Serves 6

---

1 lb/500 g mushrooms, wiped
    and thinly sliced
12 oz/350 g ready-made puff
    pastry
1 egg, beaten
5 oz/150 g Cheddar, finely
    grated
a dusting of paprika pepper
2 oz/50 g butter

2 oz/50 g flour
1 tsp mustard powder
¾ pt/450 ml milk (use a little
    bit more if the sauce seems too
    stiff for your liking)
salt and freshly ground black
    pepper
freshly grated nutmeg

Roll out the pastry, rolling in one direction only and not backwards and forwards, into an oblong about 12 × 4 in/30 × 10 cm. Lay on a greased baking sheet and bake in a hot oven – 400°F/200°C/Gas 6/top right oven in a 4 door Aga – for 12 to 15 minutes. Take it out, brush the top with beaten egg, sprinkle 2 oz/50 g of the finely grated cheese over it and dust with paprika. Put it back into the hot oven for a further 10 minutes or so, until it is well risen.

At the end of the baking time, take it out of the oven and leave to cool a bit. When it is cool enough to handle, split it in half lengthways using a serrated knife. When it is cooler still, slice each half into pieces about 2 in/5 cm wide. Trim the slices so that they are as neat as possible.

Meanwhile melt the butter in a saucepan and add the sliced mushrooms. Sauté for a minute or two, then stir in the flour and mustard powder. Cook for a further couple of minutes before gradually adding the milk, stirring until the sauce boils. Then stir in the remaining grated cheese, and season with salt, pepper and nutmeg to taste.

Sandwich two slices of pastry together with some of the mushroom and cheese filling for each person. Serve immediately on warmed plates.

The sauce can be made in advance and reheated to serve, but the pastry should be baked just before serving.

Mushroom and garlic roulade

This roulade is a great favourite here, both with us and our guests. Don't be tempted to skip the flavouring of the milk – it does make all the difference, and makes the roulade taste extra good. The filling is just cream cheese and chopped hard-boiled eggs flavoured with crushed garlic and parsley. Alternatively you can use less cream cheese and replace it with a layer of sliced red, yellow and green peppers, first sautéed until soft in olive oil. Both fillings are delicious.

Serves 6–8

FOR THE FLAVOURED
   MILK
1 pt/600 ml milk
1 onion, skinned and halved
1 celery stick, cut in 3
1 bayleaf
a few parsley stalks
½ tsp salt
8–12 black peppercorns
FOR THE ROULADE
1 lb/500 g mushrooms
3 oz/75 g butter
3 oz/75 g flour
reserved flavoured milk

4 large eggs, separated
salt and freshly ground black
   pepper
freshly grated nutmeg
FOR THE FILLING
8 oz/250 g cream cheese (or a
   low fat substitute, such as
   quark)
1 garlic clove, skinned and
   chopped
a few tbsp milk
2 rounded tbsp finely chopped
   parsley
4 hard-boiled eggs, chopped

Put all the ingredients for the flavoured milk into a saucepan, bring to scalding point over a gentle heat. Take the saucepan off the heat and leave to stand for 40 to 45 minutes. Strain the milk and reserve it for the roulade.

Wipe the mushrooms, put them into a liquidizer or food processor and blend until they are evenly pulverized. Pour the thick mushroom purée into a large sieve lined with 2 to 3 thicknesses of kitchen paper to absorb any excess moisture from the mushrooms.

Meanwhile melt the butter in a saucepan and stir in the flour. Cook for a couple of minutes. Stirring all the time, gradually add the flavoured milk. Stir until the sauce boils. Take the pan off the heat and beat in the egg yolks, one by one. Season with salt, pepper and nutmeg. Line a baking tin or Swiss roll tin, about 12 × 14 in/30 × 35 cm with siliconized greaseproof paper.

Fold the raw mushroom purée into the sauce. Whisk the egg whites until stiff, and, using a large metal spoon, fold them quickly and thoroughly into the mushroom sauce. Pour the mixture onto the lined tin and bake in a moderate oven – 350°F/180°C/Gas 4/bottom right oven in a 4 door Aga – for 20 to 25 minutes or until the roulade feels firm to touch. Take it out of the oven, cover with another piece of siliconized greaseproof paper and a damp tea towel, and leave to cool.

Put the cream cheese and garlic into a liquidizer or food processor and blend. Thin the mixture with a little milk – just enough to give the mixture a spreadable consistency. Add the chopped parsley and blend again. Turn the mixture into a bowl and mix in the hard-boiled eggs.

To assemble the roulade, first remove the tea towel and top sheet of paper. Lay a fresh piece of greaseproof paper on a table or work surface. Invert the roulade onto this. Carefully peel off the paper, tearing in strips parallel to the roulade – if you try to pull the whole sheet off at once, it tends to tear the roulade. Spread the roulade with the cream cheese and egg mixture, and roll it up lengthways, like a Swiss roll. Slip it on to a serving dish and serve in 2 in/5 cm slices.

Mushroom and walnut pâté

This quick and easy pâté can be served as a dip for crudités or as a pâté with wholemeal – granary, preferably – bread or toast. There is a good contrast of textures between the smooth mushroom pâté mixture and the chopped sautéed walnuts.

Serves 6

---

8 oz/250 g mushrooms, wiped and sliced

8 oz/250 g cream cheese (or quark if you prefer a low-fat cheese)

3 tbsp oil, sunflower if possible

juice of ½ a lemon

1 large garlic clove, skinned and chopped

3 oz/75 g walnuts, chopped

¼ tsp salt

A dash of Tabasco

freshly grated nutmeg

salt and freshly grated ground black pepper

Heat 2 tablespoons of oil in a saucepan and sauté the mushrooms for a minute. Then, with a slotted spoon remove the mushrooms from the saucepan. Put the mushrooms, cream cheese, lemon juice and garlic into a food processor (you can't really substitute a liquidizer for this recipe, the mixture is too stiff) and whizz till the ingredients are smooth.

Meanwhile, heat the remaining oil in a saucepan and add the walnuts and salt. Cook for 3–4 minutes, stirring so that the nuts cook evenly and don't burn. Then take them out of the pan. Taste the pâté in the processor, and season to your taste with Tabasco, nutmeg, salt and pepper. Scrape the pâté into a bowl, and then stir the chopped walnuts through it – and don't be tempted to add the nuts while the mixture is still in the processor, as the nuts would become pulverized to the same consistency as the pâté. Sprinkle with chopped parsley, if you like, to serve.

Spinach, tomato and garlic soup

This is one of the soups I like best, combining as it does three of my favourite flavours – spinach, tomato and garlic. It is extremely low in calories and makes a wonderful first course for a dinner party or a main course soup for lunch. It is very easy and quick to make. I use frozen chopped spinach so I don't bother to liquidize the soup, and the spinach and the pieces of tomato which are stirred through it give a nice texture. I don't think it needs a garnish – the chopped tomato does double duty as part of the soup and as garnish.

Serves 6–8

---

2 lb/1 kg frozen chopped spinach, thawed and drained
4 tomatoes, skinned, deseeded and chopped
3 tbsp olive oil
2 medium onions, skinned and very finely chopped

2 garlic cloves, skinned and finely chopped
2 pt/1.2 L chicken or vegetable stock
salt and freshly ground black pepper

Heat the olive oil in a saucepan and add the onions. Sauté for about 5 minutes, stirring occasionally to make sure that they cook evenly. Add the chopped garlic, and cook for a further minute or two before stirring in the spinach and the stock. Simmer the soup gently for 15 minutes, season to your taste and stir in the chopped tomatoes – check the seasoning again after the tomatoes have been added, and serve. You can make the soup, tomatoes and all, the day before you want to serve it, just reheating gently to serve.

Cod baked with leeks and fresh ginger

A simple dish that takes very little time to prepare and cook. If you have a steamer, you can steam the whole thing instead of sautéeing the leeks first, making it a very low-calorie dish indeed. I like to accompany it with creamy mashed potatoes and carrots or perhaps broccoli.

You can make this dish with any firm-fleshed white fish. It is particularly good made with turbot, but really fresh cod takes a lot of beating.

Serves 6

---

6 pieces of filleted cod, about 4–6 oz/100–175 g each
12 medium leeks, trimmed, washed and diagonally sliced into ½ in/1 cm pieces
2 in/5 cm piece of fresh root ginger, peeled and finely chopped

2 oz/50 g butter
1 tbsp oil (sunflower if possible)
salt and freshly ground black pepper
1 tbsp finely chopped parsley

If you are using a steamer, mix half the sliced leeks with half the ginger and arrange in the steamer, lay the cod fillets on top and season with salt and pepper. Cover with the remaining leeks and ginger, and steam until cooked, about 7 to 10 minutes. If you don't have a steamer, heat the butter and oil together in a casserole, and sauté the leeks and chopped ginger together over a fairly gentle heat, so that the leeks soften without turning in colour. Season with salt and pepper. When they are fairly soft, arrange half the leeks in a layer over the base of an ovenproof dish, lay the cod fillets on top and finish with another layer of leeks and ginger. Cover the dish and bake in a moderate oven – 350°F/180°C/Gas 4/bottom right oven in a 4 door Aga – for 20 to 25 minutes, or until the fish is cooked. If the dish is covered with foil rather than a lid, it will need longer cooking time, foil being such a bad conductor of heat. Sprinkle with chopped parsley to serve.

Marrow stuffed with curried rice and vegetables

Marrow can be deadly – often the only thing in its favour is that it contains virtually no calories because it is composed largely of water. But marrow *can* be very good, so make the most of them while they are in season in the autumn months. I like them best stuffed because they rely on accompanying vegetables or meat for flavour. The moistness of the marrow makes for a good juicy filling, and this one with curried rice and onions, peppers, garlic and mushrooms is delicious. Serve with an accompanying cheese or tomato sauce (see page 16) if you like.

Serves 6

---

1 large marrow, peeled and halved lengthways, with the seeds scooped out of each half
8 oz/250 g cooked brown rice
4 tbsp oil (I use sunflower)
2 onions, skinned and chopped
1 red and 1 yellow pepper, halved, deseeded and chopped

2 garlic cloves, skinned and chopped
1 tbsp curry powder
8 oz/250 g mushrooms, wiped and chopped
2 tsp tomato purée
salt and freshly ground black pepper

Heat the oil in a frying pan and add the onions and peppers. Sauté for about 5 minutes, stirring occasionally so that they cook evenly, then stir in the garlic and the curry powder, and cook for a further couple of minutes. Add the mushrooms and tomato purée. Season with salt and freshly ground black pepper and cook for 2 to 3 minutes. Mix this together thoroughly with the cooked brown rice.

Oil a large piece of foil, and put one half of the marrow on it. Pack the stuffing into the scooped-out hollow, mounding it up to fill the hollow in the other half which you put on top like a lid. Wrap the foil tightly around the marrow and put the foil parcel in a roasting tin. Bake in a fairly hot oven – 400°F/200°C/Gas 6/top right oven in a 4 door Aga – for 1¼ to 1½ hours; pierce the marrow with a knife to see whether it is soft and cooked. This dish keeps warm successfully for about an hour before serving. Cut the marrow into thick slices to serve, spooning the stuffing into the middle of each slice.

Roast duck with raspberry sauce

The raspberry sauce served with this roast duck makes a refreshing change from the more usual orangy sauces. Duck, domestic that is, is extremely popular when we put it on the menu here at Kinloch. I know that some people think it is difficult to deal with and are put off serving it at home, but really it is very simple to serve – the key is not to try to carve it. A duck has a broad breastbone with very little meat on it, and the best way to calculate how many ducks you will need is by allowing 1 duck per 4 diners. Then you can simply quarter each duck with strong scissors or game shears.

We buy ducks weighing approximately 5 lb/2.5 kg each. Much of the duck is fat which seeps out as the duck roasts, leaving behind the delicious crunchy skin. Don't be tempted to prick the skin at all before roasting or juices will run out during cooking and prevent the skin crisping properly – the crispy skin is the main attraction of roast duck. I like duck well done rather than fashionably pink, with revoltingly flabby skin and fat.

191

*2 ducks, weighing about 5 lb/2.5
   kg each*
                  Raspberry sauce *(see below)*

Put the ducks into a deep roasting tin and roast them in a
hot oven – 400°F/200°C/Gas 6/top right oven of a 4 door
Aga – for 2 hours. Once cooked they will keep warm until
you are ready to quarter and serve them. Accompany with
Raspberry sauce (see below).

Raspberry sauce

The raspberry sauce is tart and delicious served with rich
roast duck. It is also very easy to make, and can be made
several hours in advance and reheated to serve with the
roast duck. If you haven't got raspberry vinegar, you can
easily make your own by pushing some raspberries into a
bottle of wine vinegar and leaving it in a warm place for
several hours.

*8 oz/250 g frozen or fresh
   raspberries, thawed if frozen
¼ pint/150 ml wine vinegar
   (raspberry, if possible)
2 rounded tbsp granulated sugar
¾ pt/450 ml chicken stock, or
   stock made with the duck
   giblets*

*1 rounded tbsp arrowroot
juice of half a lemon
salt and freshly ground black
   pepper*

Put the wine vinegar and sugar into a saucepan and
simmer over a gentle heat until the sugar has dissolved.
Then boil the mixture fast until you have a caramel-like

syrup. Pour in the stock, taking care not to scald yourself on the whoosh of steam as the stock meets the caramel-like contents of the pan. Let the syrup and stock boil and reduce by about half.

Slake the arrowroot with the lemon juice and about 2 tablespoons water. Pour a little of the hot syrupy stock onto the slaked arrowroot, mix well, add more hot liquid, mix and return the arrowroot mixture to the saucepan, stirring until the sauce comes back to the boil. Stir in the raspberries and season with salt and pepper. Serve in a sauce boat or bowl.

Venison braised with beetroot

Sadly, beetroot is still synonymous with pickled beetroot to many people. Beetroot is a most delicious vegetable and makes wonderful soups. It has a special affinity with game, and in this recipe venison is cooked slowly with lots of beetroot, cut in julienne strips along with carrots and parsnips, making one of my favourite dishes for the increasingly cold autumn and winter months.

Serves 6–8

3 lb/1.5 kg venison, cut into 1 in/2.5 cm chunks	2 parsnips, peeled and cut into julienne strips
1 lb/500 g raw beetroot	2 carrots, peeled and cut into julienne strips
3 tbsp flour	
salt and freshly ground black pepper	1 garlic clove, skinned and finely chopped
2–3 oz/50–75 g beef dripping or 4–5 tbsp oil (I use sunflower)	1½ pt/1 L red wine and water mixed
2 onions, skinned and thinly sliced	2 tsp redcurrant jelly

Boil the beetroot in their skins until tender. Allow to cool a little, then peel them and cut into julienne strips.

Mix together the flour, salt and pepper. Toss the pieces of venison in this seasoned flour. Heat the dripping or oil in a casserole. When it is very hot, brown the meat all over, doing a few pieces at a time. Keep the browned meat warm while you continue browning the rest. Set the meat aside and keep warm. Add the onions to the fat in the casserole. Sauté for about 5 minutes, stirring occasionally, then add the parsnips, carrots, beetroot and garlic. Cook for a further 5 minutes, then stir in the red wine and water and the redcurrant jelly. Stir until the mixture boils, then return the meat to the casserole. Cover the casserole with a tightly fitting lid and cook in a moderate oven – 350°F/180°C/Gas 4/bottom right oven in a 4 door Aga – for 1½ hours. Take the casserole out of the oven at the end of the cooking time, allow to cool and reheat to serve. Somehow all casserole dishes taste so much better cooked and reheated. Reheat until the gravy is bubbling. I like to serve this dish with creamy mashed potatoes, and spicy red cabbage cooked with raisins and chopped apples.

Pork fillets in mushroom and soured cream sauce

This simple but ritzy main course dish can have chanterelles substituted for the mushrooms if they are available. It is very quick and easy to make, but doesn't reheat very well. Don't be put off making it, though – you can prepare the pork fillets in the morning ready to cook before your guests arrive, and slice the mushrooms all ready to pop into the frying pan. The finished dish can be kept warm for about half an hour in a low oven.

4 pork fillets (each weighing
   8–12 oz)
2 oz/50 g butter
2 tbsp oil (I use sunflower)
1 medium onion, skinned and
   finely chopped
1 lb/500 g mushrooms, wiped
   and sliced (keep their stalks
   for stock)

½ pt/300 ml single cream
¼ pt/150 ml double cream
salt and freshly ground black
   pepper
juice of half a lemon
1 tbsp finely chopped parsley to
   garnish

Start by preparing the fillets. Cut each fillet into 4 thick pieces. Sandwich each piece between two layers of clingfilm and pound gently with a rolling pin to flatten the round piece of pork fillet into an escalope. Heat the butter and oil together in a large frying pan. Brown the escalopes a few at a time so that the heat in the frying pan isn't reduced too much and the meat can really seal and cook. Cook the escalopes, turning them so that they cook evenly on both sides, for about 5 minutes each side. Test to see if they are done by sticking the point of a sharp knife into the middle of the meat – the juices should run clear. Put the escalopes into a warmed serving dish and keep them warm while you make the sauce. Add the onion to the fat in the frying pan and cook for about 5 minutes, stirring occasionally so that the onion cooks evenly. Then add the mushrooms, and cook for a minute or two before pouring in the single cream. Let the sauce simmer for 3 to 4 minutes, then add the double cream and the salt and pepper. Let the sauce boil for a few moments, then add the lemon juice and pour over the pork escalopes in the serving dish. Garnish with chopped parsley before serving.

Blackberry and lemon mousse

Lemon enhances all fruits, but particularly raspberries and blackberries. This mousse is most delicious, and makes a refreshing end to a rich dinner. If you like a more luxurious mousse, you can fold in ½ pt/300 ml whipped cream to the blackberry and lemon mixture before you fold in the stiffly whisked egg whites.

Serves 6–8

---

2 lb/1 kg blackberries
pared rind and juice of 2 lemons
1 sachet gelatine – approximately
  ½ oz/15 g

4 tbsp water
4 large eggs, separated
5 oz/150 g caster sugar

Put the blackberries into a saucepan together with the thinly pared lemon rinds and the lemon juice. Cook the blackberries over a gentle heat until they are soft. Allow to cool, then liquidize them. Sieve the liquidized blackberries for an absolutely smooth and seedless purée.

Sprinkle the gelatine on the water, leave it to sponge up, and then dissolve the gelatine granules over a very gentle heat.

Beat the egg yolks, gradually adding the caster sugar, beating until the mixture is thick and pale. Fold the lemon and blackberry purée into the yolk mixture and stir in the melted gelatine. Leave to set in a cool place until the mixture will coat the back of a metal spoon quite thickly. Then whisk the whites until they are very stiff, and, using a large metal spoon, fold them quickly and thoroughly into the blackberry mixture. Pour into a serving dish, and leave to set in a cool place.

You can make this mousse the day before serving. Decorate with whipped cream and serve with little almond or vanilla biscuits.

Brown sugar meringues with lemon and blackberry sauce

Here are the flavours of lemon and blackberry again, this time in a sauce served with brown sugar meringues. It is a very convenient pudding because the meringues can be made several days in advance and stored in an airtight container, and the sauce can be made two or three days in advance and kept in a covered bowl in the refrigerator. All you need to do to serve them is to sandwich together the meringues with whipped cream.

This sauce is also very good served with vanilla or lemon ice cream, or with hot apple pie instead of (or as well as!) cream.

Serves 6

FOR THE BROWN SUGAR
   MERINGUES
4 large egg whites
4 oz/100 g demerara sugar
4 oz/100 g granulated sugar
½ pt/300 ml double cream,
  stiffly whipped

FOR THE SAUCE
1 lb/500 g blackberries
pared rind and juice of 1 lemon
2–3 oz/50–75 g granulated
  sugar

Whisk the egg whites till fairly stiff, then gradually start to add the sugars, mixed together, spoonful by spoonful, whisking all the time until the sugar is all added. Pipe or spoon the meringue onto bakewell paper lined baking trays. I find piping much easier, that way you can get evenly sized meringues. Bake in a cool oven – 200°F/110°C/Gas ½/top left oven in a 4 door Aga. Bake for 2 to 2½ hours. Cool on a wire rack.

Make the sauce by putting the blackberries, pared lemon rind and juice into a saucepan, together with the

197

granulated sugar. Cook over a gentle heat until the black-berries are soft. Leave to cool and liquidize. Sieve the liquidized blackberries to get a seedless and smooth purée.

Before serving, sandwich together the meringues with the whipped cream, and pile them on a serving dish. Hand the lemon and blackberry sauce separately in a bowl or jug.

Damson roulade

This delicious version of a roulade was the invention of Angela Fox, who worked with us at Kinloch for three years several years ago, and from whom Pete and I learned a great deal. She usually comes and cooks with us for the month of October still, and this year came up with this winner of a pudding. I love the distinct tart flavour of damsons, far superior to that of any other plum. Like all roulades, this one has to be made ahead of time.

Serves 6–8

---

2 lb/1 kg damsons	*6 oz/175 g caster sugar*
3 oz/75 g granulated sugar	*½ pt/300 ml double cream*
4 eggs, separated	*icing sugar for dusting*

Line a 12 × 14 in/30 × 35 cm Swiss roll tin with siliconized greaseproof paper. Put the damsons into a saucepan together with the granulated sugar. Cook over a gentle heat until the juices of the damsons run and the sugar dissolves. When the damsons are soft, scoop them into a sieve with a slotted spoon and rub them through the mesh. Cool the purée.

Whisk the egg yolks, gradually adding 4 oz/100 g of the caster sugar, whisking until the mixture is pale and thick.

Fold the cooled damson purée into the yolk mixture. Whisk the egg whites until they are very stiff. With a large metal spoon, fold the whites quickly and thoroughly into the damson mixture, and pour into the lined Swiss roll tin. Bake in a moderate oven – 350°F/180°C/Gas 4/bottom right oven in a 4 door Aga – for 20 to 25 minutes, until the roulade feels firm. Take it out of the oven, cover with a fresh sheet of greaseproof paper and then a damp tea towel. Leave to stand for several hours.

Whip the cream with the remaining 2 oz/50 g caster sugar until fairly stiff. Remove the tea towel and the top sheet of greaseproof paper from the roulade. Dust a table or work surface with sieved icing sugar, and invert the roulade onto the icing sugar. Carefully peel the paper off the back of the roulade, peeling in strips parallel to the roulade. If you try to tear the paper off in one go, the roulade is inclined to tear.

Spread the surface of the roulade evenly with the whipped cream, and roll the roulade up lengthways and slip it onto a serving plate. Serve in 2 in/5 cm thick slices.

Plum compote with almond sponge cake

We have some guests – the Sanders – who stay with us every year during either August or September, and they invariably bring us a huge box full of plums from their garden. I would dearly love to see their garden, which must have dozens of plum trees, because every year Mrs Sanders has to cope with literally hundreds of basketfuls of plums! They are Victoria plums – the nicest of all for eating just as they are. I prefer to use tarter plums for cooking. In this compote the plums are cooked very slowly with orange juice and cinnamon, and are served with or without whipped cream (with for Godfrey, without for me) accompanied by *Almond sponge cake*.

Serves 6

---

2 lb/1 kg plums
3 oz/75 g granulated sugar
(more, if the plums are
particularly tart)

juice of 2 oranges
1 rounded tsp powdered
cinnamon

Put the plums, sugar, orange juice and cinnamon together into a saucepan. Cover the pan and cook the plums over a gentle heat until they are soft. Allow them to cool. Using a slotted spoon and a fork, take the stones out of the plums.

Almond sponge cake

---

4 oz/100 g softened butter or
margarine
4 oz/100 g caster sugar
2 large eggs

4 oz/100 g ground almonds,
sieved
icing sugar for dusting

Butter an 8 in/20 cm cake tin and line the base of the tin with a disc of siliconized greaseproof paper. Cream the butter or margarine, gradually adding the caster sugar. Beat together until the mixture is pale and fluffy. Beat in the eggs, one at a time. Lastly fold in the sieved ground almonds, using a metal spoon. Pour into the prepared cake tin and bake in a moderate oven – 350°F/180°C/Gas 4/bottom right oven in a 4 door Aga – for 25 to 30 minutes, until the cake is just beginning to come away from the sides of the tin. Cool on a wire rack, and dust with icing sugar before serving.

Spicy butter apple tart

This pie is very easy to make and delicious to eat. It is made with a filling of sliced apples (I use a tart eating apple, so that the slices stay as slices instead of breaking down into mush as cooking apples do) topped with a set 'custard' of butter, spices, soft brown sugar, eggs and vanilla essence. It is nicest served hot, with or without cream or Greek yoghurt.

Serves 6–8

FOR THE PASTRY
4 oz/100 g butter, hard from the refrigerator, cut in pieces
6 oz/175 g flour
1 oz/25 g icing sugar
FOR THE FILLING
4 tart eating apples
lemon juice

4 oz/100 g butter
5 oz/150 g light or dark soft brown sugar
1 rounded tsp powdered cinnamon
½ tsp grated nutmeg
a few drops of vanilla essence
4 large eggs

If you have a food processor, put all the pastry ingredients in together and process until the mixture is like fine breadcrumbs. If not, put all the ingredients in a bowl and rub in the butter with your fingertips until you have a crumb-like mixture. Pat out the mixture around the base and sides of an 8–9 in/20–22 cm flan dish. Put the flan dish into the refrigerator for about an hour, before baking in a moderate oven – 350°F/180°C/Gas 4/ bottom right oven in a 4 door Aga – for 20 to 25 minutes, or until the pastry is golden.

Peel, core and slice the apples. Brush with lemon juice to prevent the slices turning brown. Put the butter, sugar, spices and vanilla into a heatproof bowl. Beat the eggs and sieve them into the bowl. Put the bowl over a saucepan of gently simmering water until the butter melts and the sugar dissolves. Arrange the apple slices in the cooked pastry case and pour over the filling. Carefully put the flan dish into a moderate oven – 350°F/180°C/Gas 4/bottom right oven in a 4 door Aga – for 15 to 20 minutes, until the filling is just firm to the touch. Serve warm.

October

September is the run-in to autumn, and I don't feel that autumn proper begins until October. With the evenings getting darker earlier, I notice more of a change in October than in any other month, and there is nothing nicer than to sit by the fire and eat tea – crumpets, hot buttered cinnamon toast and all the delicious things which rightly belong to winter tea time.

Pheasants become available during October. Pheasants are more widely bred these days, and they can be bought from game dealers and poulterers. I have included in the main courses for this month a recipe for roast pheasant, with game chips and bread sauce. It might sound very old hat to some, but it's surprising just how many people don't realize that a slower roasted pheasant tends to be much juicier than one roasted at a high temperature, or that bread sauce can be a world apart from the gluey stuff made with steamed sliced bread. It's the same with game chips – it is so easy to make your own, and they can be done in the morning for dinner that night, much, much nicer than resorting to packets of bought potato crisps!

Winter vegetables such as celeriac become available again in October – one of my very favourite vegetables, probably because it is so versatile. All in all, October is a good month!

First Courses

Creamy celeriac soup
Curried savoury profiteroles with creamy white sauce
Game terrine with Cumberland jelly
Tomato and cheese soufflé

Main Courses

Sautéed sweetbreads with white wine and mushroom sauce
Roast pheasant with bread sauce and game chips
Sautéed chicken with sesame seeds and lemon,
parsley and horseradish sauce

Shepherd's pie with cheese and oatmeal crumble
Wild duck with apricot and lemon sauce

Puddings

Hazelnut brownies
Lime griestorte with lime curd
Prune, lemon and walnut tea bread
Oatmeal and raisin gingerbread
Pumpkin pie
Rich baked chocolate pudding with coffee cream sauce

Creamy Celeriac Soup

This delicious creamy soup, like most soups, can be made a day or even two days ahead of time, stored in a covered container in the refrigerator and reheated to serve. The creaminess of the name lies not in the ingredients but in the texture of the soup. I like to contrast the creamy texture with tiny, crunchy croûtons, fried in butter with a teaspoon of curry powder added. Make a good batch of croûtons, cool them on absorbent kitchen paper, and freeze them. Just reheat them to serve with soups.

Serves 6–8

---

1 average-sized celeriac, peeled and chopped	2 pts chicken stock
2 oz/50 g butter	salt and freshly ground black pepper
2 medium onions, peeled and chopped	2 tbsp finely chopped parsley
freshly grated nutmeg	tiny croûtons, fried in butter and 1 tsp curry powder, to garnish

---

Melt the butter in a saucepan and add the onions. Sauté for about 5 minutes, stirring occasionally to make sure that the onions cook evenly, then add the celeriac. Sauté for a further couple of minutes, then add the stock, nutmeg, salt and pepper. Simmer gently for 25 to 30 minutes, or until the celeriac is soft. Leave to cool a little. Liquidize and then sieve the soup, to get an extra creamy consistency. Reheat to serve, tasting to see if the seasoning is right for you. Just before serving stir the finely chopped parsley through the soup to prevent it looking too anaemic -- the parsley will lose its bright fresh green colour if it has to sit in the hot liquid for any length of time. If you like, add a swirl of cream to each plateful of soup and serve. Hand the croûtons separately.

Curried savoury profiteroles with creamy white sauce

The cheesey profiteroles for this dish can be made in advance and frozen, and simply defrosted, reheated and filled before serving. The filling can be made up in the morning, all ready to fill the profiteroles for dinner the same evening. These savoury profiteroles make an unusual and delicious first course or an ideal 'eat' to serve with drinks. For a first course, serve with the *Creamy white sauce* (see below) spooned over. Leave it out if people will be eating them with their fingers!

Serves 6

FOR THE PROFITEROLES
½ pt/300 ml water
5 oz/150 g butter
7 oz/200 g flour, sieved twice
2 rounded tsp mustard powder
a few drops of Tabasco
4 eggs

3 oz/75 g well flavoured
Cheddar, grated
FOR THE FILLING
1 oz/25 g butter
1 medium onion, skinned and
finely chopped
1 rounded tsp curry powder
10 oz/300 g cream cheese

First make the choux pastry for the profiteroles. Put the water into a saucepan and cut the butter into it. Over a gentle heat melt the butter in the water, then let the liquid come to the boil. As soon as it begins to bubble, take the pan off the heat and add the flour and mustard powder all at once. Beat hard until the mixture comes away from the sides of the pan. Leave to cool for 10 minutes or so. Beat in the Tabasco and the eggs, one by one, beating really well until the choux paste is glossy. Mix in the grated cheese. Pipe or spoon the pastry into small blobs about 1 in/2.5 cm across on a baking tray. Leave enough space for the profiteroles to expand during cooking. Bake in a hot oven – 450°F/220°C/Gas 7/top right oven in a 4 door Aga – for 10 to 15 minutes, until the cheese choux buns are well risen, golden brown and quite firm to the touch. Cut one in half and if there is still undercooked dough inside, pop the profiteroles back in the oven for a few more minutes. Cool them on a wire rack.

To prepare the filling, melt the butter in a saucepan and add the onion. Sauté for about 5 minutes, stirring from time to time, then stir in the curry powder and cook for a further 4 to 5 minutes. Take the saucepan off the heat and leave to cool.

Put the curried onion mixture into a liquidizer or food processor and add the cream cheese. Blend until smooth. Halve the profiteroles and spoon in the filling.

To serve, pop the filled profiteroles on a baking tray and bake in a hot oven – 425°F/220°C/Gas 7 – for 2 to 3 minutes, just long enough to heat them through.

Creamy white sauce

This creamy sauce has a million uses in the kitchen, and complements the *Curried savoury profiteroles* (see above) beautifully.

Makes ½ pt/300 ml

---

2 oz/50 g butter	*salt and freshly ground black*
1 garlic clove, skinned and very	*pepper*
finely chopped	*freshly grated nutmeg*
1 rounded tbsp flour	*1 rounded tbsp finely chopped*
½ pt/300 ml milk	*parsley*

Melt the butter in a saucepan and add the finely chopped garlic and the flour. Cook for 2 to 3 minutes, stirring continuously. Gradually add the milk, beating it in as you go. Let the sauce boil for a minute, still stirring, then take it off the heat. Season to taste with salt, pepper and nutmeg. Just before serving, stir in the finely chopped parsley.

If you are serving it with the profiteroles, spoon a little over the top of each one. Sprinkle with more parsley, if you like.

Game terrine with Cumberland jelly

This makes a delicious first course, or a main course served with baked potatoes and a salad or two. It has to be made in advance, up to 2 or 3 days ahead, and kept in the refrigerator. Cumberland jelly (see below) goes so well with it but is a purely optional accompaniment.

Serves 8 (6 as a main course)

---

1 lb/500 g game meat, such as pigeon, pheasant or hare, or a combination, cut off the bone and finely chopped
4 tbsp olive oil
¼ pt/150 ml red wine
3–4 juniper berries, crushed
pared rind of 1 orange
2 medium onions, skinned and finely chopped

8 oz/250 g lamb's liver, trimmed and finely chopped
1 lb/500 g good pork sausagemeat
salt and freshly ground black pepper
3 bayleaves
12–14 streaky bacon rashers

First prepare the marinade. Put the oil, red wine, juniper berries and orange rind in a saucepan over a moderate heat, and bring to the boil. Simmer for a minute, then draw off the heat and cool. Put the onions, game meat and liver together in a bowl and pour over the marinade. Mix

208

well and leave to marinate for several hours or overnight.

At the end of the marinating time, strain off and discard the liquid from the marinade, and fish out the orange peel. Mix the game, liver and onions together with the sausagemeat and salt and pepper. The only way to do this mixing properly is with your hands – a rather satisfyingly squelchy affair!

Line a terrine or loaf tin with foil and lay the 3 bayleaves on the bottom. Line with the streaky bacon rashers, and fill with the game and sausagemeat mixture, packing it well down. Cover with foil and stand the terrine in a roasting tin, with water coming halfway up the sides of the terrine. Bake in a moderate oven – 350°F/180°C/Gas 4/bottom right oven in a 4 door Aga – for 2 to 2½ hours, or until the juices run clear when you stick a skewer into the terrine.

Take it out of the oven, lift it out of the roasting tin, and put a weight on top – I use tins of baked beans for this purpose. Leave in a cool place until quite cold. To serve, unwrap the foil and turn out the terrine – it looks attractive with the bayleaves uppermost on the streaky bacon. Slice and serve.

Cumberland jelly

This Cumberland jelly goes very well with all cold meats, and it is delicious with hot venison dishes, too. It makes a good little present to give to friends, and it keeps well for 3 to 4 weeks in the refrigerator.

Makes ½ pt/300 ml

8 oz/250 g redcurrant jelly	*2 tsp powdered gelatine*
1 rounded tbsp mustard powder	*grated rind and juice of 1 orange*
¼ pt/150 ml port	*grated rind and juice of 1 lemon*

Put the redcurrant jelly and mustard powder into a saucepan, and gradually stir in the port. Sprinkle on the gelatine powder and add the orange and lemon rinds and juice. Over a gentle heat, stir until the redcurrant jelly and the gelatine granules have dissolved completely. Pour into warmed jars, and leave to cool and set for 2–3 hours or overnight. Store in the refrigerator until you want to serve it.

Tomato and cheese soufflé

Soufflés don't deserve the mystique with which they are surrounded – most of the preparation can be done ahead of time, leaving only the whisking and addition of the egg whites to the last minute. The one thing to remember with a soufflé is that it just won't wait once it's cooked – it has to be eaten immediately. So I reckon that soufflés are really only suitable for small and informal entertaining, for groups of friends who you can depend on not to vanish to the loo when you say that supper is ready. There is nothing sadder than watching a soufflé slowly but surely deflate!

Serves 4–5

---

3 oz/75 g butter
1 large garlic clove, skinned and crushed
3 oz/75 g flour
1 rounded tsp mustard powder
1 pt/600 ml milk
salt and freshly ground black pepper

freshly grated nutmeg
6 oz/175 g well flavoured Cheddar, grated
6 large eggs, separated
a little grated Parmesan (optional)
5 tomatoes, skinned, deseeded and chopped

Melt the butter in a saucepan, and stir in the garlic, flour and mustard powder. Cook for a couple of minutes, stirring occasionally, then gradually add the milk, stirring all the time until the sauce boils. Season with salt, pepper and nutmeg, and stir in the cheese – it sounds a lot of cheese, but you need it for a good flavour. Add the egg yolks, one at a time, beating well in. Butter a 2 pt/1.2 L soufflé dish and dust it with the Parmesan cheese if you have it. Cover the sauce with dampened greaseproof paper to prevent a skin forming.

About 45 minutes before you want to serve the soufflé, stir the chopped tomatoes into the soufflé sauce and whisk the egg whites until they are very stiff, and, using a large metal spoon, fold them quickly and thoroughly into the sauce. Pour into the buttered soufflé dish, and bake in a hot oven – 425°F/220°C/Gas 7/top right oven in a 4 door Aga – for 40 minutes (a further 5 minutes won't hurt the soufflé and it gives you and your guests time to get seated). I like to serve soufflés with hot garlic-buttered brown rolls, which have been wrapped in foil and warmed until the garlic butter soaks into the bread, and a green salad.

Sautéed sweetbreads with white wine and mushroom sauce

Sweetbreads fall into the category of food which people either love or wouldn't touch with a bargepole. Godfrey's passion for sweetbreads is such that on a recent visit to France he ordered them three nights running. When we serve them here we find the response is unpredictable – anything from 10 to 75 per cent of our guests might choose them. Sweetbreads do take a bit of time to prepare for sautéeing, but they are so delicious it is well worth the trouble. *White wine and mushroom sauce* (see below) complements the sweetbreads very well.

211

2–2½ lb/1–1.25 kg sweetbreads
(calf's are the nicest, with
lamb's coming a good second –
whichever you have, the
preparation is the same)
2 slices of lemon

½ tsp salt
1 pt/600 ml chicken stock
2 oz/50 g butter
1 tbsp oil (I use sunflower)
White wine and mushroom
   sauce (see below)

Rinse the sweetbreads well under cold running water. Put them into a saucepan and cover with fresh cold water. Add the lemon slices and salt, and bring to the boil. Drain and return to the rinsed-out pan. Pour over the chicken stock and bring to the boil. Simmer gently for 10 minutes, then drain them. Leave to cool. When they are cool enough to handle, trim each piece of sweetbread of its membranes and gristly bits. Slice the sweetbreads into pieces more or less the same size, ready for sautéeing.

When you are ready to cook the sweetbreads heat the butter and oil together in a frying pan. Fry the sliced sweetbreads until they are golden. Serve them with the *White wine and mushroom sauce* (see below), poured over.

White wine and mushroom sauce

Makes 1 pt/600 ml

1 pt/600 ml dry white wine
2 medium onions, skinned and
   very finely chopped
2 oz/50 g butter
8 oz/250 g mushrooms, wiped
   and sliced

2 rounded tbsp flour
1 pt/600 ml milk
salt and freshly ground black
   pepper
freshly grated nutmeg
finely chopped parsley to garnish

Put the wine and onions into a saucepan over a moderate heat, and simmer uncovered, until the wine has reduced by about three-quarters and the onions are very soft.

Melt the butter in another saucepan and add the sliced mushrooms. Stir in the flour and cook for a couple of minutes. Gradually add the milk, stirring continuously until the sauce boils. Stir in the salt, pepper and nutmeg, and the onion and wine liquid.

Pour over the sautéed sweetbreads in a serving dish, and sprinkle with the chopped parsley.

Roast pheasant with bread sauce and game chips

This seems rather an obvious item to include in this book – obvious, because to many people straight roast pheasant seems to be so easy. But it isn't often that you come across really good roast pheasant really properly produced with creamy bread sauce and proper game chips. Game gravy should be thin in texture and intense in flavour – it's a matter of taste, but I generally add port to mine.

Serves 6

2 pheasants approximately 2–2½ lb/1–1.25 kg each	*butter*
several rashers of streaky bacon (smoked if possible)	*salt and freshly ground black pepper*

Smear butter over the breasts of the pheasants, season with a little salt and freshly ground black pepper, and cover the pheasants with the streaky bacon. You can do all this in the morning so that the pheasants are all ready to pop into the oven before dinner that evening. Roast them in a hot oven – 400°F/200°C/Gas 6/top right oven in a 4 door Aga – for 20 minutes, then lower the temperature to 350°F/180°C/Gas 4/bottom right oven in a 4 door Aga and continue to roast the birds for about an hour. Test to see whether they are cooked by piercing a leg at the point where it joins the body – if the juices run clear, and are not tinged with pink, they are ready. I find that dropping the oven temperature prevents the pheasant flesh drying out too much. Keep the pheasants warm until you are ready to carve and serve them.

Bread sauce

Really good bread sauce needs to be made from baked bread, not the steamed, sliced sort. It freezes beautifully, so you can either make it in advance or freeze any which happens to be left over.

Makes 1 pt/600 ml

---

1 pt/600 ml milk
1 medium onion, skinned
6 cloves

salt and freshly ground black pepper
6 oz/175 g fresh breadcrumbs
1–2 oz/25–50 g butter

Put the milk into a saucepan. Stick the cloves into the onion and add to the milk. Season with salt and pepper, and heat the milk until a skin forms. Then take the pan off the heat, and leave the onion in the milk to flavour it. Allow to stand for at least an hour. Stir the breadcrumbs into the flavoured milk. Throw out the onion, reheat the milk and stir in the butter. If the sauce is too stiff for your liking, add some more milk.

214

Game chips

Game chips, either wafer thin slices or matchsticks, can be made in the morning and reheated to serve with pheasants for dinner.

To make good game chips you really need a mandoline, because you can't slice the potatoes thinly enough by hand – I know, I've tried! The slices have to be thin to stay crisp – if they are too thick, they will go flabby soon after frying. We make matchsticks here for our guests. Our mandoline has a matchstick blade, and the matchsticks don't take a minute to cook.

Serves 6

---

fat for deep frying   *salt*
1½ lb/750 g potatoes

A chip pan with a wire basket is the best utensil for cooking the chips. You can use an ordinary saucepan with a metal slotted spoon for fishing out the cooked chips or matchsticks, but you have to be quick about it so as not to burn any in the saucepan.

Pour fat into the pan to a depth of about 4 in/10 cm and heat until it sizzles when you drop a piece of potato in. Cook your chips or matchsticks, in batches if necessary, until they are golden brown. Drain them, and put them in a roasting tin lined with several thicknesses of kitchen paper to absorb excess grease. Sprinkle them with a little salt, and either leave and reheat to serve or keep warm to serve.

Sautéed chicken with sesame seeds and lemon, parsley and horseradish sauce

This is one of those dishes which is dead easy to make, but can be dressed up for the dinner party table simply by serving an unusual sauce alongside. Our children love these sautéed chicken breasts with their crispy coating of sesame seeds as much as we do!

Serves 6

---

6 chicken breasts
1 egg, beaten
2 oz/50 g sesame seeds

sunflower oil for frying
Lemon, parsley and
 horseradish sauce *(see below)*

Pat the chicken breasts dry with absorbent kitchen paper before dipping them first in the beaten egg and then in the sesame seeds. Pour sunflower oil into a frying pan to a depth of about ¼ in/5 mm and fry the chicken pieces until they are golden brown all over and cooked through. This takes about 10 minutes, turning the chicken breasts over and over during the cooking, so that they cook evenly. Keep warm on an ovenproof dish lined with two or three thicknesses of kitchen paper to absorb any excess oil. Make the sauce (see below) and hand it separately.

Lemon, parsley and horseradish sauce

This sauce is tangy and delicious, so good with both chicken and grilled fish.

¼ pt/150 ml single cream	salt and freshly ground black
¼ pt/1..0 ml milk	pepper
1 tbsp grated horseradish	grated rind of 2 lemons and juice
1 tsp flour	of 1 lemon
2 oz/50 g butter	2 rounded tbsp finely chopped
2 egg yolks	parsley

Put all the ingredients except the lemon juice and parsley into a liquidizer or food processor, and blend until smooth. Pour into a heatproof bowl. Stand the bowl in a roasting tin with water coming halfway up the sides of the bowl. Cook, with the water just about simmering, stirring from time to time with a wire whisk, for about 20 to 25 minutes. When the sauce has thickened, stir in the lemon juice and, just before serving, the finely chopped parsley. If you add the parsley too soon, so that it has to sit in the hot sauce, it will lose its bright fresh colour. Serve separately in a bowl or sauce boat.

Shepherd's pie with cheese and oatmeal crumble

Shepherd's pie features often on our family menu. We generally eat up the leftovers from the hotel kitchen larder, which usually includes joints of beef, lamb or venison waiting to be made into shepherd's pie or something similar. Sometimes I put leeks in a creamy sauce on top of shepherd's pie instead of mashed potatoes or, another alternative as in this recipe, a sort of savoury crumble of oatmeal and grated cheese.

Shepherd's pie is a rather vague name for any pie dish using leftover meat, but a real shepherd's pie is never made with raw meat – nor with shepherds. One Sunday just before Christmas last year, when shepherds were uppermost in our minds in connection with cribs and wise men, our youngest, Hugo, then aged three, hissed at me during the sermon, 'What's for lunch?' 'Shepherd's pie,' said I. '*Real* shepherds?' he asked, with glee.

Serves 6–8

FOR THE FILLING
1½–2 lb/750 g–1 kg cooked lamb, beef or venison, cut off the bone, trimmed of fat and gristle, and finely minced
2–3 oz/50–75 g dripping or 5 tbsp oil (sunflower, if possible)
2 medium onions, skinned and chopped
4 carrots, peeled and finely diced
2 parsnips, peeled and finely diced
1 rounded tbsp wholemeal flour
1 pt/600 ml water or leftover gravy
1 tbsp tomato purée
salt and freshly ground black pepper
FOR THE TOPPING
3 oz/75 g wholemeal flour
3 oz/75 g medium oatmeal or porridge oats
4 oz/100 g grated Cheddar
1 rounded tsp mustard powder

Heat the dripping or oil in a casserole and add the onions, carrots and parsnips. Sauté the vegetables for about 10 minutes, stirring from time to time so that they cook evenly. Add the minced meat and cook for another minute or two. Stir in the flour and cook for a further couple of minutes. Pour on the water or gravy and stir it in, together with the tomato purée and salt and pepper. Bring to the boil, stirring all the time. Cover with a lid and simmer gently for 20 minutes or so.

Mix all the ingredients for the crumble together well, rubbing them with your fingertips. Sprinkle the crumble over the meat filling in the casserole, and cook in a moderate oven – 350°F/180°C/Gas 4/bottom right oven in a 4 door Aga – for 30 to 35 minutes, until the crumble is golden brown. I like to serve this pie with baked potatoes and cabbage, stir-fried with grainy mustard or grated nutmeg.

Wild duck with apricot and lemon sauce

Both roast wild duck and domestic duck are good with this sauce. I like to serve a green vegetable, such as celery with walnuts and orange segments, with the duck, and perhaps sautéed potatoes.

Serves 6

---

3 mallard duck, approximately	*2 oz/50 g butter*
1½–2 lb/¾–1 kg each	Apricot and lemon sauce
2 oranges	*(see below)*

Put half an orange inside each duck, and rub the ducks all over with butter. Roast in a hot oven – 400°F/200°C/Gas 6/top right oven in a 4 door Aga – for about 45 minutes. Keep warm, then carve the breasts, and serve with the following sauce.

219

Apricot and lemon sauce

This delicious sauce can be made in advance if necessary.

Makes 1 pt/600 ml

---

6 oz/175 g dried apricots
1 rounded tbsp granulated sugar
¼ pt/150 ml red wine vinegar
1 pt/600 ml chicken stock or stock
  made with the duck giblets
  and root vegetables, scrubbed
  and chopped

1 rounded tbsp cornflour
grated rind and juice of 1 lemon
salt and freshly ground black
  pepper

Chop the apricots. Put them in a saucepan, cover with water and simmer for 40 to 45 minutes, then drain.

Put the sugar and the wine vinegar into a saucepan over a gentle heat. When the sugar has dissolved completely, boil fast until you have a caramel-like syrup. Pour on the stock, and boil fast for another 5 minutes. Slake the cornflour with the lemon juice, and stir in a little of the hot liquid from the pan. Stir the lemony mixture back into the hot liquid, and continue stirring until the sauce boils. Add the grated lemon rind and the plumped-up apricots. Season with salt and freshly ground black pepper to your taste, and reheat to serve with the roast duck.

Hazelnut brownies

Brownies are more widely known as a teatime goody, but they also make a lovely pudding, served warm with vanilla ice cream, loved by sweet-toothed child and adult alike. These brownies contain hazelnuts instead of the more usual walnuts, which makes quite a difference. I love the combination of hazelnuts and chocolate, and I can't imagine why I didn't think of putting hazelnuts in brownies years ago. These brownies keep well in an airtight container for several days. They are much nicer a little undercooked and gooey, rather than baked solid.

Makes 12–14 squares

---

2 oz/50 g hazelnuts
4 oz/100 g butter
4 oz/100 g dark chocolate
10 oz/300 g soft dark brown
   sugar

4 large eggs, beaten
8 oz/250 g self-raising flour
1 oz/25 g cocoa powder

Toast the hazelnuts and rub off their papery skins by rolling them in a tea towel – it doesn't matter if bits of skin are left on.

Melt the butter and chocolate together in a saucepan, and then stir in the brown sugar. Add the beaten eggs, beating well into the chocolate mixture. Sieve in the flour and cocoa powder, and stir in the hazelnuts.

Butter a 10 × 12 in/25 × 30 cm baking tin and line with siliconized greaseproof paper. Spoon and scrape the brownie mixture into the tin, and smooth it evenly. Bake in a moderate oven – 350°F/180°C/Gas 4/bottom right oven in a 4 door Aga – for 20 minutes. Take out of the oven and leave to cool in the baking tin. When it is cold, cut into squares and store in an airtight container.

Lime griestorte with lime curd

This is a wonderful pud for a dinner party. The semolina gives the cake a slightly grainy texture – there is no flour in it. You can use lemons instead of limes if you prefer.

FOR THE CAKE
3 eggs, separated
4 oz/100 g caster sugar
grated rind of 2 limes and juice
  of 1 lime
2½ oz/60 g fine semolina

FOR THE FILLING
Lime curd *(see below)*
½ pt/300 ml double cream,
  whipped fairly stiffly
icing sugar for decoration

Butter an 8 in/20 cm diameter cake tin and line the base with a disc of siliconized greaseproof paper.

Put the 3 yolks into a bowl and beat, gradually adding the caster sugar. Beat until the mixture is thick, pale and mousse-like – about 15–20 minutes. Add the lime juice and rind, beating in well. Fold in the semolina. Whisk the egg whites until very stiff. Using a large metal spoon, fold the egg whites quickly and thoroughly into the lime mixture. Pour and scrape into the prepared cake tin, and bake in a low to moderate oven – 325°F/170°C/Gas 3/bottom of the bottom right oven in a 4 door Aga – for 35 to 40 minutes, until the cake is springy to the touch. Take it out of the oven, leave to cool for a couple of minutes in the tin, then turn out onto a wire rack to cool completely.

To fill the cake, cut it in half with a serrated knife. Put the bottom half onto a serving plate, and spread it with *Lime curd*. Spread the cream over the *Lime curd* and replace the top half of the cake. Sieve a spoonful of icing sugar over the cake to decorate it. You can assemble the cake a couple of hours or more before serving it.

Lime curd

The lime curd can be made up to a week in advance and kept in a covered container in the refrigerator.

2 oz/50 g butter	*1 whole egg plus 2 yolks, beaten*
4 oz/100 g granulated sugar	*together and sieved*
	grated rind and juice of 3 limes

Put the butter, sugar, sieved egg and yolks, grated lime rinds and lime juice into a heatproof bowl over a saucepan of gently simmering water. Stir as the butter melts and the sugar dissolves, then stir occasionally as the curd thickens. When the curd is very thick, take the bowl off the heat and set aside to cool. When it has cooled, pour into a jar, cover and store in the refrigerator until you are ready to use it.

Prune, lemon and walnut teabread

This delicious teabread has a thin lemon-flavoured icing and, like all teabreads, it is served sliced and buttered. It doesn't keep very well – not for much more than two days – so if you want to make it in advance, freeze it and then thaw it on the day it is to be served.

4 oz/100 g prunes	*3 oz/75 g light or dark soft*
China tea for simmering the	*brown sugar*
prunes	*3 oz/75 g walnuts, chopped*
2 tbsp golden syrup	*grated rind and juice of 2 lemons*
¼ pt/150 ml milk	*1 large egg, beaten*
8 oz/250 g self-raising flour	*6 oz/175 g icing sugar*
1 rounded tsp powdered	
cinnamon	

Simmer the prunes in the China tea for 30 minutes. Drain them, allow to cool a little, then cut the prune flesh off the

223

stones and chop. The prunes won't be fully plumped up, but they aren't meant to be.

Butter a 2 lb/1 kg loaf tin and line the base and short sides with siliconized greaseproof paper. Put the golden syrup and milk into a saucepan and dissolve the syrup over gentle heat.

Sieve the flour and cinnamon into a bowl, and add the soft brown sugar, walnuts and prunes. Add the lemon rinds (not the juice) to the bowl, and beat in first the syrupy milk and then the egg. Beat all well together, then pour and scrape the mixture into the prepared loaf tin. Bake in a low to moderate oven – 325°F/170°C/Gas 3/bottom of the bottom right oven in a 4 door Aga – for about 1 hour 15 minutes, or until a skewer stuck into the middle of the loaf comes out clean. Allow to cool in the tin for 10 minutes, then turn out onto a wire rack and cool completely.

Sieve the icing sugar and mix it with enough lemon juice to make it spreadable. Cover the top of the cooled tea-bread with the lemony icing. Slice to serve.

Oatmeal and raisin gingerbread

October is the month when I begin to seek inspiration for teatime goodies. It must be something to do with it getting dark earlier in the afternoons, and the general cosiness of the fireside with the curtains drawn against the chilly dark evenings.

This gingerbread is moist and tasty. This same recipe can be made free of dairy produce, substituting granose for butter and orange juice for milk – I've done it and it is just as delicious, but it won't keep quite as well as it does when made with butter and milk.

224

3 oz/75 g treacle	*grated rind of 1 orange*
3 oz/75 g golden syrup	*grated rind of 1 lemon*
3 oz/75 g soft brown sugar	*2 rounded tsp ground ginger*
4 oz/100 g medium oatmeal	*1 rounded tsp baking powder*
7 oz/200 g wholemeal flour	*2 oz/50 g raisins*
4 oz/100 g butter	*½ pt/300 ml milk*

Put the treacle, golden syrup and soft brown sugar together in a saucepan over a gentle heat to melt and dissolve. Mix together the oatmeal and flour in a bowl. Cut in the butter and rub with your fingertips until the mixture is like breadcrumbs. Mix in the grated orange and lemon rinds, and the ground ginger and baking powder. Stir in the warm treacle, syrup and sugar mixture, and finally the raisins and milk.

Grease a shallow 12 × 10 in/30 × 25 cm baking tin and line with siliconized greaseproof paper. Pour the mixture into the prepared tin and bake in a moderate oven – 350°F/180°C/Gas 4/bottom right oven in a 4 door Aga – for 25 to 30 minutes. Take it out of the oven, cool in the tin, and when cold cut it into squares. Store in an airtight tin or container, and try to keep it for 2 days before eating – the flavour will improve with keeping!

Pumpkin pie

Halloween falls in October and gap-toothed leering-faced pumpkin lanterns, with a candle flickering inside, stare out from many windows. The scooped-out pumpkin flesh can be made into a delicious pie, very appropriate Halloween fare. An Australian friend taught me the secret of a good pumpkin pie – cooking the pumpkin flesh in milk, not in water as I had done in previous attempts to make an edible pumpkin pie.

Serves 6–8

FOR THE PASTRY
4 oz/100 g butter, hard from the
   refrigerator and cut in pieces
1 oz/25 g icing sugar
5 oz/150 g flour
a few drops of vanilla essence
FOR THE FILLING
1 lb/500 g pumpkin flesh,
   roughly chopped

1½ pt/1 L milk
a cinnamon stick
3 oz/75 g soft brown sugar
½ tsp freshly grated nutmeg
1 rounded tsp powdered
   cinnamon
2 oz/50 g butter
3 large eggs

If you have a food processor, put all the ingredients for the pastry in the bowl and process until the mixture is like fine breadcrumbs. If you are making the pastry by hand, mix the icing sugar and flour into a bowl. Rub in the pieces of butter with your fingertips until you have a crumb-like consistency. Add the vanilla essence.

Pat the pastry mixture around the sides and base of an 8–9 in/20–22 cm flan dish, and put it into the refrigerator for about 1 hour. Bake in a moderate oven – 350°F/180°C/ Gas 4/bottom right oven in a 4 door Aga – for 20 to 25 minutes, until the pastry is golden brown. Take it out of the oven and leave to cool.

Put the pumpkin flesh into a saucepan together with the milk and cinnamon stick. Simmer gently for 35 to 40 minutes, then discard the cinnamon stick and drain the pumpkin flesh well. Put the cooked pumpkin flesh into a liquidizer or food processor together with the soft brown sugar, nutmeg, cinnamon and butter and blend to a smooth purée. Add the eggs, one at a time, and blend again. Pour the pumpkin mixture into the pastry case and bake in a moderate oven – 350°F/180°C/Gas 4/bottom right oven in a 4 door Aga – until the filling is just firm to the touch, about 20 to 25 minutes. Serve warm.

Rich baked chocolate pudding with coffee cream sauce

This is an extremely rich chocolate pudding, right up my street and absolutely irresistible to all chocolate lovers. I like to serve it with *Coffee cream sauce* (see below), the two flavours complement each other so well. If the pudding looks a little sloppy still after its allotted cooking time, don't worry because it firms as it cools in its baking dish.

Serves 6–8

---

1 lb/500 g dark chocolate
2 oz/50 g caster sugar
1 tbsp flour, sieved
4 oz/100 g butter, cut into pieces

4 large eggs, separated
Coffee cream sauce *(see below)*

Butter a 2 pt/1.2 L soufflé dish. Break the chocolate into a heatproof bowl and rest it over a saucepan of very gently simmering water – don't let the water touch the bottom of the bowl. As soon as the chocolate is soft, take the bowl off the heat and stir in the sugar, flour and butter. Beat in the egg yolks, one by one. Beat well. Whisk the egg whites until stiff and, using a large metal spoon, fold them quickly and thoroughly into the chocolate mixture. Pour this into the buttered soufflé dish and bake in a fairly hot oven – 400°F/200°C/Gas 6/top right oven in a 4 door Aga – for 15 minutes, then take it out of the oven and leave the pudding to cool completely. You can warm it up to serve or alternatively serve it cold, whichever you prefer. Hand the coffee cream sauce separately.

227

Coffee cream sauce

This delicious sauce enhances any chocolate pudding, but it is specially good served with the *Dark chocolate terrine* (see page 247).

Makes ¾ pt/450 ml

½ pt/300 ml single cream
1 tbsp instant coffee granules
3 egg yolks

3 oz/75 g caster sugar
1 tsp cornflour

Put the single cream and instant coffee granules together in a saucepan and heat gently. Meanwhile beat the egg yolks in a bowl, gradually adding the sugar. Sieve in the cornflour and beat all well together. Pour in a little of the coffee-flavoured cream, mix well, then pour the contents of the bowl into the saucepan. Over a gentle to moderate heat, stir until the sauce thickens to the consistency of pouring cream. Allow to cool. Serve cold or warm, but not hot.

November

November is a month I positively relish, whether in the town or the country. Here in the depths of the Skye countryside, the weather varies from the wild and stormy to the cold and still, often great contrasts within a few hours. As I write, it is the middle of November, and there is fresh snow quite low down on the hills which surround our white house on the shores of the sea loch Loch na Dal.

At the beginning of the month there is Guy Fawkes Night to celebrate. Up here 5 November didn't feature at all at one time. Why should it – Scotland and England weren't even one country (some would say they still aren't!) when Guy Fawkes tried to blow up Parliament. All the celebrations up here focused on Halloween. But now almost equal attention is given to Bonfire Night I'm glad to say, because I do love an excuse for a party.

At the end of November it is Godfrey's birthday, when we usually have a few close friends to stay for the weekend. Beaujolais Nouveau arrives just in time and, although in the more élite foodie circles Beaujolais Nouveau is despised, we love it. I always plan the food for the birthday weekend around the wine, which virtually gives me *carte blanche* as it is such a versatile wine. We drink it with meat, game and fish.

Throughout the month of November I think ahead to Christmas. Once December comes the days fairly whizz by, and the more that can be done during November the better. We have to start our Christmas shopping much earlier because our trips to Edinburgh and Inverness aren't exactly frequent.

This month I make the mincemeat, any Christmas cakes which I haven't got round to making in October and the Christmas puddings. On the hotel side we are usually much quieter, but it is fairly unpredictable. This year, for instance, we have been kept very busy and are still half full with guests. On the food front, we have an abundance of game to be made into soups, terrines, salamis or just straight roasted. Apples are at their best in the winter months, and are excellent in all things both sweet and savoury.

First Courses

Chicken livers with cream and Calvados
Leek and bacon soup
Smoked salmon and horseradish creams
Pheasant, cumin and apricot soup

Main Courses

Game pudding with lemon suet crust
Pheasant with walnuts and grapes
Wild duck with cider and apples
Venison with soured cream and pistachios
Venison en daube
Venison and leek pie

Puddings

Apple and Calvados soufflé
Crêpes with apples and Calvados butter
Dark chocolate terrine
Kinloch mincemeat
No-butter Christmas cake

Chicken livers with cream and Calvados

This makes a delicious first course, if rather rich, and takes literally minutes to make. I like to serve it with hot garlic bread or brown rolls.

Serves 6–8

---

2 lb/1 kg chicken livers, picked over and any greenish bits removed
2 oz/50 g butter
1 tbsp oil (I use sunflower)
1 small onion, skinned and finely chopped

3 fl oz/75 ml Calvados or other apple brandy
½ pt/300 ml thick cream
salt and freshly ground black pepper
1 tbsp finely chopped parsley

Heat the butter and oil together in a saucepan or frying pan and add the finely chopped onion. Sauté for about 5 minutes, stirring occasionally, until the onion is soft and transparent. Add the chicken livers and cook for 2 to 3 minutes, continuing to stir, just long enough to seal them. Pour on the Calvados and light with a match immediately. Let it flame for a few seconds then pour on the cream. Season with salt and pepper, and let the cream bubble away for 2 to 3 minutes. Stir in the chopped parsley just before serving on warmed plates, accompanied by the garlic bread or rolls.

Leek and bacon soup

This is really one of those delicious thick soups that are ideal for lunch on a chilly winter's day. You can either liquidize it for a smooth soup or serve it with the leek and bacon chunks still identifiable. It will keep for a couple of days in the refrigerator.

Serves 6–8

---

2 oz/50 g butter
2 tbsp oil (I use sunflower)
2 onions, skinned and chopped
4 oz/100 g smoked bacon (you can use green if you like), chopped
6 good-sized leeks, washed, trimmed and fairly finely sliced

4 medium potatoes, peeled and chopped
2 × 15 oz/450 g tins of tomatoes (liquidized if you are serving a chunky, unliquidized soup)
1½ pt/1 L chicken or vegetable stock
salt and freshly ground black pepper

Heat the butter and oil in a saucepan. Add the onion and sauté for a few minutes until the onion is soft and transparent. Add the bacon and cook for a further few minutes, then stir in the leeks and potatoes. Cook for about 5 minutes, then pour on the tomatoes. Stir in the stock, season with salt and pepper, and bring to boiling point. Simmer very gently with the pan uncovered, for 30 to 40 minutes, until the pieces of potato are almost falling apart. Allow to cool a little. Liquidize the soup if you want a smooth texture. Reheat to serve.

Smoked salmon and horseradish creams

These luxurious creams don't take a minute to make. They have to be made ahead of time, to allow the gelatine to set. The flavours of horseradish, lemon and smoked salmon all go together so well. If you like, you can gild the lily by serving the creams on a few slices of smoked salmon. Serve with brown bread and butter, and lemon wedges.

Serves 6

6 oz/175 g smoked salmon
2 tsp grated horseradish
1 sachet gelatine – approximately
½ oz/15 g
juice of 2 lemons made up to ¼
pt/150 ml with cold water if
necessary

½ pt/300 ml double cream
lots of freshly ground black
pepper
finely chopped parsley and lemon
wedges to garnish

Oil the ramekins or moulds. Put the smoked salmon and horseradish into a liquidizer or food processor and blend. Sprinkle the gelatine onto the lemon juice in a small saucepan, and heat gently until the granules of gelatine have dissolved completely. Add this mixture to the smoked salmon and blend to a smooth thick paste. Pour in the double cream and season with pepper. Blend thoroughly. Pour and scrape into 6 ramekins or dariole moulds. Leave to set. To turn out, dip each mould into hot water for a few seconds, invert and shake onto a serving dish. Sprinkle finely chopped parsley over each cream and serve with lemon wedges.

Pheasant, cumin and apricot soup

This mildly spiced soup is delicious, fragrant with cumin which is complemented by the apricots. As with all soups, the stock is all-important, even more so in this recipe, if that is possible! It will keep well in the refrigerator for 1 to 2 days.

234

FOR THE PHEASANT
   STOCK

2 pheasant carcasses

*2 onions, studded with 6 cloves
   each*

*2 carrots, washed (but not
   peeled) and chopped*

2 leeks, washed and chopped

2 celery sticks

2 tsp sea salt

12–15 black peppercorns

2 bayleaves

*pared rind of 1 orange (I use a
   potato peeler to get all skin
   and virtually no pith)*

FOR THE SOUP

2 oz/50 g butter

1 tbsp oil (sunflower if possible)

*3 medium onions, skinned and
   chopped*

*2 medium potatoes, peeled and
   chopped*

*4 oz/100 g dried apricots,
   chopped*

3 tsp cumin

2 pt/1.2 L pheasant stock

*salt and freshly ground black
   pepper*

*2 tbsp finely chopped parsley, to
   be added just before serving*

First make the stock. Put all the stock ingredients together in a large saucepan and cover with water. Heat until the water boils. Cover the pan and simmer for 2½ to 3 hours. Leave the stock to cool, then strain it into a bowl.

Heat the butter and oil together in a saucepan. Add the onions and sauté for several minutes, stirring from time to time, until the onions are soft and transparent. Stir in the potatoes, apricots and the cumin. Cook for a minute or two, then pour in the pheasant stock. Simmer gently for 35 to 40 minutes. Leave to cool. Liquidize the soup, and sieve the liquidized soup. Reheat to serve. Just before serving stir the finely chopped parsley through the soup.

Game pudding with lemon suet crust

This is a useful and absolutely delicious way of using up small amounts of game. The lemony suet crust goes so well with the rich game filling. A suet pudding like this is very convenient – it doesn't take very long to put together, although it does take several hours to cook. This game version is good served with celeriac purée and spicy red cabbage.

Serves 6

FOR THE SUET PASTRY
12 oz/350 g self-raising flour
6 oz/175 g shredded suet
salt and freshly ground black pepper
grated rind of 2 lemons
FOR THE FILLING
1½ lb/750 g game meat – hare, old grouse, pheasant or a combination – stripped from the carcass and cut into ½ in/1 cm cubes

1 medium onion, skinned and finely chopped
2 tbsp flour
salt and freshly ground black pepper
½ pt/300 ml water
3 tsp redcurrant jelly
½ pt/300 ml red wine

Mix together the pastry ingredients – the self-raising flour, suet, salt, pepper and lemon rind. Stir in enough cold water to mix to a dough, about ¼ pt/150 ml. Roll out two-thirds of the dough and line a 4 pt/2.4 L pudding bowl with it. Keep the remaining third for the lid.

Mix the pieces of game, onion, flour and seasonings together well, and pack down into the pastry-lined bowl. Dissolve the redcurrant jelly in the water over heat and pour this and the red wine over the game. Top up with extra water, if necessary, to bring the liquid up to the level of the game.

Roll out the lid of suet pastry, and lay it over the top of the pudding. Trim it and pinch it into place. Cut out a piece of siliconized greaseproof paper, and lay it over the top of the pastry. Cover this with a double layer of foil, and tie it securely round the edge of the pudding bowl. Put the bowl into a large saucepan, with water coming halfway up the sides of the pudding bowl, and cover the pan with a lid. Over a low to moderate heat, let the water in the pan simmer, topping it up from time to time – don't let it boil dry. Cook the pudding like this for 3½ to 4 hours, if you are cooking it in advance for reheating, or for 5 hours if you are going to serve it straight away. Do be careful as you lift the pudding out of the saucepan at the end of the cooking time. In front of a kitchen full of eager and hungry family and friends, I once lifted a pudding like this out of its saucepan and promptly dropped it on my foot. There was an audible intake of breath from all present as I hopped around speechless with agony. Everyone relaxed visibly, however, when it became clear that the pudding was intact, which was more than could be said for my poor foot!

If you have made the pudding in advance, reheat it by cooking it in the same way for an additional 1½ hours – 5 to 5½ hours' cooking in total.

Pheasant with walnuts and grapes

A simple but rather different way of serving roast pheasant – the pheasants are covered with bacon, stuffed with walnuts, roasted and accompanied by a wine and cream-based grape sauce. I like to serve it with creamy mashed potatoes and Brussels sprouts.

2 pheasants approximately
   2–2½ lb/1–1.25 kg each
6 oz/175 g shelled walnuts
streaky bacon to cover the
   pheasants
1 rounded tbsp granulated sugar
¼ pt/150 ml dry white wine
1 pt/600 ml chicken, pheasant or
   vegetable stock

2 tsp cornflour
juice of 1 lemon
½ pt/300 ml double cream
8 oz/250 g seedless grapes,
   halved
salt and freshly ground black
   pepper

Put the pheasants into a roasting tin and stuff them with the walnuts. Lay the strips of bacon over the birds and roast for 20 minutes in a hot oven – 400°F/200°C/Gas 6/top right oven in a 4 door Aga – then for a further 1 hour at a lower temperature – 350°F/180°C/Gas 4/bottom right oven in a 4 door Aga.

Meanwhile dissolve the sugar in the white wine over a gentle heat. Boil fast until the sugar and wine reduce to a thick caramel-like consistency. Pour on the stock, and let the caramel dissolve in the hot stock, then boil the liquid until it is reduced by about three-quarters. Slake the cornflour with the lemon juice and stir a little of the hot liquid into it. Stir this back into the saucepan and stir until it boils. Allow to cool a bit, then stir in the cream and grapes – try not to let the sauce boil again once the cream has been added. Reheat it gently. Season with salt and pepper to taste, and serve with the carved pheasant, spooning a few walnuts on to each plate as you serve.

Wild duck with cider and apples

You can, if you wish, leave the cream out of this recipe, to make it a fairly low-calorie dish. But I think it is much nicer with the cream! Serve with a purée of celeriac and crunchy stir-fried cabbage, both of which complement the wild duck and apples particularly well.

Serves 6

---

2 mallard duck, approximately 2 lb/1 kg each
2 small onions, skinned, and 1 apple, halved, to stuff the ducks
3 oz/75 g butter
1 tbsp oil (I use sunflower)
2 medium onions, skinned and thinly sliced

1½ lb/750 g apples – a mixture of eating, such as Cox's, and cooking apples – peeled, cored and sliced
salt and freshly ground black pepper
1 pt/600 ml dry cider
¼ pt/150 ml double cream

Stuff each duck with a whole skinned onion and half an apple. Heat the butter and oil together in a heavy casserole, and brown the ducks well, all over. Take them out of the casserole and keep them warm. Add the onions to the casserole and sauté for about 5 minutes, stirring occasionally to prevent them sticking. Add the apples. Season with salt and pepper, and stir in the cider. Return the mallards to the casserole, pushing them down into the oniony apple mixture. Cover the casserole with a tightly fitting lid and simmer very gently for 1 hour, or until the juices run clear when you stick the point of a sharp knife into the duck flesh. The cooking apples will have become mush, but the eating apples should have retained their shape. Just before serving, stir in the cream and check the seasoning. Carve the ducks, and spoon the sauce around the slices of duck.

Venison with soured cream and pistachios

A rich and delicious dish that makes a wonderful main course. Be careful about adding any salt to the dish – the pistachios are salty enough for most tastes. I like to serve this with creamy mashed potatoes, and glazed carrots and parsnips.

Serves 6–8

2½ lb/1.25 kg venison, trimmed and cut into chips about ½ in–1 cm thick
2 oz/50 g butter
2 tbsp oil (I use sunflower)
2 medium onions, skinned and very thinly sliced

1 tbsp flour
freshly ground black pepper
1 pt/600 ml vegetable stock
¼ pt/150 ml dry white wine
juice of 1 lemon
½ pt/300 ml double cream
4 oz/100 g shelled pistachio nuts

Heat the butter and oil together in a casserole. Brown the thin chips of venison, a few at a time. Keep the browned meat warm as it is done. Add the onions to the casserole. Cook them, stirring occasionally to prevent them sticking, for about 5 minutes. Stir in the flour and pepper. Cook for a further minute or two, then gradually add the stock and white wine, stirring until the sauce boils. Add the browned meat to the sauce, cover the casserole with a tightly fitting lid and cook in a moderate oven – 350°F/180°C/Gas 4/bottom right oven in a 4 door Aga – for 45 minutes. Just before serving, stir the lemon juice into the cream and add to the casserole together with the pistachios. Reheat, being careful not to let the sauce boil once the cream has been added, and serve.

Venison en daube

This is a rich and warming dish, perfect for cold winter months. As with all casserole dishes it is much better made, cooled and reheated so that the flavour intensifies. Marinating the meat for a day or two before cooking may sound a fiddle, but it does make all the difference to the end result. The daube is even more delicious served with a purée of Brussels sprouts, and a dish of baked sliced potatoes and onions.

Serves 6–8

2½ lb/1.25 kg venison, trimmed and cut into 1½ in/3 cm chunks

FOR THE MARINADE
½ pt/300 ml red wine
4 tbsp olive oil
2 bayleaves
1 onion, skinned and roughly chopped
1 celery stick, roughly chopped

FOR THE DAUBE
3 tbsp olive oil
6 rashers of streaky bacon, cut into 1 in/2.5 cm lengths

2 medium onions, skinned and finely sliced
3 garlic cloves, skinned and chopped
2 tbsp tomato purée
1 pt/600 ml beef stock or consommé
¼ pt/150 ml strained and reserved marinade
¼ pt/150 ml red wine
salt and freshly ground black pepper
½ tsp dried thyme or a sprig of fresh
3 oz/75 g black olives, stoned

Put the marinade ingredients together in a saucepan and bring to the boil. Simmer for 5 minutes, then cool. When it is completely cold, pour the marinade into a dish and mix in the prepared venison. Leave for at least 8 hours – overnight is better, and 2 days is better still. At the end of the marinating time, strain off and reserve the marinade, discarding the bits of onion and celery, and the bayleaves. Pat the meat dry with absorbent kitchen paper.

Heat the olive oil for the daube in a heavy casserole, and add the bacon and onions. Sauté for 5 minutes, until the onions are soft and just beginning to turn colour, and the bacon is just beginning to crisp. Take the bacon and onions out of the casserole with a slotted spoon, and keep them warm. Brown the meat, a few pieces at a time so that the temperature in the casserole isn't lowered too much. Keep the batches of browned meat warm as they are done. Return all the browned meat together with the garlic, bacon and onions to the casserole. Stir the tomato purée into the stock, and stir this into the casserole, together with the marinade and the red wine. Season with salt, pepper and thyme, cover the casserole with a lid and cook in a moderate oven – 350°F/180°C/Gas 4/bottom right oven in a 4 door Aga – for 1½ hours. Stir the black olives into the casserole and cook for a further 20 to 25 minutes, with the casserole uncovered so that the liquid reduces a little. Serve on warmed deep plates.

Venison and leek pie

This is a great favourite in our family. It is really a shepherd's pie made from minced leftover venison. You can make it with fresh venison mince, too. The venison filling has steamed leeks in a white sauce on top. Served with baked potatoes and a salad or a steamed green vegetable, it makes a delicious dish for lunch or supper in the long winter months.

FOR THE MEAT FILLING
2 lb/1 kg lean venison, minced
3 oz/75 g venison or beef dripping, or 6 tbsp oil (sunflower if possible)
3 medium onions, skinned and finely chopped
3 carrots, peeled and finely diced

FOR THE TOPPING
8 medium leeks, washed, trimmed and cut into ½ in/1 cm slices
2 oz/50 g butter
1 medium onion, skinned and fairly finely chopped

3 parsnips, peeled and finely diced
1 rounded tbsp wholemeal flour
1½ pt/1 L stock or dry cider
3 tsp redcurrant jelly
4–6 tbsp Worcestershire sauce (depending on your taste)
salt and freshly ground black pepper

2 oz/50 g wholemeal flour
1 pt/600 ml milk
salt and freshly ground black pepper
freshly grated nutmeg
3 oz/75 g grated Cheddar

First make the filling. Heat the fat in a heavy casserole. Add the onions, carrots and parsnips. Sauté for 7 to 10 minutes, stirring from time to time so that the vegetables cook evenly and don't stick. Add the minced venison. Cook for a minute or two, then stir in the wholemeal flour. Cook for a further few minutes and then stir in the stock or cider, redcurrant jelly, Worcestershire sauce, and salt and pepper. Let the meaty mixture simmer for a few minutes, then take it off the heat and leave to cool completely.

To make the topping, first steam the sliced leeks for a few minutes until they are soft. Melt the butter in a saucepan and stir in the onion. Sauté for 5 minutes, stirring from time to time, then stir in the flour. Cook for a couple of minutes, then gradually add the milk, stirring until the sauce boils. Season with salt, pepper and nutmeg. Stir the steamed leeks into the sauce, and allow to cool completely before spooning it over the cooled venison mixture. Sprinkle with the grated cheese, and cook in a moderate oven – 350°F/180°C/Gas 4/bottom right oven in a 4 door Aga – for 30 to 35 minutes, or until the cheese has melted and the whole pie is bubbling and golden.

Apple and Calvados soufflé

This is the best hot sweet soufflé I know. A sweet soufflé is really very easy to make and serve – you can have everything ready, only needing to whisk the egg whites and fold them into the prepared sauce, pour it over the apples and pop it into a hot oven before you serve the main course.

Serves 6

FOR THE APPLE BASE
6 *eating apples, peeled, cored and*
   sliced (Cox's orange pippins
   are by far the best apples for
   this dish)
3 *oz/75 g softened butter*
4 *oz/100 g light or dark soft*
   brown sugar

FOR THE SOUFFLÉ
2 *oz/50 g butter*
2 *oz/50 g flour*
3/4 *pt/450 ml milk*
1/4 *pt/150 ml Calvados or other*
   apple brandy
2 *oz/50 g caster sugar*
5 *large eggs, separated*

Butter and dust with caster sugar a 3 pt/2 L soufflé dish. First make the apple base. Melt the butter and dissolve the soft brown sugar together in a saucepan, then boil for 3 to 4 minutes. Add the apples and cook for about 5 minutes. Pour into the prepared soufflé dish.

Melt the butter for the soufflé in a saucepan and stir in the flour. Cook for a moment or two then gradually add the milk, stirring all the time. Let the thick sauce boil, then take the pan off the heat and stir in the Calvados. Beat in the sugar. Beat in the yolks, one by one. You can prepare the soufflé up to this stage in the morning for dinner the same evening.

Whisk the egg whites until stiff, and with a large metal spoon, fold them quickly and thoroughly into the sauce. Pour the mixture over the apples, and bake in a hot oven – 400°F/200°C/Gas 6/top right oven in a 4 door Aga – for 40 minutes. Serve immediately!

Crêpes with apples and Calvados butter

This variation on my version of Crêpes Suzette – immodest though it undoubtedly sounds – is really very good. I came home enthused from a brief holiday in Normandy last year for cooking with apples and Calvados. November is just the right time of year for such indulgence! The Calvados butter is really just brandy butter made with Calvados.

Serves 6–8

FOR THE CRÊPES
5 oz/150 g flour
2 eggs
½ pt/300 ml milk
¼ pt/150 ml water
1 oz/25 g caster sugar
1 oz/25 g melted butter
butter for cooking the crêpes
icing sugar for dusting
5 tbsp Calvados for serving

FOR THE CALVADOS
   BUTTER
4 oz/100 g softened butter
4 oz/100 g soft brown sugar
grated rind of 1 orange
4 tbsp Calvados
FOR THE CRÊPE FILLING
8 apples (Cox's orange pippins if
   possible), peeled, cored and
   sliced
2 oz/50 g butter
3 oz/75 g soft brown sugar

245

First make the pancake batter. Put the flour and eggs into a food processor or liquidizer and blend, gradually adding the milk and water. Blend in the caster sugar and melted butter. Leave the batter to stand for an hour or two before making up into pancakes.

Next make the Calvados butter. Put the butter into a food processor if you have one and process, gradually adding the sugar, until well mixed. Add the grated orange rind and, a very little at a time, the Calvados, and process again. Alternatively, you can cream the butter in a bowl with a hand-held electric whisk, gradually adding the sugar, orange rind and Calvados.

To make the filling, melt the butter and dissolve the sugar together in a saucepan. Allow to bubble for 3 to 4 minutes, then add the sliced apples to this buttery sugary mixture and cook for about 5 minutes. Leave to cool.

Make the crêpes. Spread each one with some of the Calvados butter and put a small spoonful of the apple mixture in the centre. Roll up the crêpe, tucking the ends under. Arrange the crêpe parcels in a large shallow oven-proof dish. (Or you can freeze them at this stage – give them 3 hours to thaw.) To serve, put the dish in a hot oven – 400°F/200°C/Gas 6/top right oven in a 4 door Aga – until the butter is melted and the crêpes are hot through, about 10 minutes. Take the crêpes out and dust with a little sieved icing sugar. Warm the Calvados in a saucepan but don't let it boil. Light the Calvados (warmed, it will ignite much easier) with a match and pour it flaming over the crêpes – this is much easier than trying to ignite it once it has been poured over the crêpes. Blow out the flickering blue flames after 20 to 30 seconds, and serve.

Dark chocolate terrine

This heavenly chocolate pudding looks simple but impressive, especially when sliced and served either with a spoonful of cream at its side or in a pool of cream. It is dead easy to make, and doesn't suffer at all from being made a day or two in advance. Use the best quality dark chocolate you can find – we buy ours from an Italian delicatessen in Edinburgh – and you will get perfect results.

Serves 8–10

1½ lb/750 g good dark chocolate
1 pt/600 ml single cream
¼ pt/150 ml mixture of water
 and either Tia Maria or
 brandy, mixed half and half

1½ sachets gelatine –
 approximately ¾ oz/20 g
6 egg yolks
whipped cream, flavoured with
 vanilla, to serve

Cut a piece of siliconized greaseproof paper to fit the base and narrow sides of a terrine, or a 1 lb/500 g loaf tin if you don't have a terrine.

Heat the single cream over a gentle heat to scalding point. Meanwhile break the chocolate into a liquidizer or food processor. Put the Tia Maria mixture into a small saucepan. Sprinkle the gelatine on to the Tia Maria and let it sponge up. Warm the Tia Maria over a gentle heat until the gelatine granules have dissolved completely.

Pour the scalding cream onto the chocolate pieces. Cover the top of the liquidizer or food processor with a cloth or several pieces of absorbent kitchen paper and blend the cream and chocolate (the noise will be awful, but it doesn't last for long!). When the chocolate is melted and you have a thick smooth purée, add the egg yolks, one at a time, blending continuously. Add the gelatine and Tia Maria mixture – which will be very thick and syrupy, so scrape it all out of the saucepan with a plastic spatula –

and blend again until the mixture is thick and smooth. Scrape and pour it into the terrine, and leave it in a cool place for several hours to set.

To turn out the terrine, dip a palette knife into hot water and run it down the long (unlined) sides of the terrine, put a serving plate over it, and invert the whole thing. Pull the ends of the paper, and the terrine should come easily out of the tin. Peel the paper off the short sides and top of the chocolate terrine, and slice as thickly or as thinly as you like. Serve with whipped cream, flavoured with vanilla, and with some sugar too, if you like. It's also delicious served with the coffee cream sauce in the last chapter.

Kinloch mincemeat

I used to think that making mincemeat for mince pies and puddings around Christmas time was a real chore and not one that I was up to tackling – until one year I rolled up my sleeves and made some. I discovered that making mincemeat doesn't take very long at all, and probably the most difficult part is weighing out the ingredients. Over the years, I have juggled around with my list of ingredients and finally decided to dispense with suet altogether. I can't see the point of it in mincemeat – it only adds extra calories, it makes mincemeat non-vegetarian and the mincemeat doesn't seem to suffer without it in any way. I suspect that it may be included in recipes to bulk the mincemeat out.

It does have to be made at least a couple of weeks before you want to use it, so I try to make mine (and I make vast quantities) sometime during November, giving it an occasional stir during the weeks after it is made.

12 oz/350 g seedless raisins
6 oz/175 g chopped mixed peel
12 oz/350 g sultanas
12 oz/350 g raisins
6 oz/175 g flaked almonds,
    toasted until pale golden (the
    flavour is so good)
6 medium eating apples (Cox's
    orange pippins if possible),
    cored and finely chopped, but
    not peeled

12 oz/350 g soft dark brown
    sugar
8 oz/250 g dried apricots,
    chopped
1 tsp freshly grated nutmeg
1 rounded tsp powdered
    cinnamon
1 rounded tsp ground allspice
grated rind and juice of 2 oranges
grated rind and juice of 2 lemons
¼ pt/150 ml brandy, whisky or
    rum

Mix everything together well and leave in a large covered container, stirring once or twice a week for 3 weeks, before potting and sealing in jars.

No-butter·Christmas cake

A recipe for Christmas cake not using butter may sound strange to some, but an ever-increasing number of people can't eat dairy produce for one reason or another, and I don't see why they should go without Christmas cake. This is a variation on my carrot cake recipe. It keeps well for a couple of weeks, so I suggest making it in November and freezing it until about 10 days before Christmas, when you can thaw it, and marzipan and ice it like an ordinary Christmas cake.

10 oz/300 g soft dark brown sugar
½ pt/300 ml sunflower oil
4 large eggs
8 oz/250 g flour
1 rounded tsp ground cinnamon
½ tsp grated nutmeg
1 rounded tsp mixed spice
9 oz/275 g sultanas
9 oz/275 g raisins
6 oz/175 g currants
6 oz/175 g dried apricots, snipped into small pieces (mind your fingers)
3 oz/75 g glacé cherries, chopped
4 oz/100 g mixed peel
4 oz/100 g flaked almonds, toasted until pale golden
grated rind of 1 orange
grated rind of 1 lemon
4 tbsp brandy, whisky or rum

Rub an 8–9 in/20–22 cm cake tin with sunflower oil and line it with a double thickness of siliconized greaseproof paper. Whisk the soft brown sugar into the oil using a hand-held electric whisk, then add the eggs, one at a time, whisking each one in thoroughly. Continue whisking for 3 to 4 minutes. Sieve the flour and spices together in a bowl. Weigh all the dried fruits, glacé cherries and mixed peel into another bowl, add the flaked almonds and stir in 2 tablespoons of the sieved flour and spices. Stir this mixture into the oil, sugar and eggs, and add the grated orange and lemon rinds. Stir in the sieved flour and spices, and the brandy, whisky or rum, and mix all well together. Spoon and scrape the cake mixture into the prepared tin, and bake in a fairly low oven – 250°F/130°C/Gas 1/top left oven in a 4 door Aga – for 5 to 5½ hours, until a skewer stuck into the middle of the cake comes out clean. Take the cake out of the oven when it is done and cool it in the tin. While it is still in the tin prick it all over and right down to the bottom of the cake with a skewer and pour 3 to 4 more tablespoons of brandy, whisky or rum over the cake. Leave to stand for 24 hours, then take the cake out of the tin, wrap it in foil, and freeze it.

December

I've never got over my love of Christmas, and I hope I never do. I can't bear to hear people moaning about all the work involved in preparing for this wonderful festival. It must be a slog for people who lose sight of what it is all about, and just think of it as a vast commercial bash. We have strong family Christmas traditions. We close for hotel guests over Christmas, and fill up the spare bedrooms in this lovely old house with family and friends. How I love it! Last Christmas I think we were twenty-two sitting down to dinner on Christmas night. We have never had Christmas lunch – I don't think I could get it ready in time and I've always wondered what people do for the rest of the day. We have a candlelit dinner, served rather earlier than usual, 7.30-ish for the benefit of the younger members of the family. No one under five is allowed to stay up for dinner – food doesn't mean a great deal before that age anyway, and I don't think Christmas dinner should be spoiled by very young children.

After 1 December has been and gone, the days whizz by frighteningly fast. I do try to get presents wrapped and the ones to be posted off early, to give me time to think about, plan and make food for the holiday. I make and freeze many dishes, so that when the time comes I only have to remember to thaw them! I freeze both stuffings for the turkey – one a lemony one and the other a pork and chestnut one, and I make vast quantities of bread sauce (see page 214). Recipes for all of these are given in my first book, *Seasonal Cooking*. In this chapter I include a recipe for a stuffing for roast goose, which can also be made ahead and frozen.

An alternative and less time-consuming main course for Christmas lunch or dinner is the *Baked glazed ham*, served with tomato and Madeira sauce. I've included my recipe for *Vegetable lasagne* as a December dish, because it freezes very well, tastes good, and is one of those useful all-in-one dishes that just need garlic bread to accompany them.

My way of making sure I enjoy the Christmas and New Year celebrations along with the rest of the household is to be prepared, like the proverbial boy scout. I make menu plans and stick them on the refrigerator door, alongside an equally important list of what items to get out of the deep freeze and when! Panic is thus eliminated from the kitchen, and there are always plenty of willing hands to set tables, to clear and wash up. I hope some of the recipes and ideas will enable those of you who anticipate this holiday season with dread in your hearts to relax and enjoy it, too.

First Courses

Celeriac and egg mousse
Leek and tomato soup
Smoked salmon roulade
Spinach and garlic terrine
Stilton and celery profiteroles

Main Courses

Baked glazed ham with tomato and Madeira cream sauce
Roast goose with apricot, chestnut, lemon and thyme stuffing
Cod and smoked haddock puffed pie
Sausage and lentil hot-pot
Vegetable lasagne

Puddings

Chocolate and coffee roulade
Chocolate cream pavlova
Ginger iced cream with hot chocolate sauce
Lime and grape mousse
Pineapple sorbet

Celeriac and egg mousse

This mousse can conveniently be made a day or two in advance and kept in the refrigerator. The grated celeriac is delicious combined with eggs and mayonnaise, and provides a good contrasting texture. You can decorate the top of the mousse with black olives and anchovies, or do as my sister Camilla does, and serve it with black olive pâté – fairly easily obtainable from delicatessens – spread on slices of toasted French bread. The mousse makes a very good first course, or a supper dish to follow a hot soup.

Serves 8

---

8 hard-boiled eggs, chopped
1 lb/500 g celeriac, peeled
juice of 1 lemon
1 sachet gelatine – approximately
    ½ oz/15 g
½ pt/300 ml chicken stock

½ pt/300 ml double cream
1 tbsp anchovy essence
a good dash of Tabasco
freshly ground black pepper
6 tbsp mayonnaise
black olives or parsley to garnish

Grate or very finely shred the celeriac, and toss it in the lemon juice to prevent the celeriac from discolouring. Sprinkle the gelatine over the chicken stock and heat gently (watch that it doesn't boil) until the gelatine granules have dissolved completely. Leave to cool. When it is quite cold, stir the chopped eggs and the celeriac into the stock, and leave until the mixture begins to set. Then whip the cream and fold together with the anchovy essence, Tabasco, pepper and mayonnaise. Fold this mixture and the egg and celeriac mixture together thoroughly. Pour into a serving dish and leave to set. If you don't want to bother with the black olives, sprinkle some finely chopped parsley over the mousse and serve.

Leek and tomato soup

This soup tastes wonderful, combining the flavours of leeks, tomatoes, onions and garlic! It doesn't take a second to make and is low in calories, so it makes a good first course around Christmas time when so much of what we eat traditionally is filling and rich.

Serves 6–8

8 medium leeks, washed, trimmed and thinly sliced

2 tbsp olive oil

2 medium onions, skinned and chopped fairly small

2 garlic cloves, skinned and finely chopped (optional for non-garlic lovers)

1 pt/600 ml chicken or vegetable stock

2 × 15 oz/450 g tins of tomatoes

salt and freshly ground black pepper

Heat the oil in a saucepan and add the onions. Sauté for about 5 minutes, stirring once or twice so that they cook evenly, then add the leeks and garlic. Cook for another 5 minutes, then pour on the stock. Liquidize and sieve the tinned tomatoes and add to the saucepan. Season with salt and pepper, cover the pan with a lid and simmer gently for 30 minutes. Serve with warm garlic-buttered rolls.

Smoked salmon roulade

This roulade consists of a filling of smoked salmon and finely diced cucumber in whipped cream wrapped in a roulade made with a deliciously flavoured sauce. It is easy to prepare, makes a rather special first course for a party, and yet it isn't wildly extravagant with the smoked salmon.

FOR THE FLAVOURED
  MILK
1 pt/600 ml milk
1 onion, skinned and halved
2 celery sticks, washed
2 bayleaves
12 black peppercorns
1 tsp sea salt
FOR THE ROULADE
2 oz/50 g butter
2 oz/50 g flour
strained flavoured milk
4 large eggs, separated

freshly grated nutmeg
salt and freshly ground black
  pepper
FOR THE FILLING
8 oz/250 g smoked salmon, finely
  shredded
1/2 pt/300 ml double cream
grated rind and juice of 1 lemon
freshly ground black pepper
1 cucumber, peeled and halved,
  deseeded and diced
finely chopped parsley to garnish

Gently heat all the ingredients for the flavoured milk together until the milk reaches scalding point. Take the pan off the heat and leave the milk with the vegetables steeping in it for 1 to 2 hours – the nearer to 2 hours the better.

Line a baking tray or Swiss roll tin with siliconized greaseproof paper. To make the roulade, melt the butter in a saucepan and stir in the flour. Cook for a minute or two, gradually add the strained milk, stirring all the time until the sauce boils. Let it boil for a minute, then take the saucepan off the heat and beat in the egg yolks, one at a time. Add some grated nutmeg, and check the seasoning, adding more salt or pepper if necessary. Whisk the egg whites until stiff and, with a large metal spoon, fold them quickly and thoroughly into the sauce. Pour the sauce into the prepared baking tin and bake in a moderate oven – 350°F/180°C/Gas 4/bottom right oven in a 4 door Aga – for 20 to 25 minutes. Take it out of the oven, cover with first a fresh piece of greaseproof paper and then a damp tea towel, and leave for several hours.

For the filling, whip the cream together with the lemon

rind and juice. Fold in the smoked salmon and cucumber. Season with black pepper.

Remove the tea towel and greaseproof paper from the roulade. Lay a fresh sheet of greaseproof paper on a table or work surface, and turn out the roulade onto it. Carefully peel the paper off the roulade, tearing it in strips parallel to the roulade, so that you don't tear the roulade itself. Spread the smoked salmon filling over the roulade and roll it up lengthways, like a Swiss roll, slipping it onto a serving plate. Dust with finely chopped parsley to garnish.

You can make the roulade a day in advance, filling and assembling it on the day.

Spinach and garlic terrine

A really useful recipe which tastes good – this can be used as a first course, served with tomato salad, or it can be a main course loved by vegetarians and carnivores alike. It's useful for a buffet lunch or supper party because it's easy to serve and easy to eat with just a fork, and looks appetizing. It can be made 2 to 3 days in advance. All in all, it's a winner. Adjust the amount of garlic to suit your own taste.

Serves 8

1½ lb/750 g frozen chopped spinach, thawed and squeezed of any excess liquid	4 oz/100 g well-flavoured Cheddar, grated
4 large eggs	salt and freshly ground black pepper
2 garlic cloves, skinned and chopped	lots of freshly grated nutmeg
	a good dash of Tabasco

Line the short sides and base of a terrine or loaf tin with siliconized greaseproof paper. Put the spinach into a liquidizer or food processor and blend. Add the eggs, one at a time, blending continuously. Add the garlic, cheese and seasonings. Pour the mixture into the prepared terrine and cover with a piece of siliconized greaseproof paper. Stand the terrine in a roasting tin with water coming halfway up the sides of the terrine. Bake in a moderate oven – 350°F/180°C/Gas 4/bottom right oven in a 4 door Aga – for 1½ hours. Take it out of the oven and leave to cool completely.

To serve, run a wetted palette knife down the long sides of the terrine, put a serving plate over the top and invert the whole thing. The terrine should come out with no trouble. Peel off the lining paper. Slice the terrine to scrve. Serve with a tomato salad, perhaps with a sweet and mustardy vinaigrette dressing.

Stilton and celery profiteroles

These little cheesy choux buns make perfect finger food for parties. The celery in the stuffing gives a good crunchy texture and the Stilton and celery flavours go so well together. The profiteroles can be made in advance and frozen, and reheated for a few moments in a hot oven before being filled. The filling itself can be made 2 to 3 days in advance and kept in a covered bowl in a cool place.

Serves 8

FOR THE PROFITEROLES
½ pt/300 ml water
5 oz/150 g butter
6 oz/175 g flour
2 rounded tsp mustard powder
4 large eggs
3 oz/75 g Cheddar, grated

FOR THE FILLING
6 oz/175 g Stilton
3 celery sticks, washed, trimmed and thinly sliced
a little milk
a little paprika for dusting

First make the profiterole pastry. Put the water into a

258

saucepan and cut the butter into it. Gently heat until the butter melts, without letting the water boil. When the butter has melted, allow to come to the boil. Sieve the flour twice, and as soon as the first signs of boiling show in the saucepan, add the flour and mustard powder all at once. With a wooden spoon beat hard until the mixture comes away from the sides of the saucepan. Leave to cool for 10 minutes, then beat in the eggs, one by one. Beat in the cheese, until the mixture is glossy and the cheese more or less melted. With a large star nozzle, pipe the choux pastry into blobs about 1 in/2.5 cm across on a baking tray. Bake in a fairly hot oven – 400°F/200°C/Gas 6/top right oven in a 4 door Aga – for 15 to 20 minutes, until the profiteroles are well risen and golden brown. Cool on a wire rack. You can freeze them at this stage.

Crumble the Stilton into a liquidizer or food processor and blend, adding a very small amount of milk to let down the mixture and to make it less stiff. Scrape the smooth Stilton mixture into a bowl and stir in the celery. Don't be tempted to put the celery into the blender or processor, or you will lose the contrast in texture.

When you are ready to assemble the profiteroles, halve them and put a small amount of the filling in each. Put the tops back on, dust with a little paprika and put the profiteroles into a hot oven for 3 minutes before serving.

Baked glazed ham with tomato and Madeira cream sauce

For those who have family and friends to stay over the Christmas holiday, I can think of no better main course to welcome their arrival. It is endlessly useful afterwards, served for breakfast, sliced thinly with scrambled eggs or with baked potatoes and salads for lunch. It is so delicious too, first served hot, with this wonderful *Tomato and Madeira cream sauce* (see below).

259

I buy smoked ham, off the bone, which makes carving much easier. Half a smoked ham weighs about 7–8 lb/ 3.5–4 kg. Soak it first for 24 hours in water. Then put it in a large saucepan or ham pan and cover with fresh cold water. Add halved onions, carrots, a couple of leeks and a few sticks of celery, bring to the boil and simmer gently for 2 hours. Let it cool a bit in the liquid (which you can strain off and make into wonderful lentil soup). Then take out the ham, skin it, score the fat to make a diamond pattern and spread it with this glaze.

| FOR THE GLAZE | 3 tbsp Dijon or grainy mustard |
| 6 oz/175 g demerara sugar | cloves for studding the ham |

Mix the sugar with the mustard to make a smooth paste. Spread evenly over the fat. Stick a clove in the centre of each diamond.

Roast the glazed ham in a hot oven – 400°F/200°C/ Gas 6/top right oven in a 4 door Aga – for 20 minutes, then lower the temperature to 350°F/180°C/Gas 4/ bottom right oven in a 4 door Aga and cook it for a further 25 minutes. Carve and serve with *Tomato and Madeira cream sauce* (see below).

Tomato and Madeira cream sauce

The idea for this sauce came from Brigadier Ley, a neighbour of my parents and a great cook and gourmet. The onion and tomatoes in the sauce are my embellishment, but it is the Madeira which makes it so special. It can be made a day in advance and reheated to serve.

¾ pt/450 ml Madeira	4 tomatoes, skinned, deseeded
1 medium onion, skinned and	and chopped
very finely chopped	a very little salt and freshly
2 oz/50 g butter	ground black pepper
2 oz/50 g flour	freshly grated nutmeg
1 pt/600 ml milk	1 tbsp finely chopped parsley

Simmer the onion and Madeira together in a saucepan, until the Madeira has reduced by about three-quarters and the onion is cooked. Melt the butter in another saucepan and stir in the flour. Cook for a couple of minutes, then gradually add the milk, stirring all the time, until the sauce boils. Stir in the onion and Madeira mixture, the tomatoes and the salt, pepper and nutmeg. Just before serving, stir the parsley through the sauce – by adding it at the last minute you keep the bright fresh colour of the parsley. If it sits too long in the hot sauce, it will go dull and brownish.

Roast goose with apricot, chestnut, lemon and thyme stuffing

Roast goose makes a traditional alternative to turkey for dinner on Christmas Day. A goose has a broad breast bone, like a domestic duck, and its size is deceptive. There isn't a great deal on a goose, but it is much richer than turkey and your guests won't want huge helpings. Goose needs a sharp and fruity stuffing, like this one combining the flavours of apricot, chestnut, lemon and thyme. You can make the stuffing two or three weeks ahead and freeze it. Give it 24 hours to defrost before stuffing the goose.

Halfway through the cooking time, carefully pour off the goose fat which has collected in the roasting tin. Don't throw it away, though – it is the best fat there is for roasting or frying potatoes. Its value varies from place to place – where my mother and father live in the north-west of England, goose fat is much prized for pouring around the rose bushes!

The best accompaniments to your Christmas Day goose are roast potatoes, spicy red cabbage cooked with onions, apples and allspice, and celeriac purée.

Serves 8–10

a goose weighing about 11 lb/5.5 kg

FOR THE STUFFING
8 oz/250 g dried apricots, soaked in water overnight, drained and snipped into bits
2 tbsp oil (I use sunflower)
2 onions, skinned and finely chopped
1 × 15 oz/450 g tin of whole chestnuts, drained of their juice
1 lb/500 g cooked brown rice
grated rind of 2 lemons

½ tsp dried thyme or a good sprig of fresh thyme
salt and freshly ground black pepper

FOR THE GRAVY
3 fl oz/75 ml goose fat
2 heaped tbsp flour
1 pt/600 ml chicken stock
¼ pt/150 ml port
2 tsp redcurrant jelly
salt and freshly ground black pepper

Heat the oil in a saucepan and sauté the onions for 5 to 7 minutes, until they are soft and transparent. Mix together the cooked onions, apricots, chestnuts, brown rice, lemon rind, thyme, salt and pepper. Stuff the goose with this mixture, and roast the bird in a deep roasting tin in a hot oven – 425°F/220°C/Gas 7/bottom right oven in a 4 door Aga – for 1½ hours. Carefully pour off the fat which has collected in the roasting tin, then lower the temperature to 350°F/180°C/Gas 4/bottom right oven in a 4 door Aga and cook for a further 1¼ hours. Keep the goose warm for half an hour or so before serving.

To make the gravy, tip the measured goose fat into a saucepan. Stir in the flour and cook for a couple of minutes. Gradually add the chicken stock and port, stirring all the time, and bring to the boil. If the gravy looks too thick, add more chicken stock. Add the redcurrant jelly, and season with salt and pepper. Strain and keep warm until you are ready to serve.

Cod and smoked haddock puffed pie

Fish makes a welcome change from the meat and rich game dishes which are traditionally served around Christmas and New Year. You can use any firm-fleshed white fish for this pie. I like to serve it with a green salad and a purée of parsnips and carrots.

Serves 6–8

---

1 lb/500 g puff pastry
2 lb/1 kg cod (or other
  firm-fleshed white fish)
2 lb/1 kg smoked haddock
2 onions, skinned and left whole
1 celery stick
1 bayleaf
a few peppercorns

2 pt/1.2 L milk
3 oz/75 g butter
3 oz/75 g flour
freshly grated nutmeg
freshly ground black pepper
1 egg, beaten, for glazing the
  pastry

Put all the fish into a large saucepan, together with the onions, celery, bayleaf and peppercorns, and pour on the milk. Add enough water so that the liquid covers the fish, and put the pan on a gentle heat. Bring very slowly to simmering point, simmer for 3 to 4 minutes, then take off the heat and let the fish cool in the liquid. When it is quite cold, strain off and set aside the liquid. Flake the fish, removing all skin and bones.

263

Melt the butter and stir in the flour. Cook for a couple of minutes, then gradually add the reserved strained liquid, stirring all the time until the sauce boils. Season with nutmeg and pepper. Stir in the flaked fish, and pour into a large pie dish. Roll out the puff pastry to cover the pie. Crimp the edges (I always think a set of false teeth would do this job perfectly) and slash the surface of the pastry in 4 or 5 places, to let the steam escape as the pie cooks. Brush the pastry with beaten egg and bake in a hot oven – 400°F/200°C/Gas 6/top right oven in a 4 door Aga – for about 35 minutes, until the pastry is well risen and golden brown. Keep the pie warm until you are ready to serve it.

Sausage and lentil hot-pot

This is a kind of soupy stew – one of those convenient all-in-one dishes. It is very warming, just the thing for cold winter days. It is very quick to put together, and can be made a day in advance and reheated to serve. You can substitute beef sausages for the pork listed in the ingredients – it is a matter of personal taste.

Serves 6–8

1 lb/500 g pork sausages, cut into 1 in/2.5 cm chunks
2–3 tbsp oil (I use sunflower)
3 onions, skinned and chopped
4 carrots, scraped and chopped into smallish chunks
4 parsnips, peeled and chopped into smallish chunks

4 medium potatoes, peeled and chopped
1 large garlic clove
8 oz/250 g red lentils
2 pt/1.2 L chicken or vegetable stock
salt and freshly ground black pepper

Grill the chunks of sausage until they are brown all over (I personally can't bear an unbrowned sausage, however well cooked it is). Heat the oil in a saucepan or large casserole and add the onions. Sauté for 4 to 5 minutes, then stir in the carrots, parsnips, potatoes and garlic. Cook for several minutes, then stir in the lentils and the pieces of sausage, the stock and the seasoning. Cover the saucepan or casserole with a tightly fitting lid, and simmer gently over a low heat for about 45 minutes or until the pieces of vegetable are tender. Serve, or cool and reheat to serve the next day.

Vegetable lasagne

A useful dish to have made up and in the deep freeze, ready to go on the menu around Christmas time. Don't make it much more than two to three weeks in advance, though – it doesn't improve with weeks of freezing. Alternatively you can make it two days before baking it, and keep it in the refrigerator. Vegetable lasagne can be dreary or delicious, and one made in the summer is quite different from one made in December. The summery dish is full of new courgettes, fresh peas and broad beans, and the winter version uses cauliflower, carrots, parsnips, red peppers, haricot beans and chopped Brussels sprouts, all stirred into a cheesy parsley sauce.

If you have a steamer, use it to cook the vegetables to the point where they have a bit of crunch to them. If you haven't got a steamer (yet!), cook them for a very short time in a small amount of water, in a pan with a tightly fitting lid. Steamed vegetables retain so much more flavour than those cooked in even the smallest amount of water. Don't worry if you can't get all the vegetable ingredients – make up the weight with whatever is available.

12 oz/350 g green lasagne (the
ready-to-bake variety, which
needs no pre-cooking)
1 small cauliflower, washed and
broken into florets
8 oz/250 g Brussels sprouts,
washed and trimmed
8 oz/250 g green haricot beans,
ends cut off and cut into
1 in/2.5 cm lengths
1 lb/500 g carrots, scraped and
cut into 1 in/2.5 cm strips
1 lb/500 g parsnips, scraped and
cut into 1 in/2.5 cm strips
1 red pepper, halved, deseeded
and cut into thin strips
3 oz/75 g butter
2 tbsp oil (sunflower if possible)
2 medium onions, skinned and
thinly sliced

2 large garlic cloves, skinned and
finely chopped
4 leeks, washed, trimmed and
fairly thinly sliced
8 oz/250 g mushrooms, wiped
and sliced
3 oz/75 g flour
2 rounded tsp mustard powder
2 pt/1.2 L milk or milk and
chicken stock mixed
salt and freshly ground black
pepper
freshly grated nutmeg
8 oz/250 g Cheddar, grated
(keep 2 oz/50 g aside, for
sprinkling on the top of the
lasagne)
2 tbsp finely chopped parsley

Steam the cauliflower, sprouts, beans, carrots, parsnips and lastly the strips of red pepper. Quarter the cooked sprouts.

Heat the butter and oil together in a large saucepan. Add the onions and sauté for about 5 minutes, until they are soft and transparent. Stir in the garlic and leeks. Sauté for another 5 minutes, stirring occasionally so that the leeks cook evenly. Then stir in the mushrooms and cook for a couple of minutes before stirring in the flour and mustard. Gradually stir in the milk (or milk and stock), stirring continuously until the sauce boils. Season with salt, freshly ground black pepper and nutmeg. Stir in 6 oz/175 g of the grated cheese.

Add the steamed vegetables to this sauce, and stir in the chopped parsley. Butter a large shallow ovenproof dish and first put in a layer of the vegetable sauce. Cover with a layer of pasta, 2 to 3 sheets thick. Layer up like this, finishing with a vegetable sauce layer. Sprinkle with grated cheese.

At this stage you can cover and freeze the lasagne. Or you can bake it in a moderate oven – 350°F/180°C/Gas 4/bottom right oven in a 4 door Aga – for 40 to 45 minutes, until the sauce is bubbling and the cheese on top is melted and golden brown, and the lasagne feels soft when you stick a knife into it. Serve with a green salad tossed in vinaigrette, and warmed garlic-buttered rolls.

Chocolate and coffee roulade

I can't resist including this delicious, high-calorie roulade with the December recipes – it is loved by all who taste it. It can be made a couple of weeks before Christmas, and kept in the deep freeze – it won't spoil at all – and all you need to do before serving is dust it with a little more sieved icing sugar.

Serves 8

FOR THE ROULADE
8 oz/250 g good quality dark
*   chocolate*
2 tbsp strong black coffee
5 large eggs, separated
5 oz/150 g caster sugar

FOR THE FILLING
½ pt/300 ml double cream
5 tbsp Tia Maria
sieved icing sugar for dusting

Line a 12 × 14 in/30 × 35 cm baking tray with siliconized greaseproof paper.

Break the chocolate into a heatproof bowl with the

coffee. Rest the bowl over a saucepan of gently simmering water, and melt the chocolate in the coffee. Stir to a thick cream, being careful not to overheat the chocolate or it will seize up. Leave to cool a little.

Whisk the egg yolks, gradually incorporating the caster sugar. Whisk until the mixture is very pale and thick, then fold in the melted chocolate. Whisk the egg whites until they are very stiff, then, using a large metal spoon, fold them quickly and thoroughly into the chocolate mixture. Pour and scrape this onto the lined baking tray, and bake in a moderate oven – 350°F/180°C/Gas 4/bottom right oven in a 4 door Aga – for 20 minutes, or until firm to the touch. Take out of the oven, and cover first with a sheet of greaseproof paper, then with a damp tea towel. Leave for several hours or overnight.

To assemble the roulade, lay a fresh sheet of grease-proof paper on a table or work surface and dust liberally with sieved icing sugar. Turn the roulade out onto this, and carefully peel the paper off the back, tearing in strips parallel to the roulade to prevent the roulade tearing. Whip the cream together with the Tia Maria. Spread the cream smoothly and evenly over the roulade. Roll up the roulade lengthways, and slip it on to a serving dish. Dust it with more sieved icing sugar to serve.

Chocolate cream pavlova

This pudding has a history. I invented it late one after-noon for dinner the same evening because the chocolate pudding I had made earlier was not destined for the table. It was inadvertently put on a low shelf in the larder by someone who was working with us that year, a fact which did not go unnoticed by Florence, our sleek black whippet, who scoffed the lot. And she did so without being sick.

Such a capacity – to eat a pudding intended for 16 people – can only be respected if not exactly admired.

I promptly devised a chocolate version of my vanilla pavlova, and realized while eating the leftovers that here was a winner, and we've been making it ever since. It is wonderful, perhaps the best chocolate pudding I know, and that's saying something – I must rate as one of the country's greatest self-confessed chocolate lovers.

Serves 6–8

FOR THE PAVLOVA
6 large egg whites
10 oz/300 g caster sugar
1 tsp vanilla essence
2 rounded tbsp cocoa powder (not drinking chocolate), sieved

FOR THE FILLING
½ pt/300 ml double cream
4 oz/100 g dark chocolate, grated (chill the chocolate in the refrigerator first, that way it grates more easily)

Line a baking tray with a sheet of siliconized greaseproof paper. Whisk the egg whites in a large, clean bowl until fairly stiff. Then, still whisking, gradually incorporate the caster sugar, a spoonful at a time, until the meringue mixture is very thick. Measure in the vanilla essence and, with a very large metal spoon, quickly and thoroughly fold the sieved cocoa into the meringue – watch out for little pockets of cocoa, and try to get it all smoothly mixed in. Pour and scrape this mixture onto the lined baking tray and gently smooth it into the shape you want – round or oblong. Bake in a moderate oven – 350°F/180°C/ Gas 4/bottom right oven in a 4 door Aga – for 2 minutes (5 minutes if you're cooking in an Aga), then lower the temperature to 200°F/110°C/Gas ½/top left oven in a 4 door Aga, and cook for a further hour. Take the pavlova out of the oven and leave to cool.

To assemble the pavlova, carefully turn the meringue onto a serving plate and peel off the paper. Whip the cream and spread over the meringue. Strew the grated chocolate evenly over the surface. Don't assemble the pavlova much more than 2 hours before dinner.

Ginger iced cream
with hot chocolate sauce

This is one of my very favourite puddings. The smooth iced cream is flavoured with ginger and has pieces of ginger through it. Chocolate and ginger go so well together that the sauce is an essential accompaniment.

The iced cream can be made and frozen a couple of weeks in advance, and the chocolate sauce can be made and kept in the refrigerator for 7 to 10 days. All you need to do to serve it is thaw the iced cream (take it out of the freezer just before you sit down to dinner and keep it in the refrigerator, then bring it out to room temperature when you dish up the main course, and it won't be too rock-like to serve) and warm up the *Hot chocolate sauce* (see below).

Serves 6–8

4 eggs, separated	*2 tsp ground ginger*
4 oz/100 g icing sugar, sieved	*about 10 pieces of preserved*
½ pt/300 ml double cream	*ginger, drained and chopped*

Whisk the egg whites until stiff. Gradually whisk in the icing sugar, a spoonful at a time, until it is all incorporated. Whisk the egg yolks until pale. Whip the cream, whipping in the ground ginger. Fold the 3 mixtures together – the yolks into the cream, and then the stiff meringue and chopped ginger into the yolks and cream mixture, and pour into a polythene container. Cover and freeze.

Hot chocolate sauce

Makes ½ pt/300 ml

6 oz/175 g soft brown sugar
¼ pt/150 ml water
1 tsp vanilla essence
3 rounded tbsp cocoa powder,
   sieved

3 tbsp golden syrup (dip your
   tablespoon in very hot water
   before dipping it into the
   syrup, and the syrup will slip
   easily off the spoon)

Put all the ingredients together in a saucepan and heat gently to melt and dissolve them. Then boil fast for about 5 minutes. Keep warm to serve.

Lime and grape mousse

The grapes provide a good contrast in texture in this refreshing mousse. Limes are widely available nowadays – we can buy them in Portree, the main town on Skye, 52 weeks a year, and they do have a distinct and wonderful flavour, quite different from lemons. You can make this mousse a day before it is wanted if you like.

Serves 6–8

5 limes
8 oz/250 g black or green grapes,
   halved and seeded
4 large eggs, separated

1 sachet gelatine – approximately
   ½ oz/15 g
4 oz/100 g caster sugar
½ pt/300 ml double cream

Grate the rind of the limes into a bowl. Add the egg yolks. Squeeze the juice from the limes into a small saucepan, and sprinkle the gelatine over. Heat gently until the gelatine granules dissolve, then raise the temperature until the lime juice is very hot, but not actually boiling.

Meanwhile whisk the egg yolks and rind, gradually incorporating the caster sugar, until the mixture is very thick and pale. Still whisking, add the very hot lime juice and gelatine mixture in a thin stream (not too fast – rather like adding the oil to mayonnaise). Whisk in well, and leave the mixture until it is very thick. Whip the cream and fold it in.

Whisk the egg whites until very stiff and, using a large metal spoon, fold them quickly and thoroughly into the mousse, along with the grapes. Pour into a glass or china serving dish and leave in a cool place. If you like, gild the lily and top with more whipped cream and more halved grapes.

Pineapple sorbet

A delicious pud to end a rich lunch or dinner at this time of year, when we seem to suffer from a gastronomic onslaught. It is a convenient dish because it can be made two to three weeks in advance and kept in the deep freeze until needed.

Serves 6–8

---

1 average-sized pineapple
1½ pt/1 L water
8 oz/250 g granulated sugar

pared rind and juice of 2 lemons
2 egg whites

Put the water, sugar and pared lemon rind into a saucepan over a gentle heat until the sugar has dissolved completely. Then boil fast for 5 minutes, take the saucepan off the heat and stir in the lemon juice. Leave to cool.

Cut the skin off the pineapple, and put the flesh into a liquidizer or food processor. Blend to a smooth purée.

Strain the lemony syrup and stir it into the pineapple purée. Pour the mixture into a polythene container and put in the freezer for 2 to 3 hours. Then take the container out of the freezer, and whisk the pineapple mixture thoroughly. Return it to the freezer and repeat the process, this time also folding in the egg whites, stiffly whisked. Put the container back into the freezer, freeze for another hour or two then beat and whisk for the last time. All this whisking and freezing really does make the sorbet light, and gives it a good, smooth texture. Take the container out of the freezer about half an hour before serving – as you dish up the main course. At the same time put the serving bowl in the refrigerator, so that when you spoon the sorbet into it the sorbet stays firm.

Index

277

278

THE CLAIRE MACDONALD COOKBOOK
by Claire Macdonald of Macdonald

Clarissa Dickson Wright, now famous for her role in *Two Fat Ladies*, has described Kinloch Lodge on the Isle of Skye as 'the hotel where Claire Macdonald and her husband Godfrey cheerfully dispense peace, good humour and wonderful food'. Distilled from Claire's years of cooking at Kinloch Lodge, this is a celebratory collection of the best of the recipes from her many books together with much new material.

Revised and updated to take account of the health- and weight-conscious Nineties, the recipes range exhaustively across soups, first courses, fish, poultry and game, meat, eggs, vegetables (both as a main course and a side dish), salads, pasta and rice, stocks, sauces and a selection of delicious breads, cakes and puddings in every shape and form.

Claire Macdonald, whose hallmarks are the use of seasonal, fresh country ingredients, and practical, down-to-earth methods, is justly renowned for her cookery writing. Whether providing ideas for informal family fare, intimate gourmet meals or special occasion dishes, Claire is a remarkably reliable source of foolproof and marvellous recipes. *The Claire Macdonald Cookbook* is an indispensable addition to every cook's *batterie de cuisine*.

0 593 04268 9

NOW AVAILABLE AS A BANTAM PRESS HARDBACK

CELEBRATIONS
by Claire Macdonald of Macdonald

Celebrations is written for anyone who likes to eat and drink well, and to celebrate the milestones in their lives. Almost any event can be an excuse for a party or a feast – birthdays, Christmas, anniversaries, christenings or even just a summer party or barbecue – and Claire Macdonald, who runs a family hotel at Kinloch Lodge on the Isle of Skye, offers a host of delicious recipes to help even the most hard-pressed cook to celebrate life.

Menus range from romantic dinners for two to lunch or dinner parties for twenty or more. *Celebrations* also includes a stunning selection of the puddings for which Claire Macdonald is so justly famous.

Above all, the recipes are supremely practical and many can be prepared in advance; *Celebrations* is aimed at those of us who love to entertain but have to cope with busy lives as well.

'Claire Macdonald of Macdonald is plainly one of nature's hostesses . . . the recipes are many of them novel as well as practical'
Glasgow Herald

0 552 99436 7

OTHER CLAIRE MACDONALD COOKERY TITLES AVAILABLE FROM CORGI BOOKS AND BANTAM PRESS

THE PRICES SHOWN BELOW WERE CORRECT AT THE TIME OF GOING TO PRESS. HOWEVER TRANSWORLD PUBLISHERS RESERVE THE RIGHT TO SHOW NEW RETAIL PRICES ON COVERS WHICH MAY DIFFER FROM THOSE PREVIOUSLY ADVERTISED IN THE TEXT OR ELSEWHERE.

All Transworld titles are available by post from:

Bookpost, P.O. Box 29, Douglas, Isle of Man IM99 1BQ

Credit cards accepted. Please telephone 01624 836000,
fax 01624 837033, Internet http://www.bookpost.co.uk or
e-mail: bookshop@enterprise.net for details.

Free postage and packing in the UK. Overseas customers allow
£1 per book (paperbacks) and £3 per book (hardbacks).